Better Homes and Gardens®

1993 Best Recipes YEARBOOK

First Edition. Printing Number and Year: 5 4 3 2 1 97 96 95 94 93
ISSN: 8755-3090
ISBN: 0-696-04632-6

Better Homes and Gardens Books®

An Imprint of Meredith® Books
President, Book Group: *Joseph J. Ward*
Vice President and Editorial Director: *Elizabeth P. Rice*
Executive Editor: *Connie Schrader*
Art Director: *Ernest Shelton*
Test Kitchen Director: *Sharon Stilwell*

1993 Best Recipes Yearbook

Editorial Project Managers: *Jennifer Darling and Shelli McConnell*
Contributing Designer: *Lyne Neymeyer*
Contributing Editor: *Joyce Trollope*
Production Editor: *Paula Forest*
Production Manager: *Randy Yontz*

Meredith Corporation

Corporate Officers: Chairman of Executive Commitee: *E.T. Meredith III*
Chairman of the Board, President, and Chief Executive Officer: *Jack D. Rehm*
Group Presidents: *Joseph J. Ward,* Books; *William T. Kerr,* Magazines;
Philip A. Jones, Broadcasting; *Allen L. Sabbag,* Real Estate
Vice Presidents: *Leo R. Armatis,* Corporate Relations;
Thomas G. Fisher, General Counsel and Secretary; *Larry D. Hartsook,* Finance;
Michael A. Sell, Treasurer; *Kathleen J. Zehr,* Controller and Assistant Secretary

Our seal assures you that every recipe in the *1993 Best Recipes Yearbook*
has been tested in the Better Homes and Gardens® Test Kitchen.
This means that each recipe is practical and reliable, and meets
our high standards of taste appeal. We guarantee your satisfaction
with this book for as long as you own it.

WE CARE!

All of us at Better Homes and Gardens® Books are dedicated to
providing you with the information and ideas you need to create tasty foods.
We welcome your comments and suggestions.
Write us at:
Better Homes and Gardens® Books,
Cookbook Editorial Department,
RW-240, 1716 Locust St.,
Des Moines, IA
50309-3023

*If you would like to order additional copies of any of our books,
call 1-800-678-2803 or check with your local bookstore.*

Contents

January   *Fabulous Family Meals Under $10* 6   *Prize Tested Recipes* 18

February   *Victorian Valentines* 22   *Prize Tested Recipes* 30

March   *Make-Over Magic* 34   *Prize Tested Recipes* 44

April   *Spring Delicious* 48   *Prize Tested Recipes* 62

May   *Chicken* 66   *Prize Tested Recipes* 78

June   *8 Great Recipes for Summer Cookouts* 82   *Prize Tested Recipes* 92

July   *Summer Fun Outdoor Eats* 96   *Prize Tested Recipes* 106

August   *Garden Fresh Recipes* 110   *Prize Tested Recipes* 130

September   *Eat Smart on the Run* 134   *Prize Tested Recipes* 144

October   *Simple Pleasures of Home Baking* 148   *Prize Tested Recipes* 166

November   *Light Appetizers & Desserts* 170   *Prize Tested Recipes* 186

December   *Delicious Memories* 190   *Prize Tested Recipes* 208

Index   211

Introduction

Looking up recipes in old *Better Homes and Gardens®* magazines or clippings that you've stashed away can have delicious consequences. But without some organization, it's a time-consuming job, even for those of us who work on the magazine.

It was your letters and pleas for just such a time-saving alternative that brought about the annual tradition of collecting and publishing our year's best recipes in a cookbook. No more clipping, or sorting, or filing. In this yearbook, you'll find 1992's cream-of-the-crop recipes and their tempting photographs, organized month by month as they appeared in the magazine.

We're certain you'll enjoy paging through this rich compendium of good taste—from our personal moneywise favorites in " Fabulous Family Meals Under $10" to the prizewinning reader recipes in "8 Great Recipes for Summer Cookouts," to "Light Appetizers and Desserts" from America's top chefs, and more. We created every story especially with your many cooking and serving needs in mind. Each recipe has been meticulously tested and tasted in the  Better Homes and Gardens® Test Kitchen so it works perfectly the first time or the nth time you make it.

And now with the organizing all done, you can spend your precious time on the fun part—preparing and serving these luscious foods to your family and friends.

The Editors—Kristi, Lisa, Nancy, Julia, and Joy

January

Fabulous
Family Meals Under $10

Editors' Choice Menus

Prize Tested Recipes®

Chicken-Artichoke Pizza, Four-Cheese and Peppers Pizza, Broccoli-Noodle Stir-Fry, Broccoli-Sausage Quiche

Fabulous family meals under $10

Editors' Choice Menus

Clipping coupons, reading grocery ads, shopping with a list. Sound familiar? Like you, food editors also search for ways to save money on groceries. That's why we challenged ourselves to come up with tasty family meals, while spending no more than $10. Our menus show how we—and you— can cook more for less.

Lois White, senior food editor, with husband, Shawn, and baby, Robert. "Squeeze a dinner for four, plus lunch, out of $10."

Lois' plan
◆ Shop where prices are rock bottom, such as warehouse supermarkets.
◆ Ground beef is still one of the best budget meats around. Buy the leanest beef you can afford.
◆ Purchase in-season produce like apples and oranges in 3- to 5-pound (or even larger) bags to get a better produce price per pound.
◆ Fix thrifty homemade mixes.
◆ Try store-brand products, which are often lower-priced than national brands.

Dinner For Four
Oriental Meatballs and Vegetables
Hot Cooked Rice
Citrus-Greens Salad
Cherry-Apple Cobbler

$6.45

Lunch For Four
Meatball and Bean Soup
Cornmeal Biscuits

$3.50

Oriental Meatballs and Vegetables

LOIS CAN FIX THIS HOMEY DISH ON BUSY weeknights, thanks to meatballs that she's made ahead and kept in the freezer until needed—

¾ cup water
2 tablespoons soy sauce
2 teaspoons cornstarch
½ teaspoon ground ginger
½ teaspoon instant beef bouillon granules
¼ teaspoon pepper
3 cups loose-pack frozen broccoli cuts
2 medium carrots, bias-sliced ¼-inch thick
(1 cup)
1 tablespoon cooking oil
16 1½-inch Freezer Meatballs (see recipe, page 8), thawed
2 cups hot cooked rice

For sauce, stir together water, soy sauce, cornstarch, ginger, bouillon granules, and pepper. Set aside.

In a large skillet cook broccoli and carrots in hot oil over medium-high heat
continued on page 8
Oriental Meatballs and Vegetables ◆

continued from page 6
for 5 to 6 minutes or till vegetables are crisp-tender. Remove vegetables from skillet. Stir sauce; add to skillet. Cook and stir over medium heat till thickened and bubbly. Stir in vegetables and thawed meatballs; cover and cook about 5 minutes or till meatballs are heated through. Serve with hot cooked rice. Makes 4 servings.

Nutrition information per serving: 409 cal. (38% from fat), 17 g fat, 79 mg chol., 22 g pro., 42 g carbo., 2 g fiber, 812 mg sodium. RDA: 11% calcium, 26% iron, 146% vit. A, 60% vit. C, 27% thiamine, 21% riboflavin, and 37% niacin.

Freezer Meatballs

TO USE THE FROZEN MEATBALLS, LET them stand, covered, in the refrigerator for 8 hours or overnight to thaw. Or, defrost them in the microwave oven just before using—

1 beaten egg
¾ cup soft bread crumbs (1 slice)
⅛ cup milk
1 teaspoon Worcestershire sauce
¼ teaspoon onion powder
¼ teaspoon salt
¼ teaspoon garlic powder
1½ pounds ground beef

In a large bowl combine egg, bread crumbs, milk, Worcestershire sauce, onion powder, salt, and garlic powder. Add beef. Mix well. Shape *half* of the meat mixture into 16 1½-inch meatballs; shape remaining beef mixture into 24 1-inch meatballs. Place all of the meatballs in a single layer in a 15x10x1-inch baking pan.

Bake in a 350° oven for 20 minutes or till meatballs are no longer pink in center. Remove with slotted spoon and drain on paper towels. Cool meatballs for 15 minutes.

Place the 16 1½-inch meatballs in one freezer container for the Oriental Meatballs and Vegetables recipe. Place the 24 1-inch meatballs in another freezer container for the Meatball and Bean Soup recipe. Seal, label, and freeze containers of meatballs for up to 6 months. Makes 40 meatballs.

Nutrition information per four 1 ½ - inch meatballs (⅛ of recipe): 198 cal. (63% from fat), 13 g fat, 79 mg chol., 15 g pro., 3 g carbo., 0 g fiber, 143 mg sodium. RDA: 11% iron, 12% riboflavin, 20% niacin.

Citrus-Greens Salad

2 medium oranges
½ cup plain yogurt
2 teaspoons sugar
¼ head iceberg lettuce, cut into 4 wedges

Finely shred enough orange peel to measure ¼ teaspoon; set aside. Working over a small bowl, peel and section oranges, reserving orange juice.

For dressing, in a small bowl stir together orange peel, reserved orange juice, yogurt, and sugar. Place a lettuce wedge on each salad plate; arrange orange sections on top. Spoon dressing atop salads. Makes 4 servings.

Nutrition information per serving: 61 cal., (8% from fat), 1 g fat, 2 mg chol., 2 g pro., 12 g carbo., 2 g fiber, 23 mg sodium. RDA: 11% calcium, 61% vit. C.

Cherry-Apple Cobbler

WHAT APPLE VARIETY WORKS BEST IN baked recipes? Some varieties to look for are Golden Delicious, Granny Smith, or Jonathan apples—

½ cup Homemade Biscuit Mix (see recipe, page 9)
2 tablespoons whole wheat flour
1 tablespoon sugar
1 egg
1 tablespoon milk
2 cooking apples, peeled, cored, and thinly sliced
1½ cups frozen unsweetened pitted tart red cherries
¼ cup sugar
2 tablespoons water
1 tablespoon cornstarch
1 teaspoon sugar
¼ teaspoon ground cinnamon
¼ cup light cream or half-and-half (optional)

In a medium mixing bowl combine biscuit mix, whole wheat flour, and the 1 tablespoon sugar. Beat egg slightly; combine with milk. Set aside.

In a medium saucepan combine apples, frozen cherries, the ¼ cup sugar, and *1 tablespoon* of the water. Bring to boiling; reduce heat. Cover and simmer for 5 minutes or till apples are almost tender, stirring occasionally. Combine cornstarch with remaining 1 tablespoon water; add to fruit. Cook and stir over medium heat till thickened and bubbly. Transfer hot cherry-apple mixture to a 1-quart casserole.

Add egg-milk mixture all at once to dry ingredients, stirring just till moistened. Immediately spoon biscuit topping into 4 mounds onto hot fruit mixture. Stir together the 1 teaspoon sugar and cinnamon. Sprinkle mixture over dough.

Bake in a 400° oven about 15 minutes or till toothpick inserted into biscuits comes out clean. Serve warm with cream. Makes 4 servings.

Nutrition information per serving: 245 cal. (20% from fat), 6 g fat, 54 mg chol., 4 g pro., 47 g carbo., 3 g fiber, 143 mg sodium. RDA: 10% vit. A, 14% thiamine, 13% riboflavin.

Homemade Biscuit Mix

TO MEASURE, LIGHTLY SPOON THE MIX into a measuring cup for dry ingredients; level off with the flat side of a knife—

1¾ cups all-purpose flour
1 tablespoon baking powder
1 tablespoon sugar
½ teaspoon salt
⅓ cup shortening

In a bowl stir together flour, baking powder, sugar, and salt. Cut in shortening till mixture resembles coarse crumbs. Store in an airtight container for up to 6 weeks at room temperature or for up to 6 months in the freezer. Use to make Cherry-Apple Cobbler and Cornmeal Biscuits. If frozen, bring mix to room temperature before using. Makes about 2¼ cups mix.

Meatball and Bean Soup

IF YOU'RE RESTRICTING SODIUM IN YOUR diet, use low-sodium tomatoes and add only 2 teaspoons bouillon granules. You'll save 600 milligrams of sodium per serving of soup—

Meatball and Bean Soup ◆

4 cups water
1 16-ounce can tomatoes, cut up
1 15-ounce can dark red kidney beans, rinsed and drained
1 carrot, thinly sliced
4 teaspoons instant beef bouillon granules
½ teaspoon dried oregano, crushed
¼ teaspoon dried thyme, crushed
Several dashes bottled hot pepper sauce
½ cup elbow macaroni
24 1-inch Freezer Meatballs (see recipe, page 8), thawed
Grated Parmesan cheese (optional)

In a 3-quart saucepan combine water, *undrained* tomatoes, beans, carrot, bouillon granules, oregano, thyme, and hot pepper sauce. Bring to boiling. Add macaroni. Return to boiling; reduce heat. Cover and simmer for 5 minutes. Add meatballs. Return to boiling; reduce heat. Simmer about 5 minutes more or till meatballs are heated through. Sprinkle each serving with Parmesan, if desired. Makes 4 main-dish servings.

Nutrition information per serving: 374 cal. (33% from fat), 14 g fat, 79 mg chol., 26 g pro., 39 g carbo., 7 g fiber, 1,384 mg sodium. RDA: 12% calcium, 30% iron, 74% vit. A, 36% vit. C, 25% thiamine, 36% riboflavin, 32% niacin.

Cornmeal Biscuits

1½ cups Homemade Biscuit Mix (see
recipe, page 9)
½ cup cornmeal
½ cup milk
Margarine and/or honey (optional)

In a medium mixing bowl combine
biscuit mix and cornmeal. Make a well
in the center; add milk all at once. Stir
just till dough clings together.

On a lightly floured surface, knead
dough gently for 10 to 12 strokes. Roll
or pat dough to a 6-inch circle. Cut into
eight wedges. Arrange wedges 1 inch
apart on ungreased baking sheet; sprinkle with additional cornmeal.

Bake in a 400° oven for 10 to 12
minutes or till golden. Serve warm with
margarine and honey. Makes 4 servings.

Nutrition information per serving:
321 cal. (36% from fat), 13 g fat, 2 mg
chol., 6 g pro., 45 g carbo., 2 g fiber,
388 mg sodium. RDA: 21% calcium,
16% iron, 38% thiamine, 23%
riboflavin, 20% niacin.

Lisa Holderness, senior magazine
editor (right) and her husband,
Peter (left), enjoy a cozy meal with
Lisa's parents.

Lisa's strategies:

◆ Center a company meal around a
main-course soup. It's a wonderful way
to stretch meat and make the most of
inexpensive beans and vegetables. For
the broth base, use bouillon granules
mixed with water.
◆ Make a quick bread from scratch,
using best-buy ingredients—flour, milk,
and eggs. Use any leftover bread for
toast at another meal.
◆ For a tossed salad, look through the
produce department for the lowest
prices on salad greens. Then, top them
with a homemade dressing.
◆ Ask your dinner guests to bring the
dinner wine!

Sherried Black Bean Soup

IF YOU CAN'T FIND CANNED BLACK BEANS
in your supermarket, you can use
canned kidney beans instead—

½ cup thinly sliced carrot
1 small onion, chopped
4 cloves garlic, minced
1 tablespoon cooking oil
2 teaspoons ground cumin
4 cups water
2 15-ounce cans black beans, rinsed and
drained
1 cup cubed, fully cooked ham
¼ cup dry sherry or water
1 teaspoon instant beef or chicken
bouillon granules
2 bay leaves
1 teaspoon dried oregano, crushed
⅛ teaspoon ground red pepper
¼ cup dairy sour cream
¼ cup frozen peas, thawed

In a 3-quart Dutch oven cook carrot,
onion, and garlic in hot oil over medium-low heat for 3 minutes. Add cumin
and cook till carrots are tender. Stir in
water, the beans, ham, sherry, bouillon
granules, bay leaves, oregano, and
ground red pepper. Bring to boiling;
reduce heat.

Simmer, uncovered, for 25 minutes.
Remove bay leaves. To serve, ladle into
bowls; top with sour cream and a few
peas. Makes 4 main-dish servings.

Nutrition information per serving:
295 cal. (25% from fat), 9 g fat, 17 mg
chol., 23 g pro., 36 g carbo., 11 g fiber,
1,170 mg sodium. RDA: 17% calcium,
30% iron, 69% vit. A, 24% vit. C, 52%
thiamine.

Fresh Greens with Honey-Jalapeño Dressing

THE HOTNESS OF THE DRESSING DEPENDS
on whether 1 or 2 teaspoons of jalapeño
pepper is added—

¼ teaspoon finely shredded lime peel
2 tablespoons lime juice
1 tablespoon honey

continued on page 12
Sherried Black Bean Soup, Fresh Greens with Honey-
Jalapeño Dressing, Whole Wheat Brick Alley Bread ◆

continued from page 10

Dash ground nutmeg
¼ cup salad oil
1 to 2 teaspoons chopped fresh or canned
jalapeño pepper
4 cups torn salad greens (such as Bibb,
leaf lettuce, or iceberg)
1 large orange
2 tablespoons sliced almonds, toasted

In a blender container combine lime peel, lime juice, honey, and nutmeg. With blender running, add salad oil in a steady stream through opening in lid. Add jalapeño pepper; blend just till combined. Cover and chill.

At serving time, place greens in a bowl. Using a sharp knife, remove and discard peel and white membrane from orange. Thinly slice orange; quarter each slice. Add orange and almonds to greens. Drizzle with dressing; toss. Makes 4 side-dish servings.

Nutrition information per side-dish serving: 188 cal. (73% from fat), 16 g fat, 0 mg chol., 2 g pro., 11 g carbo., 2 g fiber, 25 mg sodium. RDA: 26% vit. A, 51% vit. C.

Whole Wheat Brick Alley Bread

THIS WHOLE WHEAT QUICK BREAD IS dotted with raisins and lightly sweetened with honey—

1 cup whole wheat flour
1 cup all-purpose flour
1½ teaspoons baking powder
¾ teaspoon salt
½ teaspoon baking soda
1 beaten egg
1 cup buttermilk or sour milk

3 tablespoons honey
1 cup raisins
1 beaten egg white

In a large bowl combine flours, baking powder, salt, and baking soda. Combine the 1 beaten egg, buttermilk, and honey. Add egg mixture to flour mixture; stir just till moistened. Stir in raisins. Turn dough out onto a greased baking sheet; pat with wet fingers to an 8-inch round (dough will be wet). Brush with egg white.

Bake in a 350° oven about 25 minutes or till golden brown and toothpick comes out clean. If necessary, cover with foil the last 5 minutes to prevent over-browning. Serve warm. Makes 1 loaf (16 servings).

Nutrition information per serving: 108 cal., (8% from fat), 1 g fat, 14 mg chol., 3 g pro., 23 g carbo., 2 g fiber, 178 mg sodium.

Kristi Fuller, associate magazine editor, enjoys cooking with husband, Peter. "Seasonings are a shrewd way to add rich taste."

Kristi's ideas:
◆ Stock up on modestly priced flavor boosters such as dried basil, lemon-pepper seasoning, and fresh garlic.
◆ Compare prices when buying chicken. If boneless breasts are only a dollar more per pound than bone-in pieces, buy the boneless cut for just a few extra pennies.
◆ Fill up on a cheap carbohydrate like pasta. Healthful, too!
◆ Use up leftovers instead of tossing them out.

Chicken Provençale
PROVENÇALE (pro-vahn-SAHL) Describes dishes prepared in the style of Provence—a region in southern France. These dishes include tomatoes, olives, and garlic. Kristi loves this dish because it's fresh tasting and easy to fix—

continued on page 14
Chicken Provençale ◆

Using a vegetable peeler, cut carrot and zucchini lengthwise into long, thin slices. Cook fettuccine according to package directions, adding carrot and zucchini for the last minute of cooking. Drain pasta and vegetables. Toss with remaining margarine.

To serve, divide fettuccine mixture between two dinner plates. Top each with a chicken breast and tomato sauce. Sprinkle with cheese. Makes 2 servings.

Nutrition information per serving: 573 cal. (36% from fat), 23 g fat, 62 mg chol., 34 g pro., 58 g carbo., 3 g fiber, 828 mg sodium. RDA: 39% iron, 160% vit. A, 51% vit. C.

Grilled Honey-Soy Chicken Sandwiches

3 tablespoons orange juice
1 tablespoon reduced-sodium soy sauce
1 tablespoon honey
1 teaspoon lemon-pepper seasoning
½ teaspoon ground ginger
⅛ teaspoon garlic powder
2 skinless, boneless chicken breast halves
(8 ounces total)
2 whole wheat hamburger buns
Lettuce leaves
1 plum tomato, sliced

In a shallow, nonmetallic dish combine orange juice, soy sauce, honey, lemon-pepper seasoning, ginger, and garlic powder. Set aside.

Place chicken breasts between two sheets of plastic wrap. Pound each with a meat mallet until ½ inch thick; place in marinade. Cover; refrigerate for 4 to 6 hours or overnight.

At serving time, remove chicken from marinade, reserving marinade. Place

◆ Grilled Honey-Soy Chicken Sandwiches
continued from page 12

4 plum tomatoes, chopped
½ of a 6-ounce can pitted
ripe olives, sliced
1 tablespoon olive oil or cooking oil
2 teaspoons dried basil, crushed
2 cloves garlic, minced
1 beaten egg white
1 teaspoon water
¼ cup fine dry bread crumbs
2 tablespoons snipped parsley
¼ teaspoon lemon-pepper seasoning
2 skinless, boneless chicken breast halves
(8 ounces total)
2 teaspoons margarine, melted
1 medium carrot
1 medium zucchini

3 ounces fettuccine
1 teaspoon margarine
Grated Parmesan cheese

For sauce, combine tomatoes, olives, olive oil, basil, and garlic. Let stand at room temperature for 1 hour.

In a small bowl combine egg white and water. In a shallow bowl combine bread crumbs, parsley, and lemon-pepper seasoning. Dip chicken in the egg mixture, then roll in crumbs. Place chicken in a shallow baking pan. Drizzle with the 2 teaspoons melted margarine. Bake in a 350° oven 30 to 40 minutes or till no longer pink.

Meanwhile, in a skillet cook tomato mixture, uncovered, over medium heat for 5 to 7 minutes. Keep warm.

chicken on an uncovered grill directly over *medium-hot* coals. Grill about 10 minutes or till tender and no longer pink, turning chicken once. (*Or*, place chicken on the unheated rack of a broiler pan. Broil 4 to 5 inches from heat for 6 to 7 minutes, turning once.) During the last 2 minutes of grilling or broiling, brush chicken with reserved marinade.

Split buns and place on grill rack or broiler pan for 1 to 2 minutes to toast. Serve chicken breasts on toasted buns. Top each with lettuce and tomato slices. Makes 2 servings.

Nutrition information per serving: 318 cal. (16% from fat), 5 g fat, 73 mg chol., 32 g pro., 34 g carbo., 2 g fiber, 1,107 mg sodium. RDA: 19% iron, 29% vit. C, 28% thiamine, 21% riboflavin, 94% niacin.

Mediterranean Pasta Salad

3 ounces fettuccine, broken
1 medium carrot, cut into julienne strips
½ of a 6-ounce can pitted ripe olives, halved
2 tablespoons vinegar
1 tablespoon olive oil or cooking oil
1 tablespoon water
¾ teaspoon dried basil, crushed
½ teaspoon sugar
⅛ teaspoon onion powder
1 clove garlic, minced
Dash pepper

Cook fettuccine according to package directions, adding carrots strips the last 1 to 2 minutes of cooking. Drain pasta and carrots; rinse with cold water. Drain again and place in a medium bowl; add halved olives.

In a screw-top jar combine vinegar, oil, water, basil, sugar, onion powder, garlic, and pepper. Cover; shake well. Pour dressing over pasta mixture; toss. Cover; chill. Stir occasionally and before serving. Makes 4 side-dish servings.

Nutrition information per serving: 150 cal. (36% from fat), 6 g fat, 0 mg chol., 3 g pro., 22 g carbo., 1 g fiber, 191 mg sodium. RDA: 65% vit. A.

Colleen Weeden, a home economist from our Test Kitchen, and husband, Kent, keep busy with little Kelly. "Meatless recipes let us enjoy delicious and nutritious meals for a song."

Dinner For Four
Tofu-Cheese-Stuffed Shells
Romaine and Walnut Salad
Chocolate-Peanut Butter Pudding
Iced Tea
$8.20

Colleen's methods:
◆ Create a main dish using low-fat and low-cost ingredients such as tofu, part-skim cheeses, and pasta.

◆ Serve pudding for dessert—made from scratch with peanut butter, a thrifty staple to keep on hand.
◆ Cook more than you need for any one meal. Leftovers can be your box lunch the next day.
◆ Sip penny-wise hot or iced tea.

Tofu-Cheese-Stuffed Shells
TOFU AND CHEESE PROVIDE MOST OF the protein for this meatless main dish—

12 jumbo pasta shells
¼ cup shredded carrot
2 tablespoons sliced green onion
8 ounces tofu
½ cup low-fat ricotta cheese
½ cup shredded cheddar cheese (2 ounces)
½ cup shredded mozzarella cheese (2 ounces)
1 beaten egg white
¼ teaspoon salt
¼ teaspoon pepper
1 16-ounce can tomatoes, cut up
½ of a 6-ounce can tomato paste
1 teaspoon dried basil, crushed
1 teaspoon dried oregano, crushed
½ teaspoon sugar
¼ teaspoon garlic powder
¼ teaspoon fennel seed, crushed (optional)

Cook pasta shells according to package directions. Drain. Rinse with cold water. Drain and set aside. Meanwhile, in a small saucepan cook carrot and green onion in a small amount of water till tender. Drain.

For filling, in a medium mixing bowl mash tofu with a fork. Stir in the carrot-onion mixture, ricotta cheese, cheddar cheese, ¼ cup of the mozzarella, the egg white, salt, and pepper.

continued on page 17

continued from page 15

For sauce, in a saucepan combine *undrained* tomatoes, tomato paste, basil, oregano, sugar, garlic powder, and fennel seed. Bring to boiling; reduce heat. Simmer, uncovered, 10 minutes.

Stuff each cooked shell with *about 1 rounded tablespoon* of filling. Place shells in an ungreased 8x8x2-inch baking dish. Pour sauce over shells. Top with remaining mozzarella cheese. Bake, covered, in a 350° oven for 25 minutes or till hot. Makes 4 servings.

Nutrition information per serving: 316 cal. (36% from fat), 13 g fat, 32 mg chol., 21 g pro., 31 g carbo., 2 g fiber, 714 mg sodium. RDA: 49% calcium, 39% iron, 55% vit. A, 48% vit. C, 25% thiamine, 28% riboflavin.

Romaine and Walnut Salad

SAVE A FEW DISHES BY SERVING THE salad on the same plate as the stuffed pasta shells—

4 cups torn romaine lettuce
2 plum tomatoes, sliced
½ cup sliced fresh mushrooms
¼ cup chopped walnuts
¼ cup red wine vinegar
2 tablespoons salad oil
2 tablespoons honey
¼ teaspoon dry mustard

In a mixing bowl toss together romaine, tomatoes, mushrooms, and walnuts. In a screw-top jar combine vinegar, oil, honey, and dry mustard. Cover and shake well. Pour over romaine mixture. Toss the salad to coat. Makes 4 servings.

◆ Tofu Cheese Stuffed Shells

Nutrition information per serving: 159 cal. (62% from fat), 12 g fat, 0 mg chol., 2 g pro., 14 g carbo., 2 g fiber, 9 mg sodium. RDA: 21% vit. A, 33% vit. C, 10% riboflavin.

Chocolate-Peanut Butter Pudding

IN THE SPRINGTIME, SERVE THE PUDDING with fresh berries—

½ cup sugar
¼ cup unsweetened cocoa powder
3 tablespoons cornstarch
2 cups skim milk
½ cup peanut butter
1 teaspoon vanilla
1 banana, sliced

In a medium saucepan combine the sugar, cocoa powder, and cornstarch. Stir together milk, peanut butter, and vanilla; add to sugar mixture. Cook and stir over medium heat till thickened and bubbly. Cook and stir 2 minutes more. Remove from heat. Pour into a bowl. Cover surface with plastic wrap. Chill till set or up to 24 hours.

To serve, spoon *half* of the pudding into four individual dessert cups; top each using *half* of the banana. Spoon remaining pudding over bananas; arrange remaining banana slices atop. Serve immediately. Makes 4 servings.

Nutrition information per serving: 372 cal. (40% from fat), 17 g fat, 2 mg chol., 15 g pro., 43 g carbo., 2 g fiber, 214 mg sodium. RDA: 28% calcium, 33% niacin.

How we figured the cost of recipes

The costs for the menus on pages 6-15 were based on prices in a Des Moines, Iowa, supermarket during June 1991. Prices for the menus on page 6 were figured using store brands while prices for the remaining three menus were figured using nationally advertised brands. For all menus, we did not include the price of these staples: seasonings, cornstarch, vanilla, Worcestershire sauce, sugar, and baking powder. Optional ingredients also were not figured into the total cost.

Prize Tested Recipes.

Chicken-Artichoke Pizza

THE 12-INCH ITALIAN BREAD SHELL makes a convenient crust for this top-prize pizza—

1 6-ounce jar marinated artichoke hearts
2 medium zucchini and/or yellow summer
squash, sliced
1 small red sweet pepper, chopped
1 tablespoon olive oil or cooking oil
1½ cups sliced fresh mushrooms
2 green onions, sliced
1 pound skinless, boneless chicken
breasts, cut into cubes
2 plum tomatoes, sliced
1 2¼-ounce can sliced pitted ripe olives
3 tablespoons vinegar
½ teaspoon garlic powder
½ teaspoon seasoned salt
½ teaspoon dried oregano, crushed
½ teaspoon dried basil, crushed
1 tablespoon cornstarch
1 16-ounce Italian bread shell
(Boboli brand)
1½ cups shredded Monterey
Jack cheese (6 ounces)
¼ cup grated Parmesan cheese

Drain artichokes; reserve liquid. Cut artichokes into bite-size pieces; set aside.

In a large skillet cook squash and sweet pepper in hot oil till crisp-tender; remove. Add mushrooms and onion to skillet. Cook till just tender; remove. Cook chicken, *half* at a time, for 2 to 3 minutes or till no longer pink. Return all chicken to skillet. Stir in the artichoke liquid and hearts, tomatoes,

Chicken-Artichoke Pizza ◆

olives, vinegar, garlic powder, seasoned salt, oregano, and basil. Combine cornstarch and 1 tablespoon *cold water;* add to skillet. Cook and stir till bubbly; cook 1 minute more. Return all vegetables to skillet; stir. Place bread shell on a greased baking sheet; top with chicken mixture and cheeses. Bake in a 425° oven 10 to 12 minutes. Let stand 5 minutes. Makes 6 to 8 servings.

Nutrition information per serving: 496 cal. (41% from fat), 23 g fat, 46 mg chol., 33 g pro., 42 g carbo., 3 g fiber, 964 mg sodium.

$200 WINNER
Anji Pickett, Seattle, Wash.

Four-Cheese and Peppers Pizza

CHEESE PIZZA ENTHUSIASTS WILL SAVOR every bite of Julie's scrumptious tomato-topped pizza—

1 16-ounce loaf frozen bread dough,
thawed
2 large green and/or red sweet peppers,
chopped (2 cups)
1 cup shredded mozzarella cheese (4
ounces)
¾ cup shredded fontina cheese (3 ounces)
½ cup grated Parmesan cheese (2 ounces)
½ cup crumbled feta cheese (2 ounces)
2 tablespoons snipped parsley or
2 teaspoons dried parsley flakes

*1 tablespoon snipped fresh basil or 1
teaspoon dried basil, crushed
3 medium plum tomatoes or 1 medium
tomato, thinly sliced
1 tablespoon olive oil or cooking oil
2 cloves garlic, minced*

Press bread dough evenly into a greased 12-inch pizza pan. Prick generously with a fork. Bake in 375 ° oven for 20 to 25 minutes or till crust is light brown.

To assemble pizza, top crust in this order: sweet pepper, mozzarella, fontina, Parmesan, feta, parsley, basil, and tomatoes. In a small bowl combine oil and garlic. Brush tomatoes with oil-and-garlic mixture. Bake pizza in a 375 ° oven about 15 to 20 minutes or till cheese is melted and the pizza is heated through. Let stand 5 minutes before cutting. Makes 6 servings.

Nutrition information per serving: 376 cal. (40% from fat), 17 g fat, 42 mg chol., 19 g pro., 37 g carbo., 1 g fiber, 447 mg sodium. RDA: 52% calcium, 16% iron, 18% vit. A, 55% vit. C, 34% thiamine, 32% riboflavin, 20% niacin.

$100 WINNER
Julie Hill, Tujunga, Calif.

Broccoli-Noodle Stir-Fry

*1 3-ounce package chicken
oriental noodle mix
2 teaspoons cornstarch
1½ teaspoons reduced-sodium soy sauce
1 teaspoon rice vinegar or white vinegar
¼ teaspoon crushed red pepper
1 tablespoon toasted sesame oil
1 tablespoon cooking oil
4 cups broccoli flowerets
Bias-sliced carrots (optional)*

Four-Cheese and Peppers Pizza, *above left* ◆
Broccoli-Noodle Stir-Fry ◆

Break noodles into pieces; reserve seasoning packet. Place noodles in a 1-quart microwave-safe casserole. Add 1 cup *warm water.* Micro-cook, uncovered, on 100% power (high) for 2½ to 3 minutes or till noodles are softened, stirring twice; drain.

For sauce, in a small bowl combine seasoning packet, ⅔ cup *cold water,* cornstarch, soy sauce, vinegar, and red pepper. Set aside.

continued on page 20

Broccoli-Sausage Quiche

SERVE THIS WINNING MEAL-IN-A-QUICHE with fresh fruit or a tossed salad—

1 9-inch unbaked pie shell
4 brown-and-serve sausage links,
cut into ½-inch slices
½ cup sliced fresh mushrooms
2 beaten eggs
1 10¾-ounce can condensed
cream of broccoli soup
2 tablespoons dried minced onion
⅛ teaspoon pepper
1 10-ounce package frozen chopped
broccoli, thawed and well drained
1 cup shredded Swiss cheese (4 ounces)

Line unbaked pie shell with double thickness of foil. Bake in a 450° oven for 8 minutes; remove foil. Bake for 4 to 6 minutes more or till golden. Remove from oven; set aside. Reduce oven temperature to 375°.

Meanwhile, in a large skillet cook sausage and mushrooms about 5 minutes or till sausage is brown; drain. In a medium bowl combine the eggs, soup, onion, and pepper. Stir in the sausage mixture, broccoli, and ¾ *cup* of the cheese. Pour into the baked shell.

Bake in a 375° oven for 40 to 45 minutes or till knife inserted near center comes out clean. Sprinkle with remaining cheese. Let stand about 20 minutes. Makes 6 main-dish servings.

Nutrition information per serving: 370 cal. (57% from fat), 24 g fat, 96 mg chol., 14 g pro., 27 g carbo., 1 g fiber, 635 mg sodium. RDA: 28% calcium, 13% iron, 20% vit. A, 31% vit. C, 28% thiamine, 28% riboflavin, 15% niacin.
$100 WINNER
Julie DeMatteo, Clementon, N.J.

◆ Broccoli-Sausage Quiche
continued from page 19

In a large skillet heat sesame and cooking oil over medium-high heat. Add broccoli; stir-fry 3 to 4 minutes or till crisp-tender. Stir sauce; add sauce and noodles to skillet. Cook and stir till bubbly; cook and stir 1 minute more. Makes 4 to 6 side-dish servings.

Nutrition information per serving: 213 cal. (46% from fat), 12 g fat, 0 mg chol., 7 g pro., 23 g carbo., 4 g fiber, 456 mg sodium.
$200 WINNER
Doreen Firouzbakht
Friendswood, Tex.

February

Victorian Valentines
Sweets Homemade with Love

Prize Tested Recipes®
Blackberry Frozen Yogurt, Chocolate-Mint Cheesecake, Island Swordfish, Spicy Ginger-Garlic Chicken

Victorian Valentines

Sweets Homemade with Love

Cherry-Champagne Ice

ENJOY A REFRESHING, LOW-FAT DESSERT ice spiked with some bubbly—

⅔ cup sugar
½ cup unsweetened cherry juice or white grape juice
1 16-ounce package frozen unsweetened pitted tart red cherries, slightly thawed, or 1¼ pounds fresh tart red cherries, pitted (2½ cups)
⅔ cup champagne or white grape juice
½ teaspoon finely shredded lemon peel
⅓ cup semisweet chocolate or milk chocolate pieces (optional)
1 tablespoon shortening (optional)
Fresh mint sprigs (optional)

In a medium saucepan combine sugar and cherry juice or white grape juice. Cook and stir over medium-high heat just till sugar dissolves. Remove from heat. Cover and cool.

Meanwhile, in a blender container or food processor bowl, combine cherries, champagne or grape juice, and lemon

Cherry-Champagne Ice ◆

peel. Cover and blend or process till mixture is almost smooth. Stir cherry mixture into the cooled sugar mixture. Freeze in a 1- to 2-quart ice-cream maker according to manufacturer's directions.

To decorate dishes with chocolate, in a small, heavy saucepan combine chocolate and shortening. Melt over low heat till smooth, stirring constantly. Transfer melted chocolate to a small, self-sealing plastic bag with a corner snipped off (opening should be very small) or a pastry bag, fitted with a small, round tip.

Lightly pipe chocolate on the inside of 4 chilled dessert goblets or wine glasses to make a design. Chill glasses to allow chocolate to set. Scoop cherry mixture into goblets or glasses. Top with mint, if desired. Makes 4 servings.

Nutrition information per serving: 214 cal. (3% from fat), 1 g fat, 0 mg chol., 1 g pro., 49 g carbo., 1 g fiber, 3 mg sodium.

Rum Truffles

*6 squares (6 ounces) semisweet chocolate,
coarsely chopped
¼ cup margarine or butter
3 tablespoons whipping cream
1 beaten egg yolk
3 tablespoons rum, brandy,
or whipping cream
1 pound semisweet chocolate, tempered,
(see box, right) or chocolate-flavored
candy coating, chopped
Vanilla-flavored or pink candy coating,
melted, for decorating (optional)*

In a heavy 2-quart saucepan combine the 6 squares semisweet chocolate, margarine or butter, and the 3 tablespoons

Tempering Chocolate

Tempering means to melt chocolate and then to cool it to the correct dipping temperature. Without tempering, melted chocolate often speckles or develops gray streaks as it hardens. This speckling, called blooming, affects only the appearance, not the quality or flavor, of the candy. Tempering is not needed for candy coating.

In a 1½-quart glass mixing bowl or 4-cup glass measure combine 1 pound chopped *semisweet chocolate or semisweet chocolate pieces* and 3 tablespoons *shortening*. Pour very warm tap water (100° to 110°) into a large mixing bowl to a depth of 1 inch. Place the container of chocolate inside the larger bowl. (The water should cover the bottom half of the chocolate container.) Stir the chocolate *constantly* with a rubber spatula for 15 to 20 minutes or until completely melted and smooth.

If the water begins to cool, replace it with warm water. (Avoid getting *any* water in the chocolate. Water causes chocolate to become thick and grainy. If this happens, stir in additional shortening, *1 teaspoon* at a time, until chocolate becomes shiny and smooth again.)

whipping cream. Cook over low heat, stirring constantly, till chocolate is melted. This should take about 10 minutes. Remove saucepan from heat.

Gradually stir about *half* of the hot mixture into the beaten egg yolk. Return egg mixture to saucepan. Cook over medium heat, stirring constantly, till slightly thickened. This should take about 2 minutes. Remove from heat.

Stir in rum, brandy, or whipping cream. Transfer chocolate mixture to a small mixing bowl. Chill about 1 hour or till mixture is room temperature and smooth, stirring occasionally.

Beat the cooled mixture with an electric mixer on medium speed about 2 minutes or till slightly fluffy. Chill about 15 minutes or till mixture holds its shape. Drop mixture from a *rounded teaspoon* onto a baking sheet lined with waxed paper. Chill about 30 minutes more or till firm. If desired, with hands, shape into smooth balls, working quickly so the truffles don't get too soft.

If using chocolate-flavored candy coating for dipping, in the bottom of a double boiler or a saucepan bring water to boiling. Remove from heat. Place chopped coating in top of double boiler or in a heatproof bowl and set over, but not touching, pan of water. Stir frequently till coating melts. *Or,* to melt coating in the microwave, in a 2½-quart microwave-safe bowl micro-cook coating on 100% power (high) 2 minutes. Stir. If necessary, micro-cook for 30 seconds more or till almost melted. Coating may not look melted until stirred.

Drop truffles, one at a time, into the melted, tempered chocolate or chocolate-flavored candy coating; turn truffles with a large, long-tined fork to coat. Lift
continued on page 24

continued from page 23

truffle out with the fork without piercing the centers; draw fork across rim of pan to remove excess chocolate. Invert truffles onto a waxed-paper-lined baking sheet. Twist fork slightly, as candy falls, to make a swirl on top. Let dipped truffles dry till chocolate hardens.

If the candy coating becomes too thick while dipping, reheat it in the microwave. *Or,* for coating that's been melted in a double boiler or for tempered chocolate, replace the cooled water with warm water. Stir the chocolate constantly until it once again reaches dipping consistency.

To decorate truffles, if desired, place melted vanilla-flavored or pink candy coating in a small, self-sealing plastic bag with a corner snipped off (opening should be very small) or a pastry bag, fitted with a small, round tip. Pipe coating in a design atop truffles. *Or,* drizzle coating atop truffles with a spoon. Let dry. Store truffles, tightly covered, in a cool, dry place for up to 2 weeks. Makes about 30 pieces.

Note: For quicker results, after chilling the shaped truffles for 30 minutes, roll them into *finely chopped nuts* or sifted *powdered sugar* instead of dipping them into melted chocolate. When using powdered sugar, you may need to roll truffles more than once since they tend to soak up the powdered sugar.

Nutrition information per chocolate-dipped truffle: 129 cal. (61% from fat), 10 g fat, 9 mg chol., 1 g pro., 12 g carbo., 0 g fiber, 19 mg sodium.

◆ Rum Truffels, Marzipan Treasures

Marzipan Treasures

MARZIPAN IS A CONFECTION MADE WITH almond paste or ground almonds, often tinted and molded into shapes. You can buy marzipan but you'll find this home-made version, with its rich, buttery flavor, worth making yourself—

1 8-ounce can almond paste
(see note, right)
¼ cup butter, softened
1 cup sifted powdered sugar
1 tablespoon amaretto, orange liqueur,
rum, or orange juice
2 teaspoons light corn syrup
1½ to 2 cups sifted powdered sugar
Food coloring (optional)*
Granulated sugar (optional)

Crumble almond paste into a small mixing bowl. Add butter. Beat with an electric mixer on medium speed till combined. Add the 1 cup powdered sugar; liqueur, rum, or orange juice; and corn syrup. Beat till mixture is thoroughly combined.

Shape mixture into a ball. Knead in as much of the remaining powdered sugar as needed till mixture is firm enough to hold its shape.

Divide into smaller portions to color (1 portion for each desired color). Add enough food coloring to each portion to get desired color. Shape right away or wrap each portion separately in foil or plastic wrap and chill till ready to shape, up to 24 hours. (If you chill longer, the candy mixture may start to dry out.)

For heart shapes, chill pink-colored and/or plain marzipan for 1 hour. If desired, knead pink and plain marzipan together to form a marbled effect.

Press into heart-shape candy molds. To remove hearts from molds, tap edge

To remove marzipan hearts from molds, tap the edge of the mold against a hard surface. If necessary, use a toothpick to gently loosen hearts.

With a toothpick, prick holes all over each marzipan strawberry to resemble seeds.

of mold against a hard surface. If needed, use a toothpick to gently loosen hearts (see how-to photo, *above*). Or, to omit chilling step, roll pieces of marzipan in granulated sugar, then mold. The sugar will help keep marzipan from sticking to mold.

For strawberries, roll red-colored marzipan into strawberry shapes (ovals with one end tapering to a point). With a toothpick, prick tiny holes all over each berry to resemble seeds (see how-to photo, *above*). Cut strawberry tops out of green-colored marzipan. Attach a top to wide end of each berry.

For apricot shapes, roll orange-colored marzipan into balls. Press 2 opposite ends to slightly flatten for top and bottom of apricot. With the blunt edge of a knife, make a vertical dent, from top to bottom, on rounded side of each ball. Use green-colored marzipan to make stems. Attach a stem to the top of each ball, pressing gently to make it stick.

Store, covered, in refrigerator for up to 7 days. Makes about 70 candies.

Note: Look for almond paste that does not contain glucose or syrups, as it may be too soft to shape.

*For richer-colored marzipan, use paste food coloring instead of the liquid form of food coloring.

Nutrition information per candy: 35 cal. (38% from fat), 2 g fat, 2 mg chol., 0 g pro., 5 g carbo., 7 mg sodium.

Lemon Tea Cakes

2½ cups all-purpose flour
2 cups sugar
1 teaspoon baking powder
½ teaspoon baking soda
⅛ teaspoon salt
1¼ cups buttermilk or sour milk
½ cup shortening, margarine,
or butter, softened
1 teaspoon vanilla
4 egg whites
1 tablespoon finely shredded lemon,
lime, or orange peel
1 tablespoon lemon, lime, or orange juice
Lemon Satin Icing (see recipe, page 26)
Candied violets and lilacs, edible flowers,
silver decorative candies, and/or
multicolored decorative candies (optional)
Semisweet chocolate, melted (optional)

continued on page 26

continued from page 25

Grease and lightly flour a 13x9x2-inch baking pan and set aside. In a large mixing bowl stir together flour, sugar, baking powder, baking soda, and salt. Add buttermilk or sour milk; shortening, margarine, or butter; and vanilla. Beat mixture with an electric mixer on low speed for 30 seconds or till ingredients are combined.

Beat on medium-high speed for 2 minutes, scraping sides of bowl occasionally. Add the egg whites, citrus peel, and juice; beat for 2 minutes more. Pour batter into prepared pan.

Bake in a 350° oven 35 to 40 minutes or till a wooden toothpick inserted near center comes out clean. Cool cake on wire rack for 10 minutes. Remove from pan; cool completely.

Using a serrated knife, trim edges and top of cake so that edges and top are smooth and straight. Cut cake into 1½-inch squares, diamonds, hearts, and/or circles. Brush off crumbs.

Place cake pieces on wire racks over waxed paper. Insert a 2- or 3-pronged, long-handled fork into the side of one cake piece. Holding cake piece over pan of Lemon Satin Icing, spoon enough icing over the cake to cover sides and top (see how-to photo, *right*). Place the iced cake back on the wire rack, making sure cake pieces do not touch. Repeat with remaining cake pieces; let dry .

Repeat with a second layer of icing, *except* place cake piece on top of the fork prongs (do not spear cake). If necessary, reuse icing that has dripped onto waxed paper, straining to remove crumbs.

To decorate, let icing dry. Top with candied violets and lilacs, edible flowers, silver decorative candies, and/or multi-colored decorative candies, if desired.

Edible Flowers

Before garnishing food with flowers, make sure that the flowers are not a poisonous variety and that they are pesticide-free. Your best option is to use garden-grown flowers or those commercially raised especially for eating.

Just because a flower is considered edible, or nontoxic, doesn't mean it tastes good. If you are using edible flowers as an ingredient rather than a garnish, sample the flowers first to make sure that they complement your dish.

Below are some common edible flowers and what they taste and/or smell like.

- Pansies—lettuce
- Squash Blossoms—sweet nectar
- Roses—floral
- Violets—very floral
- Carnations—bland and somewhat bitter
- Bachelor's Buttons—bland
- Lilacs—light floral
- Lavender—lemon perfume
- Nasturtiums—pepper, radish, watercress

Or, transfer any remaining icing or melted chocolate to a small, self-sealing plastic bag with a corner snipped off (opening should be very small) or a pastry bag, fitted with a small, round tip. Pipe icing or melted chocolate atop cakes to decorate.

Store cakes in a covered storage container for up to 48 hours. If storing for

To ice cakes, spear one cake piece with a fork and hold it over the pan of icing. Spoon icing over cake piece, covering sides and top. Repeat with the remaining cake pieces and icing.

more than an hour, wait till just before serving to decorate with edible flowers. Makes about 40 tea cakes.

Nutrition information per frosted cake: 184 cal. (13% from fat), 3 g fat, 0 mg chol., 1 g pro., 40 g carbo., 0 g fiber, 38 mg sodium.

Lemon Satin Icing

3 cups sugar
1½ cups hot water
¼ teaspoon cream of tartar
2 teaspoons lemon juice or ¼ teaspoon almond extract
1 teaspoon clear vanilla or vanilla

4 to 4½ cups sifted powdered sugar
Food coloring (optional)

In a medium 2-quart saucepan combine sugar, hot water, and cream of tartar. Bring the mixture to boiling over medium-high heat, stirring constantly for 5 to 9 minutes or till the sugar dissolves. Reduce heat to medium-low. Clip a candy thermometer to the side of the saucepan. Cook till thermometer registers 226° (takes about 12 minutes), stirring only when necessary to prevent sticking.

Remove pan from heat. Cool at room temperature, without stirring, to 110° (allow about 1 hour).

Add lemon juice or almond extract and vanilla to icing. Stir in enough of the powdered sugar to make the icing of drizzling consistency. If necessary, beat the icing with a rotary beater or wire whisk to remove any lumps. If desired, stir in a few drops of food coloring. Makes about 3½ cups icing.

Note: If icing gets too thick to drizzle, beat in a few drops of hot water.

Pecan Cake with Tangerine Cream Filling

2½ cups broken pecans, toasted
3 tablespoons all-purpose flour
4 teaspoons baking powder
6 eggs
1 cup granulated sugar
1 8-ounce package cream cheese, softened
¼ cup margarine or butter
½ cup packed brown sugar

continued on page 28
Lemon Tea Cakes ◆

continued from page 27
1 teaspoon finely shredded tangerine
peel or orange peel
1 teaspoon vanilla
Whipped Cream Frosting

In a blender container or food processor bowl place *half* of the pecans. Cover; blend or process till coarsely ground. Repeat with remaining nuts.

In a mixing bowl combine pecans, flour, and baking powder. In blender container or food processor bowl place eggs and sugar. Cover; blend or process till smooth. Add nut mixture. Cover; blend or process till smooth, stopping and scraping sides as needed to mix evenly (mixture may be foamy).

Spread in 2 greased and floured 8x1½-inch round baking pans. Bake in a 350° oven for 25 to 30 minutes or till light brown and top springs back when lightly touched (center may dip slightly). Cool on rack for 10 minutes. Remove from pans; cool thoroughly.

For tangerine filling, in a small mixing bowl beat cream cheese and margarine with an electric mixer on medium-high speed till fluffy. Gradually add brown sugar, beating for 3 to 4 minutes or till smooth. Stir in citrus peel and vanilla.

To assemble, with a serrated knife cut cakes in half horizontally. Place 1 split cake layer, cut side up, on a platter. Spread *one-third* of the filling atop cake. Place another split cake layer, cut side down, atop filling. Spread top with another *one-third* of the filling. Repeat with remaining cake layers and filling; end with a cake layer on top.

Frost top and sides of cake with Whipped Cream Frosting, reserving some of the frosting for piping, if desired. To decorate top of cake with piped frosting, place reserved frosting in a pastry bag, fitted with a large star tip. Pipe frosting atop cake in a ring. If desired, decorate with edible roses (see Edible Flowers tip box, *page 26*). Store frosted cake, covered, in the refrigerator for up to 4 hours. Makes 12 servings.

Whipped Cream Frosting: In a small chilled mixing bowl combine 1½ cups *whipping cream,* 2 tablespoons *sugar,* and ¾ teaspoon finely shredded *tangerine* or *orange peel.* Beat with chilled beaters on medium speed till soft peaks form. Use frosting immediately.

Nutrition information per serving: 507 cal. (68% from fat), 40 g fat, 178 mg chol., 7 g pro., 34 g carbo., 2 g fiber, 238 mg sodium.

Bittersweet Chocolate Torte With Raspberries

DUST THE BERRY TOPPING LIGHTLY WITH powdered sugar—

14 ounces bittersweet or semisweet
chocolate, coarsely chopped
½ cup margarine or butter
¼ cup milk
5 eggs
1 teaspoon vanilla
½ cup sugar
¼ cup all-purpose flour
¼ cup seedless red raspberry jam
1½ to 2 cups fresh red raspberries
powdered sugar (optional)

Grease the bottom of an 8-inch heart-shape cake pan with a removable bottom or an 8-inch round springform pan.

In a heavy medium saucepan combine chocolate, margarine, and milk. Cook and stir over low heat till chocolate melts. Remove from heat and cool 20 minutes.

In a mixing bowl beat eggs and vanilla with an electric mixer on low speed till well combined. Add sugar and flour; beat on high speed 10 minutes. Stir chocolate mixture into egg mixture. Transfer to prepared pan.

Bake in a 325° oven for 30 minutes (if using a springform pan, bake for 35 minutes) or till torte is slightly puffed on the outer one-third of the top. (Because this torte is so dense, you cannot use a traditional cake doneness test. It should be done after 30 minutes, even though center will still appear underbaked.)

Cool the torte on a wire rack about 20 minutes. While cooling, the torte may fall about ¼ inch in the center and may develop a brownielike, crusty surface on top. This is normal and will look fine when the torte is topped with the jam and fresh raspberries. With a knife, carefully loosen the torte from the sides of the pan. Cool completely (about 2 to 3 hours more). Remove the sides of the pan. Wrap the torte in foil and chill overnight or for up to 2 days. To serve, bring the torte to room temperature.

In a small saucepan melt raspberry jam; cool. Spread jam atop torte. Cover jam layer with raspberries, stem side down. If desired, using a sifter, dust berries lightly with powdered sugar just before serving. To cut, use a knife dipped in hot water. Serves 16.

Nutrition information per serving: 253 cal. (55% from fat), 17 g fat, 67 mg chol., 3 g pro., 27 g carbo., 1 g fiber, 89 mg sodium. RDA: 13% vit. A, 10% riboflavin.

Bittersweet Chocolate Torte with Raspberries ◆

Prize Tested Recipes.

Blackberry Frozen Yogurt

2 cups frozen or fresh unsweetened
blackberries or one 16 ½-ounce can
blackberries, drained
⅓ to ½ cup sugar
1 teaspoon unflavored gelatin
½ cup skim milk
¼ cup water
1 8-ounce carton plain nonfat yogurt
1 tablespoon finely shredded orange peel
¼ cup orange juice

Thaw berries, if frozen. In saucepan mix sugar and gelatin; stir in milk and water. Heat just till gelatin dissolves. Set aside to cool.

In a food processor bowl process berries till smooth. Press through sieve; discard seeds. Stir puree, yogurt, orange peel, and juice into gelatin mixture. Turn into a 2-quart electric ice-cream freezer. Freeze according to manufacturer's directions. (*Or,* pour into a 9x5x3-inch pan. Cover; freeze about 6 hours. Break into chunks. Transfer to a chilled bowl. Beat with an electric mixer till smooth but not melted. Return to cold loaf pan. Cover; freeze about 8 hours.) Makes six ½-cup servings.

Nutrition information per serving: 106 cal. (3% from fat), 0.3 g fat, 1 mg chol., 4 g pro., 24 g carbo., 41 mg sodium. RDA: 15% vit. C, 15% calcium.
$200 WINNER
Georgia Baciu, Friday Harbor, Wash.

Blackberry Frozen Yogurt ◆

Chocolate-Mint Cheesecake

SAVE ABOUT 520 CALORIES AND 32 GRAMS of fat compared to a higher-fat cheese-cake recipe—

½ cup crushed chocolate wafers (about 7)
1 cup low-fat cottage cheese
1 8-ounce package light cream cheese (Neufchâtel)
1 cup sugar
⅓ cup unsweetened cocoa powder
3 tablespoons crème de menthe liqueur
1 teaspoon vanilla
½ cup (4 ounces) frozen egg product, thawed
3 tablespoons miniature semisweet chocolate pieces
Halved, fanned whole strawberries or other fresh fruit (optional)

Sprinkle chocolate wafer crumbs evenly in the bottom of an 8-inch springform pan. Set aside.

In a food processor bowl or blender container, cover and process or blend cottage cheese till smooth. Add cream cheese, sugar, cocoa powder, liqueur, and vanilla. Process or blend till combined. (Mixture will be thick; scrape the sides of the bowl, if necessary.) Transfer mixture to a large mixing bowl. Stir in egg product and chocolate pieces. Pour into prepared pan.

Bake in a 300° oven for 35 to 40 minutes or till cheesecake appears nearly set when shaken. Cool on a wire rack for 10 minutes. *Loosen sides of pan. Cool 30 minutes more; remove sides of pan. Cool completely. Cover; chill several hours or overnight. Garnish with straw-berries or other fruit, if desired. Makes 12 servings.

*Note: Follow 10-minute cooling time before loosening from pan. Otherwise, the cheesecake may crack.

Nutrition information per serving: 175 cal. (34% from fat), 7 g fat, 16 mg chol., 6 g pro., 22 g carbo., 0 g fiber, 176 mg sodium.
$100 WINNER
Gloria Bellew, Oneonta, Ala.

Chocolate-Mint Cheesecake, *above left* ◆
Island Swordfish, *above* ◆

Island Swordfish

½ cup chopped fresh or canned mango or thawed, frozen peaches
¼ cup chopped avocado
¼ cup chopped red sweet pepper
2 tablespoons chopped red onion
1 teaspoon finely shredded lime or lemon peel (set aside)
2 tablespoons lime or lemon juice
1 tablespoon snipped fresh cilantro or parsley
1 teaspoon grated gingerroot or ¼ teaspoon ground ginger
2 cloves garlic, minced
Dash bottled hot pepper sauce (optional)
¼ cup lime or lemon juice
3 tablespoons dry white wine
1 tablespoon orange liqueur (optional)
½ teaspoon pepper

continued on page 32

continued from page 31

4 4-ounce swordfish steaks
(about ¾ inch thick)
Nonstick spray coating

In bowl stir together mango or peaches, avocado, red pepper, onion, the 2 tablespoons lime or lemon juice, cilantro or parsley, ginger, garlic, and hot pepper sauce. Cover and chill. (Let salsa stand at room temperature 20 minutes before serving with the fish.)

For marinade, in small bowl stir together the lime or lemon peel, remaining lime or lemon juice, wine, liqueur, and pepper. Place fish steaks in a shallow dish; pour marinade over fish steaks. Cover and chill 1 hour; drain fish steaks, discarding marinade.

Spray the unheated rack of a broiler pan with nonstick spray coating; place fish on rack. Broil 4 to 5 inches from heat for 8 to 12 minutes or till fish flakes easily with a fork, turning once during cooking. To serve, top fish with fruit salsa. Makes 4 servings.

Nutrition information per serving: 198 cal. (32% from fat), 7 g fat, 45 mg chol., 23 g pro., 9 g carbo., 0 g fiber, 112 mg sodium. RDA: 19% vit. A, 42% vit. C.

$200 WINNER
Laurie Watson, St. Louis, Mo.

Spicy Ginger-Garlic Chicken

THE SPECIAL MIX OF GINGER, GARLIC, cinnamon, and cardamom gives Purveen's aromatic dish its mouthwatering appeal—

4 cloves garlic, minced
1½ teaspoons grated gingerroot
½ teaspoon salt

¼ to ¾ teaspoon ground red pepper
¼ teaspoon black pepper
¼ teaspoon ground cinnamon
¼ teaspoon ground cardamom
1 tablespoon catsup
1 tablespoon red wine vinegar
1 teaspoon water
8 skinless, boneless, chicken breast halves
(2 pounds)

In a small bowl combine garlic, gingerroot, salt, red pepper, black pepper, cinnamon, and cardamom. Stir in catsup, vinegar, and water. Brush both sides

Spicy Ginger-Garlic Chicken ◆

of each chicken breast with garlic mixture. Place chicken in a shallow baking pan. Bake, uncovered, in a 375° oven for 45 to 55 minutes or till no longer pink. Makes 8 servings.

Nutrition information per serving: 126 cal. (24% from fat), 3 g fat, 59 mg chol., 21g pro., 1 g carbo., 0 g fiber, 210 mg sodium. RDA: 58% niacin.

$100 WINNER
Purveen Canteenwala, San Jose, Calif.

March

Make-Over Magic
Your Favorite Recipes Made Lighter

Prize Tested Recipes®
Honey Anise Bread, Wheat Swirl Bread,
South-of-the-Border Pie, Mideastern Cashew Salad Pitas

Make-Over Magic

Your Favorite Recipes Made Lighter

"Please make my recipe healthier!" wrote Jennifer Spencer of Romeo, Michigan, as did hundreds of readers in similar letters. So, we took a sampling of their recipes to our Test Kitchen and slashed calories, fat, cholesterol, and sodium—without sacrificing flavor.

Taco Salad

CATHIE ELIAS-WEST OF MISSION VIEJO, California, now bakes her tortilla bowls rather than frying them—

Tortilla Cups
Tomatillo Guacamole
½ pound lean ground beef
3 cloves garlic, minced
1 15-ounce can dark
red kidney beans, drained
¾ cup frozen whole kernel corn
1 8-ounce jar taco sauce
1 tablespoon chili powder
1 small head lettuce, torn into pieces
(about 8 cups)
2 medium tomatoes, chopped
1 large green pepper, chopped
¾ cup shredded reduced-fat sharp cheddar
cheese (3 ounces)

4 green onions, thinly sliced
Salsa (optional)

◆ Taco Salad

Prepare Tortilla Cups; set aside. Prepare Tomatillo Guacamole; chill.

In a medium skillet cook beef and garlic till beef is brown. Drain off fat. Stir in kidney beans, corn, taco sauce, and chili powder. Bring to boiling; reduce heat. Cover; simmer for 10 minutes.

Meanwhile, in a large bowl combine lettuce, tomatoes, green pepper, cheese, and green onions. Add beef mixture; toss to mix. To serve, divide lettuce mixture among Tortilla Cups. Top each with Tomatillo Guacamole and salsa, if desired. Makes 6 servings.

Tortilla Cups: Lightly brush six 9- or 10-inch *flour tortillas* with a small amount of *water* or spray *nonstick coating* onto one side of each tortilla.

Spray nonstick coating into 6 small oven-safe bowls or 16-ounce individual casseroles. Press tortillas, coated side up, into casseroles. Place a ball of foil in each tortilla cup to help hold its shape. Bake in a 350° oven for 15 to 20 minutes or till light brown. Remove foil. Cool; remove Tortilla Cups from bowls or casseroles. If desired, cups can be made ahead and stored in an airtight container for up to five days.

Tomatillo Guacamole: Rinse, drain, and finely chop 4 *canned tomatillos* (about ⅓ cup). (*Or,* simmer 2 husked tomatillos, about 3½ ounces, in boiling water for 10 minutes. Drain and chop.) In a small mixing bowl combine tomatillos; ½ of a small seeded, peeled, and chopped avocado (about ½ cup); 2 tablespoons chopped canned *green chili peppers;* and ⅛ teaspoon *garlic salt.* Cover and chill up to 24 hours. Makes about ¾ cup.

Nutrition information per serving: 361 cal., 13 g fat, 41 mg chol., 24 g pro., 44 g carbo., 479 mg sodium, 8 g fiber. RDA: 25% calcium, 30% iron, 24% vit. A, 77% vit. C, 19% thiamine, 30% riboflavin, 19% niacin.

Spaghetti Alla Carbonara

LINDA COLUCCI OF STANFORD, Connecticut, enjoys evaporated skim milk as a flavorful substitute for cream—

> 8 ounces linguine or spaghetti
> Nonstick spray coating
> 2 slices turkey bacon, sliced
> crosswise into strips
> 1 beaten egg
> 1 cup evaporated skim milk
> ½ cup frozen peas

continued on page 36
Spaghetti Alla Carbonara ◆

hot, cooked pasta; toss to coat. Transfer to a warm serving platter. Sprinkle with black pepper and remaining Parmesan cheese. Serve immediately. Makes 4 main-dish servings.

Nutrition information per serving: 383 cal., 7g fat, 71 mg chol., 22 g pro., 56 g carbo., 362 mg sodium, 1 g fiber. RDA: 41% calcium, 20% iron, 17% vit. A, 38% thiamine, 36% riboflavin, 21% niacin.

Greek Spanakopita

LORI KELTON OF GERMANTOWN, New York, saves fat by using less cheese and phyllo dough than in her original recipes—

2 pounds fresh spinach leaves or two 10-ounce packages frozen chopped spinach, thawed
1¼ cups chopped onion
2 cups low-fat cottage cheese, well drained
1 cup crumbled feta cheese (4 ounces)
1 8-ounce carton frozen egg product, thawed (1 cup)
⅓ cup quick-cooking rice
2 tablespoons snipped fresh basil or 2 teaspoons dried basil, crushed
¼ teaspoon salt
⅛ teaspoon ground nutmeg
⅛ teaspoon pepper
Nonstick spray coating
3 sheets frozen phyllo dough (18x14-inch rectangles), thawed
2 teaspoons margarine or butter, melted

Wash, stem, and chop spinach, if using fresh. In a large saucepan cook fresh spinach, covered, in a small amount of boiling water 3 to 5 minutes. (Do not cook frozen spinach.)

Drain fresh-cooked or frozen-thawed

◆ Greek Spanakopita
continued from page 35

¼ cup chopped red sweet pepper
¼ teaspoon crushed red pepper
½ cup freshly shredded or grated Parmesan cheese (about 2 ounces)
Black pepper

Cook linguine or spaghetti according to package directions.

Meanwhile, spray a medium saucepan with nonstick coating. Cook bacon in saucepan till crisp and light brown. Drain bacon on paper towels. Wipe saucepan clean with paper towel. For sauce, in same saucepan combine egg, evaporated skim milk, peas, sweet pepper, and crushed red pepper.

Cook and stir over medium heat just till the mixture coats a metal spoon (about 6 minutes). *Do not boil.* Stir in bacon and *half* of the Parmesan cheese. Heat through. Immediately pour over spinach well in a colander, pressing with the back of a spoon to force out excess liquid; set aside.

In a small skillet cook onion in small amount of boiling water, covered, till crisp-tender; drain. In a large mixing bowl combine the spinach, onion, drained cottage cheese, feta, egg product, *uncooked* rice, basil, salt, nutmeg, and pepper. Spray a 13x9x2-inch baking dish with nonstick coating. Spread the spinach mixture in the dish. Spray one sheet of phyllo with nonstick coating; fold in half crosswise. Place atop spinach mixture. Spray the top of the sheet again lightly with nonstick coating. Repeat with remaining sheets of phyllo dough. Brush the top layer with melted margarine or butter. Bake in a 375° oven for 40 to 45 minutes or till golden. Let stand for 5 to 10 minutes before cutting into triangles or squares. Makes 8 main-dish or 16 to 20 appetizer servings.

Nutrition information per main-dish serving: 167 cal., 5 g fat, 15 mg chol., 16 g pro., 16 g carbo., 596 mg sodium, 0 g fiber. RDA: 30% calcium, 28% iron, 96% vit. A, 18% vit. C, 15% thiamine, 29% riboflavin.

Turkey Enchiladas

JENNY SPENCER'S ENCHILADAS CHECK in with 22 grams less of fat—

½ cup chopped onion
Nonstick spray coating
½ of an 8-ounce package light cream cheese (Neufchâtel), softened
1 tablespoon water
¾ teaspoon ground cumin

continued on page 38
Turkey Enchiladas ◆

about ¼ *cup* turkey mixture on *each* tortilla; roll up. Place, seam side down, in the baking dish. For sauce, in a medium mixing bowl combine soup, sour cream, milk, and chili peppers; pour over enchiladas. Bake, covered, in a 350° oven about 40 minutes or till heated through. Sprinkle enchiladas with cheddar cheese. Bake, uncovered, for 4 to 5 minutes more or till cheese is melted. Top with snipped *cilantro or parsley, tomatoes,* and *green pepper,* if desired. Makes 12.

Nutrition information per enchilada: 256 cal., 10 g fat, 44 mg chol., 21 g pro., 21 g carbo., 271 mg sodium, 1 g fiber. RDA: 18% calcium, 11% iron, 16% riboflavin, 27% niacin.

Beef Stew with Sour Cream Biscuits

DRAINING THE MEAT AND USING reduced-fat sour cream mean less fat in this family-favorite stew of Esther R. Bowring's of Arlington, Virginia—

¾ pound boneless beef top round steak, cut
into ½-inch cubes
1 tablespoon all-purpose flour
Nonstick spray coating
1 cup chopped onion
3 medium potatoes, cubed
1 14½-ounce can Italian-style
stewed tomatoes
½ of a 6-ounce can low-sodium
tomato paste (⅓ cup)
2½ cups water
2 teaspoons instant beef bouillon granules
1 tablespoon sugar
1 teaspoon dried thyme, crushed
1 teaspoon Worcestershire sauce
1 bay leaf
1 cup cubed eggplant, peeled, if desired
Sour Cream Biscuits

◆ Beef Stew With Sour Cream Biscuits
continued from page 37
4 cups chopped cooked turkey or chicken
¼ cup chopped pecans, toasted
12 6-inch flour tortillas
1 10¾-ounce can reduced-sodium
condensed cream of chicken soup
1 8-ounce carton reduced-calorie
dairy sour cream
1 cup skim milk
1 or 2 tablespoons pickled jalapeño pepper
strips, finely chopped
½ cup shredded reduced-fat sharp cheddar
cheese (2 ounces)

In a small skillet cook onion, covered, in a small amount of water over medium heat till tender; drain. For enchiladas, spray a 13x9x2-inch baking dish with nonstick coating. In a small bowl stir together cream cheese, water, cumin, and *salt* to taste, if desired. Stir in cooked onion, turkey, and pecans.

Meanwhile, wrap tortillas in foil. Heat in a 350° oven for 10 to 15 minutes or till softened. (*Or,* wrap tortillas in microwave-safe paper towels and microcook on 100% power [high] for 30 to 60 seconds or till softened.) Spoon

⅓ cup reduced-fat dairy sour cream
1 tablespoon all-purpose flour
2 teaspoons milk
1 teaspoon sesame seed (optional)
Fresh thyme (optional)

In a plastic bag combine meat and the 1 tablespoon flour; shake to coat meat. Spray a 4½-quart Dutch oven with nonstick coating. Add meat and onion; cook till meat is brown and onion is tender. Drain off any fat. Add potatoes, *undrained* tomatoes, tomato paste, water, bouillon, sugar, thyme, Worcestershire sauce, and bay leaf. Bake, covered, in a 350° oven for 1 hour. Add eggplant. Cover and bake for 30 minutes more.

Meanwhile, prepare Sour Cream Biscuits. Remove stew from oven; increase oven temperature to 425°. Discard bay leaf. Combine sour cream and remaining 1 tablespoon flour; stir into stew. Brush biscuits with milk. Sprinkle biscuits with sesame seed, if desired.

Arrange cutout biscuits atop meat mixture. Bake, uncovered, for 20 to 25 minutes or till biscuits are golden. If desired, garnish each serving with fresh thyme. Makes 6 servings.

Sour Cream Biscuits: In a large mixing bowl stir together 1¼ cups *all-purpose flour* and 1½ teaspoons *baking powder*. Cut in ¼ cup *margarine or butter* till mixture resembles coarse crumbs. Stir in ⅓ cup *reduced-fat dairy sour cream* and ¼ cup skim *milk*. On a lightly floured surface knead dough 8 to 10 times. Roll or pat to ½-inch thickness. With a 2-inch biscuit cutter, cut dough into circles. Makes 12 biscuits.

Nutrition information per serving: 408 cal., 13 g fat, 40 mg chol., 22 g pro., 53 g carbo., 757 mg sodium, 2 g fiber. RDA: 17% calcium, 25% iron, 28% vit. A, 39% vit. C, 36% thiamine, 29% riboflavin, 40% niacin.

Breakfast Casserole ◆

Breakfast Casserole

TURKEY SAUSAGE AND AN EGG SUBSTITUTE cut the cholesterol for Elizabeth Ming Cooper of Redmond, Washington—

6 slices whole wheat bread
Nonstick spray coating
½ pound ground turkey sausage
1 medium red or green sweet pepper,
  chopped (about ¾ cup)
½ cup chopped fresh mushrooms
4 ounces shredded reduced-fat sharp
  cheddar cheese (1 cup)
1 10¾-ounce can reduced-sodium
  condensed cream of mushroom soup

1 8-ounce carton frozen egg product
  (1 cup), thawed
1 cup evaporated skim milk
¾ teaspoon dry mustard
⅛ teaspoon pepper

Cut bread into cubes; place in a large, shallow pan. Bake in a 350° oven for 8 to 10 minutes or till toasted, stirring once. Spray a 12x7½x2-inch baking dish with nonstick coating. Place *half* of the toasted bread cubes in the dish; set aside.

Meanwhile, in a large skillet cook sausage, sweet pepper, and mushrooms over medium-high heat till sausage is brown. Drain off fat. Pat vegetable mixture with a paper towel to remove excess fat. Spoon mixture atop bread cubes in dish. Sprinkle with *half* of the shredded cheese. Top with remaining bread.

In a medium mixing bowl combine soup, egg product, evaporated milk, mustard, and pepper. Pour over bread, pressing down cubes with back of spoon, to moisten. Cover; chill for at least 2 hours or for up to 24 hours.

To serve, bake in a 350° oven for 30 minutes or till a knife inserted near the center comes out clean. Sprinkle with remaining cheese. Bake 2 to 3 minutes more. Let stand for 5 to 10 minutes before serving. Makes 6 to 8 servings.

Nutrition information per serving: 322 cal., 14 g fat, 32 mg chol., 25 g pro., 23 g carbo., 932 mg sodium, 3 g fiber. RDA: 39% calcium, 19% iron, 23% vit. A, 20% vit. C, 34% riboflavin.

Dutch oven cook onion in margarine till tender. Stir in curry powder; cook and stir 1 minute over medium-low heat. Stir in carrots, water, and bouillon. Bring to boiling. Cook, uncovered, 10 minutes or till carrots are just tender.

In a small mixing bowl stir together the evaporated milk, buttermilk, and cornstarch; add to saucepan. Stir in lemon juice, salt, and pepper. Cook and stir till thickened and bubbly. Add shrimp and green pepper; return to boiling. Cook and stir 2 minutes more or till shrimp turn pink. Serve over rice with desired condiments. Makes 8 servings.

Nutrition information per serving: 303 cal., 4 g fat, 133 mg chol., 22 g pro., 45 g carbo., 431 mg sodium, 4 g fiber. RDA: 27% calcium, 22% iron, 137% vit. A, 29% vit. C,18% thiamine, 21% riboflavin, 26% niacin.

◆ Shrimp Curry

Shrimp Curry

BERYL MANLEY WAUSON OF CENTENNIAL, Wyoming, can flavor her recipe with buttermilk to save fat—

2 pounds fresh or frozen large
shrimp in shells
½ cup chopped onion
1 tablespoon margarine or butter
1 tablespoon curry powder
4 medium carrots, bias-sliced
¼ inch thick
½ cup water
1 teaspoon instant chicken
bouillon granules
1 12-ounce can evaporated skim milk

¾ cup buttermilk
3 tablespoons cornstarch
2 tablespoons lemon juice
¼ teaspoon salt
⅛ teaspoon pepper
½ cup chopped green pepper
Hot cooked brown rice
Assorted condiments, such as
2 bananas, sliced; ½ cup drained
pineapple chunks, coarsely chopped; ¼ cup
golden raisins; ½ cup chutney and/or ¼ cup
unsweetened coconut (chopped if pieces are
large) or coarsely chopped peanuts

Thaw shrimp, if frozen. Peel and devein. Cut down the back of each shrimp, cutting completely in half. Meanwhile, in a large saucepan or

Basil-Potato Soup

NANCY RICE OF WHITE BEAR LAKE, Minnesota, finds her soup more healthful with buttermilk and Canadian-style bacon—

1 large onion, finely chopped
4 fresh shiitake or button
mushrooms, sliced (about ½ cup)
2 teaspoons olive oil or cooking oil
3 large potatoes, peeled and thinly sliced
(about 4½ cups)
1 14½-ounce can beef broth
1 14½-ounce can reduced-sodium
chicken broth
½ cup buttermilk
1 tablespoon cornstarch
2 slices (1½ ounces) Canadian-style bacon,
chopped (about ⅓ cup)
1 tablespoon snipped fresh basil or
1 teaspoon dried basil, crushed

¼ cup reduced-calorie dairy sour
cream or plain low-fat yogurt
Fresh basil leaves (optional)

Cook onion and mushrooms in hot
oil over medium-high heat till onion is
tender and light brown. Add potatoes,
beef broth, and chicken broth. Bring to
boiling; reduce heat. Cover and simmer
30 minutes or till potatoes are tender.

In a small bowl stir together buttermilk and cornstarch; stir into broth mixture. Stir in bacon and basil. Cook and
stir till thickened and bubbly. Cook and
stir for 2 minutes more. Top each serving with sour cream or yogurt. If
desired, garnish with basil. Makes 6
side-dish servings.

Microwave directions: In a 2-quart
microwave-safe casserole combine
onion, mushrooms, and oil. Micro-
cook, covered, on 100% power (high)
for 2 to 4 minutes or till onion is tender.
Add potatoes and chicken and beef
broth. Cook, covered, on high for 15 to
18 minutes (low-wattage ovens: 20 to 25
minutes) or till potatoes are tender, stirring once.

Stir together buttermilk and cornstarch; stir into casserole. Stir in bacon
and basil. Cook, uncovered, on high
about 5 minutes (low-wattage ovens: 7
minutes) or till mixture is slightly thickened and bubbly, stirring after every
minute. Cook for 2 minutes more, stirring once. Serve as directed.

*Nutrition information per 1-cup
serving:* 162 cal., 4 g fat, 6 mg chol., 7 g
pro., 26 g carbo., 565 mg sodium, 1 g
fiber. RDA: 19% vit. C, 17% thiamine,
10% riboflavin.

Basil Potato Soup ◆

◆ Creamy Potluck Potatoes

Creamy Potluck Potatoes

REDUCED-CALORIE SOUR CREAM AND reduced-fat cheese let Brenda Hudson of Springfield, Oregon, enjoy the richness without the guilt—

5 large (2½ pounds) potatoes, peeled and
    chopped (7½ cups)
1 10¾-ounce can reduced-sodium
    condensed cream of chicken soup
½ cup reduced-calorie dairy sour cream
½ of an 8-ounce package light cream cheese
    (Neufchâtel), softened
½ of a ½-ounce package butter-flavored
    mix (about 1 tablespoon)
¾ cup shredded reduced-fat sharp cheddar
    cheese (3 ounces)
¼ cup sliced green onion
¼ cup skim milk
1 tablespoon dried parsley flakes
¼ teaspoon garlic salt

Cook potatoes in boiling water for 10 to 12 minutes or till tender. Drain. Rinse with cold water. Drain again.

In a large mixing bowl stir together the soup, sour cream, cream cheese, and the dry butter-flavored mix. Add ¼ cup of the shredded cheese, 3 tablespoons of the green onion, the skim milk, parsley, garlic salt, and ¼ teaspoon pepper; stir mixture to combine. Stir in the cooked potatoes. Transfer the mixture to a 2-quart shallow casserole or 12x7½x2-inch baking dish.

Bake, uncovered, in a 350° oven for 30 to 35 minutes or till heated through. Sprinkle with remaining cheese. Bake 5 minutes more or till cheese melts. Sprinkle with remaining green onion. Makes 10 servings.

Nutrition information per serving: 174 cal., 5 g fat, 16 mg chol., 6 g pro., 26 g carbo., 205 mg sodium, 0 g fiber. RDA: 12% calcium, 10% vit. A, 15% vit. C, 10% thiamine, 10% niacin.

Fall Apple Cake

WE SUBSTITUTED EGG WHITES FOR EGGS in spiced cake from Marie Ann Donovan of Chicago, Illinois—

1¼ cups sugar
½ cup cooking oil
2 egg whites
1 egg
2 teaspoons vanilla
1 cup apple juice
2 cups all-purpose flour
¾ cup whole wheat flour
2 teaspoons baking powder
2 teaspoons ground cinnamon
1 teaspoon ground nutmeg
½ teaspoon baking soda
3 cups peeled, cored, and sliced cooking
    apples (such as Golden
    Delicious or McIntosh)
½ cup finely chopped walnuts, toasted
Powdered sugar (optional)
Vanilla yogurt (optional)

In a large mixing bowl beat sugar and oil on medium speed of an electric mixer till combined; add egg whites, egg, and vanilla. Beat on medium speed for 1 minute or till creamy. Stir in juice.

In a medium mixing bowl stir together all-purpose flour, whole wheat flour, baking powder, cinnamon, nutmeg, and baking soda. Stir flour mixture into egg mixture. Gently stir in the apples and the walnuts. Pour into a greased and floured 10-inch tube pan.

Bake in a 350° oven for 60 to 65 minutes or till wooden pick inserted comes out clean. Cool in pan for 10 minutes. Remove from pan; cool on a wire rack for 30 minutes. Serve warm. If desired, sprinkle with powdered sugar; serve with vanilla yogurt and additional nutmeg. Makes 12 servings.

Nutrition information per serving:
323 cal., 13 g fat, 17 mg chol., 5 g pro.,
49 g carbo., 99 mg sodium, 2 g fiber.
RDA: 49% calcium, 11% iron, 19%
thiamine, 13% riboflavin.

Fall Apple Cake ◆

Carrot-Raisin Muffins ◆

Carrot-Raisin Muffins

CORN SYRUP REPLACES THE OIL IN THIS
muffin recipe. from Mary Dunneback of
Chicago, Illinois—

1½ cups all-purpose flour
½ cup whole wheat flour
½ cup sugar
2 teaspoons baking powder
½ teaspoon ground cinnamon
¼ teaspoon ground ginger
2 beaten eggs
1 8-ounce can crushed pineapple (juice pack)
¼ cup finely shredded carrot
¼ cup raisins
2 tablespoons light corn syrup
1 teaspoon vanilla
Nonstick spray coating
¼ cup finely chopped walnuts

In a large mixing bowl stir together
flours, sugar, baking powder, cinnamon,
and ginger. Make a well in the center;
set aside. In a small mixing bowl stir
together eggs, *undrained* pineapple, carrot, raisins, corn syrup, and vanilla; add
all at once to flour mixture. Stir just till
moistened. Spray 12 standard-size muffin cups with nonstick coating or line
cups with paper bake cups. Divide batter
evenly among muffin cups. Sprinkle
with nuts. Bake in a 400° oven about 20
minutes or till golden. Serve warm.
Makes 12 muffins.

Nutrition information per muffin:
162 cal., 3 g fat, 36 mg chol., 4 g pro.,
31 g carbo., 63 mg sodium, 1 g fiber.

Low-Fat Products—What to Look for

Many of the Make-Over Magic
recipes call for low-fat products.
For recipe testing and for the nutri-
tional analyses that accompany the
recipes, the following products
were used. Note the fat content of
these ingredients so that when you
grocery shop, you can buy similar
products to use in the recipes.

Food	Grams of Fat
Reduced-calorie	
dairy sour cream (1 oz.**)	.2.0
Reduced-fat cheese (1 oz.)	5.0
Light cream cheese (1 oz.)	7.0
Low-fat* yogurt (1 oz.**)	0.4
Non-fat* yogurt (1 oz.**)	0.1
Skim milk (1 cup)	0.4
Lean ground beef,	
90% lean (1 oz.)	.2.7
Evaporated skim milk (1 cup)	0.8
Ground turkey sausage (1 oz.)	4.2
Turkey bacon (1 slice)	2.4
1% Low-fat cottage	
cheese (1 cup)	.2.3

*You may use either non-fat or
low-fat yogurt in these recipes.
**1 oz. sour cream or yogurt =
about 2 tablespoons.

Honey Anise Bread

ANISEED GIVES THIS TOP-NOTCH BREAD A light licorice flavor—

5¼ to 5¾ cups all-purpose flour
2 packages active dry yeast
2¼ cups water
½ cup honey
3 tablespoons margarine or butter
1 teaspoon salt
1 cup whole wheat flour
½ cup cracked wheat
3 tablespoons aniseed, crushed

In a mixing bowl combine *2 cups* of the all-purpose flour and the yeast. In a saucepan heat water, honey, margarine, and salt, stirring constantly, till mixture is warm (120° to 130°). Add to flour mixture. Beat with an electric mixer on low speed 30 seconds; scraping bowl constantly. Beat on high speed for 3 minutes more.

Using a large spoon, stir in whole wheat flour, cracked wheat, and aniseed. Stir in as much of the remaining all-purpose flour as you can. Turn out onto a floured surface. Knead in enough of the remaining all-purpose flour to make a moderately stiff dough (6 to 8 minutes). Shape into a ball. Place in a lightly greased bowl; turn once to grease surface. Cover; let rise in a warm place till double (about 45 minutes). Punch dough down. Turn out onto a floured surface; divide in half. Cover; let rest 10 minutes.

◆ Honey Anise Bread

Lightly grease two 8x4x2- or 9x5x3-inch loaf pans. Shape each half into a loaf; place into prepared pans. Cover; let rise in a warm place till nearly double (30 to 40 minutes).

Bake in a 375° oven 40 to 45 minutes or till bread sounds hollow when lightly tapped. Cover with foil the last 15 minutes of baking to prevent over-browning, if necessary. Immediately remove from pans. Cool on racks. Makes 2 loaves (32 servings).

Nutrition information per serving: 115 cal., 1 g fat, 0 mg chol., 3 g pro., 23 g carbo., 81 mg sodium, 1 g fiber. RDA: 16% thiamine, 14% riboflavin, 10% niacin.
$200 WINNER
Rendi A. Hahn, Grand Prairie, Tex.

Wheat Swirl Bread

IF YOU LIKE LARGER LOAVES, YOU CAN make this honey-sweet bread in four 8x4x2-inch pans, baking until bread tests done—

4½ to 5 cups all-purpose flour
2 packages active dry yeast
2 cups milk
½ cup honey
¼ cup margarine or butter
1 teaspoon salt
1 egg
1 cup whole wheat flour
½ cup rye flour
½ cup toasted wheat germ
¼ cup margarine or butter, softened
⅔ cup packed brown sugar

In a mixing bowl combine *2 cups* of the all-purpose flour and the yeast. Heat milk, honey, ¼ cup margarine, and salt till warm (120° to 130°). Add to flour mixture; add egg. Beat with electric mixer on low speed 30 seconds, scraping bowl constantly. Beat on high 3 minutes. Stir in wheat and rye flours, wheat germ, and as much remaining all-purpose flour as you can. Turn out onto a floured surface. Knead in enough all-purpose flour to make a moderately stiff dough (6 to 8 minutes). Place into a greased bowl. Cover; let rise in a warm place till nearly double (1¼ hours).

Punch dough down. Turn out onto a floured surface; divide in half. Cover; let rest 10 minutes. Roll *each* half to a 15-inch square. Spread with softened margarine; sprinkle with brown sugar. Roll up jelly-roll style; cut into thirds. Seal ends; place into six greased 5½x3x2-inch pans. Cover; let rise in a warm place till double (about 45 minutes). Bake in a 350° oven about 30 minutes or till

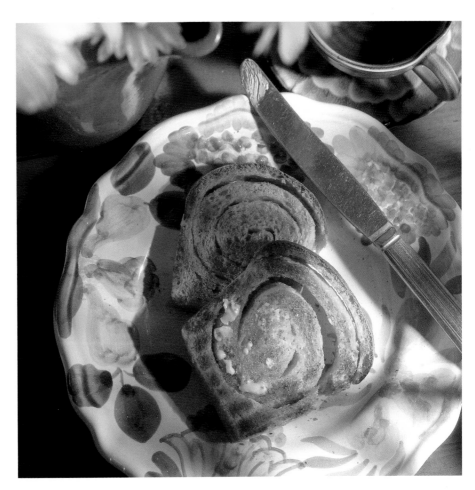

loaves sound hollow when tapped. Remove from pans. Makes 6 small loaves (48 servings).

Nutrition information per serving: 98 cal., 2 g fat, 5 mg chol., 3 g pro., 19 g carbo., 19 mg sodium, 1 g fiber. RDA: 12% thiamine

$100 WINNER
Arlene Samuelson, Oelwein, Iowa

South-of-the-Border Pie

RICE, BEANS, CHEESE, AND SEASONINGS make up this microwave chili-like pie—

continued on page 46

Wheat Swirl Bread, *top* ◆
South-of-the-Border Pie, *above* ◆

continued from page 45

1 cup chopped onion
1 tablespoon olive oil or cooking oil
1 to 2 teaspoons chili powder
1 teaspoon ground cumin
½ teaspoon garlic powder
¼ teaspoon salt
1 15-ounce can red kidney beans, drained
1½ cups cooked brown rice
1 cup shredded cheddar cheese
¾ cup milk
2 beaten eggs
Nonstick spray coating
Chopped green sweet pepper (optional)
Salsa (optional)

In a saucepan cook onion in hot oil till tender. Stir in chili powder, cumin, garlic powder, and salt. Cook 1 minute more. Cool. Stir in beans, rice, cheese, milk, and eggs. Spray a 10-inch microwave-safe pie plate with nonstick spray coating; add rice mixture.

Micro-cook, uncovered, on 50% power (medium) for 22 to 24 minutes or till center is just set, giving dish a quarter turn twice. (Or, bake, uncovered, in a 350° oven about 25 minutes or till center is just set.) Let stand 10 minutes. Garnish with chopped green sweet pepper and serve with salsa, if desired. Makes 6 servings.

Nutrition information per serving: 257 cal., 12 g fat, 93 mg chol., 14 g pro., 27 g carbo., 366 mg sodium, 5 g fiber. RDA: 27% calcium, 11% iron.

$200 WINNER
Jennifer Summers, Fayetteville, Ariz.

Mideastern Cashew Salad Pitas ◆

Mideastern Cashew Salad Pitas

CRUNCHY CASHEWS, CUCUMBER, SWEET pepper, and a curry-yogurt sauce make up this winning sandwich—

1 8-ounce carton plain yogurt
1 to 2 tablespoons snipped fresh cilantro or parsley
¼ teaspoon curry powder
1 cup dry roasted cashews
1 cup chopped cucumber
1 cup chopped red and/or green sweet pepper
½ cup chopped red onion
4 pita bread rounds, split

In medium mixing bowl stir together yogurt, cilantro or parsley, and curry powder. Stir in cashews, cucumber, sweet pepper, and red onion. Spoon evenly into split pita rounds. Makes 4 servings.

Note: To tote this sandwich for lunch, pack the cashew salad in an airtight container. Place container in an insulated lunch box with a frozen ice pack. (Cashew salad will hold for up to 6 hours.) Spoon the salad into the pita just before eating.

Nutrition information per serving: 345 cal., 17g fat, 3 mg chol., 13 g pro., 38 g carbo., 262 mg sodium, 4 g fiber. RDA: 20% calcium, 19% iron, 65% vit. C, 34% thiamine, 21% riboflavin, 15% niacin.

$100 WINNER
Maureen Valentine, Seatac, Wash.

April

Spring Delicious

20 Fresh Recipes for Brunch and Outdoor Parties

Prize Tested Recipes®

Portuguese-Style Turkey Steaks, Midwestern Baked Chili, Hot Mexican

Potato Salad, Scalloped Potatoes and Spinach

Spring Delicious

20 Fresh Recipes for Brunch and Outdoor Parties

Brunch Menu Suggestions

Strawberry-Melon Soup
with Ginger Melon Balls

◆ ◆ ◆

Scrambled Eggs with Smoked Salmon
and Rosemary Roasted New Potatoes

◆ ◆ ◆

Spinach-Feta Tart

◆ ◆ ◆

Steamed Asparagus Bundles

◆ ◆ ◆

Assorted Homemade Breads

◆ ◆ ◆

Juice, Tea, Coffee

Strawberry-Melon Soup with Ginger Melon Balls

PUREE THIS APPETIZER THE NIGHT before—

1 small cantaloupe
½ of a small honeydew melon
½ cup unsweetened pineapple juice
⅛ cup sugar
1 tablespoon grated gingerroot
4 cups fresh or frozen unsweetened
strawberries
1 8-ounce carton vanilla yogurt
1 8-ounce carton dairy sour cream
2 cups milk

Using a small melon baller scoop *half* of the cantaloupe and the honeydew into balls (see how-to photo, *right*), or use a knife to cut melon into cubes. (You should have about 4 cups cantaloupe and 2 cups honeydew.) Set aside 2 cups of the cantaloupe.

In a small saucepan combine pineapple juice, sugar, and gingerroot. Bring to boiling, stirring till sugar is dissolved. Reduce heat; simmer, uncovered, over medium heat for 5 to 7 minutes or till the mixture is the consistency of a thin syrup. Remove from heat; cool.

Transfer syrup to a storage container. Add the 2 cups cantaloupe pieces and 2 cups honeydew pieces. Cover and chill the melon overnight.

To make melon balls, plunge the melon baller into the melon till covered. Then, turn the baller in a complete circle.

Meanwhile, in a blender container or food processor bowl cover and blend or process strawberries till smooth; remove puree and set aside. Cover and blend or process reserved 2 cups cubed cantaloupe till smooth.

In a large mixing bowl stir together yogurt and sour cream. Add strawberries, blended melon, and milk; stir till combined. Cover and chill overnight.

To serve, drain melon balls, reserving syrup; stir reserved syrup into chilled soup. Ladle soup into bowls; top with melon balls. Makes 8 to10 servings.

Cost per serving: 69 cents

Nutrition information per serving: 211 cal., 8 g fat, 19 mg chol., 5 g pro., 32 g carbo., 71 mg sodium, 3 g fiber. RDA: 21% calcium, 38% vit. A, 126% vit. C, 10% thiamine, 20% riboflavin.

Spinach-Feta Tart

BAKE THE PASTRY SHELL AHEAD, THEN finish the tart the day of your brunch—

Pastry for Single-Crust Pie
(see recipe, page 50)
2 eggs

continued on page 50
Strawberry-Melon Soup with Ginger Melon Balls ◆

purpose flour and ¼ teaspoon *salt.* Cut in ⅓ cup *shortening* till pieces are the size of small peas. Sprinkle 1 tablespoon of *cold water* over part of the mixture; gently toss with a fork. Push to side of bowl. Repeat with 2 to 3 tablespoons more *cold water* till all is moistened. Form into a ball.

Make-ahead directions for tart shell: Bake the pastry shell the day before; store in a cool, dry place.

Cost per serving: 43 cents

Nutrition information per serving: 234 cal., 15 g fat, 71 mg chol., 9 g pro., 16 g carbo., 239 mg sodium, 1 g fiber. RDA: 21% calcium, 10% iron, 15% vit. A, 15% thiamine, 19% riboflavin.

Scrambled Eggs with Smoked Salmon

ROSEMARY ROASTED NEW POTATOES (recipe, *opposite*) go well with this egg dish—

12 eggs
⅔ cup milk, half-and-half, or light cream
½ cup sliced green onion or ¼ cup snipped chives
¼ teaspoon salt
¼ teaspoon pepper
1 tablespoon olive oil or cooking oil
1 cup chopped smoked salmon (lox style) or fully cooked ham (5 ounces)
1 cup shredded provolone or fontina cheese
1 tomato, seeded and chopped

In a mixing bowl beat eggs with a fork. Add milk or cream, green onion or chives, salt, and pepper.

In a large skillet cook egg mixture in hot oil. Cook, without stirring, till eggs begin to set on bottom and around edge. Using a spatula, lift and fold partially

◆ Spinach-Feta Tart
continued from page 48

continued from page 48

1 cup chopped fresh spinach
1 cup ricotta cheese
½ cup crumbled feta cheese
¼ cup milk
2 teaspoons snipped fresh oregano or ¾ teaspoon dried oregano, crushed
2 tablespoons grated Parmesan cheese
Red sweet pepper (optional)
Yellow sweet pepper (optional).
Crumbled feta cheese (optional)
Fresh herbs (optional)

Prepare pastry dough. On a lightly floured surface flatten dough with your hands. Roll from center to edge, forming a 12-inch circle.

Loosely wrap pastry around a rolling pin. Unroll onto a 10-inch tart pan with a removable bottom, easing into pan. Trim pastry even with rim of pan. *Do not prick.* Line pastry with a double thickness of heavy foil. Bake in a 450° oven for 8 minutes. Remove foil. Bake for 5 to 7 minutes more or till golden. Remove from oven. Reduce oven temperature to 325°.

Meanwhile, in a mixing bowl beat eggs slightly. Stir in spinach, ricotta, the ½ cup feta, milk, and oregano. Sprinkle pastry with Parmesan; top with egg mixture. Bake in a 325° oven about 20 minutes or till a knife inserted near the center comes out clean.

Let stand about 5 minutes. If desired, top with red pepper rings, chopped yellow pepper, feta cheese, and fresh herbs. Makes 8 servings.

Pastry for Single-Crust Pie: In a mixing bowl stir together 1¼ cups *all-*

cooked eggs so uncooked portion flows underneath. Fold in salmon or ham. Cook over medium heat for 2 to 3 minutes more or till eggs are cooked throughout but are still glossy and moist. Transfer to a warm serving platter. Top with cheese and tomato. Makes 8 servings.

Cost per serving with salmon: $1.24
Cost per serving with ham: 62 cents
Nutrition information per serving: 212 cal., 14 g fat, 335 mg chol., 17 g pro., 3 g carbo., 435 mg sodium, 0 g fiber. RDA: 22% calcium, 10% iron, 27% vit. A, 38% riboflavin.

Rosemary Roasted New Potatoes

BROWN THE POTATOES IN A SKILLET OR follow the no-watch oven method—

2 pounds new potatoes, scrubbed and quartered
1 tablespoon olive oil or cooking oil
2 cloves garlic, minced
2 teaspoons snipped fresh rosemary or ½ teaspoon dried rosemary, crushed
2 teaspoons snipped fresh thyme or ½ teaspoon dried thyme, crushed
¼ teaspoon salt
⅛ teaspoon pepper

In a 12-inch skillet or Dutch oven bring 3 cups *water* to boiling. Add potatoes; return to boiling. Reduce heat; cook, covered, over medium heat for 8 minutes. Drain; return to pan. Add oil, garlic, rosemary, thyme, salt, and pepper. Cook, uncovered, for 10 to 12 minutes or till tender and brown, stirring occasionally. Makes 8 servings.

Roasting directions: In a greased 13x9x2-inch baking dish arrange raw

potatoes. In a bowl stir together oil, garlic, rosemary, thyme, salt, and pepper. Pour over potatoes; toss to coat. Bake, uncovered, in a 450° oven about 25 minutes or till brown and tender.

Cost per serving: 25 cents
Nutrition information per serving: 126 cal., 2 g fat, 0 mg chol., 3 g pro., 25 g carbo., 75 mg sodium, 1 g fiber. RDA: 13% iron, 25% vit. C, 11% thiamine, 12% niacin.

Steamed Asparagus Bundles

TIE THE BUNDLES THE DAY BEFORE—

8 green onion tops
2 pounds asparagus spears, trimmed
Fresh thyme sprigs (optional)

In a Dutch oven bring a small amount of water to boiling. Add onions; remove from heat. Let stand for 1

Scrambled Eggs with Smoked Salmon, Rosemary Roasted New Potatoes, Steamed Asparagus Bundles Spiced Pita Crisps with Creamy Strawberry Spread◆

minute. Remove onions, reserving water. When cool, tie each green onion around 4 or 5 raw asparagus spears (see how-to photo, *below*).

Using softened green onion tops, gently tie bundles of asparagus spears.

continued on page 53

continued from page 51

Return water to boiling; add asparagus bundles. Reduce heat; cover and simmer for 4 to 8 minutes or till crisp-tender. Before serving, tuck a thyme sprig under each green onion, if desired. Makes 8 servings.

Cost per serving: 36 cents

Nutrition information per serving: 28 cal., 0 g fat, 0 mg chol., 3 g pro., 5 g carbo., 4 mg sodium, 0 g fiber. RDA: 14% vit. A, 51% vit. C, 10% thiamine, 10% riboflavin.

Walnut Easter Bread

6 to 6½ cups all-purpose flour
2 packages active dry yeast
1⅔ cups milk
½ cup sugar
⅔ cup margarine or butter
½ teaspoon salt
½ teaspoon ground nutmeg
1 egg
¾ cup finely chopped walnuts
10 walnut halves
1 beaten egg yolk
1 tablespoons water

In a large mixing bowl stir together *3 cups* of the flour and the yeast. In a saucepan heat and stir milk, sugar, margarine or butter, salt, and nutmeg till warm (120° to 130°) and margarine is almost melted. Add to flour mixture. Add whole egg. Beat with an electric mixer on low speed for 30 seconds, scraping bowl constantly. Beat on high

◆ Applesauce-Rhubarb Muffins, *top;* Walnut Easter Bread, *center;* Apricot-Pecan Hot Cross Buns *lower right;* Crunchy Parmesan Corn Bread, *lower left*

speed for 3 minutes. Using a spoon, stir in the chopped nuts and as much remaining flour as you can.

Turn dough out onto a lightly floured surface. Knead in enough of the remaining flour to make a moderately stiff dough that is smooth and elastic (6 to 8 minutes total). Shape into a ball. Place in a lightly greased bowl; turn once. Cover; let rise in a warm place till double (about 1 hour).

Punch dough down. Turn out onto a lightly floured surface. Divide into 3 portions. Cover; let rest 10 minutes.

Shape 2 dough portions into balls. Place on 1 or 2 greased baking sheets, allowing 4 inches between balls. Flatten each to a 5½-inch diameter. Divide the remaining portion of dough into 16 pieces. Roll each piece into a 10-inch-long rope. Loosely twist 2 ropes together; repeat with remaining ropes, making 8 twisted ropes total.

Place two of the twisted ropes in a cross atop each flattened ball of dough; tuck rope ends under balls. Place two more twisted ropes around the base of each ball stretching the ropes if necessary so ends will meet (see how-to photo, *above*). Brush ends with water; pinch together to seal. Also, brush water onto centers and ends of crossed ropes. Press a walnut half in center and at ends of ropes. Cover and let rise in a warm place till almost double (about 30 minutes).

In a mixing bowl stir together yolk and the 1 tablespoon water; brush onto loaves. Bake in a 350° oven for 45 to 50 minutes or till bread sounds hollow, covering loosely with foil after 25 minutes. (If using 2 baking sheets, refrigerate 1 loaf while the other bakes.) Remove from pan; cool on a wire rack. Makes 2 loaves (32 servings).

Place two of the twisted ropes in a cross atop each flattened ball of dough.

Make-ahead directions: Bake the loaves as directed; cool thoroughly. Wrap in freezer wrap or foil; freeze for up to 8 months. To serve, thaw, covered, overnight in the refrigerator.

Cost per serving: 9 cents

Nutrition information per serving: 168 cal., 8 g fat, 14 mg chol., 4 g pro., 21 g carbo., 87 mg sodium, 1 g fiber. RDA: 19% thiamine, 13% riboflavin, 10% niacin.

Apricot-Pecan Hot Cross Buns

THESE EASTER ROLLS GET THEIR NAME from the cross that's scored or frosted on top. Though they traditionally contain currants, raisins, or candied fruit, this version has pecans and dried apricots—

3½ to 4 cups all-purpose flour
1 package active dry yeast
¾ cup apricot nectar
½ cup margarine or butter
⅓ cup sugar

continued on page 54

continued from page 53

¼ teaspoon salt
3 eggs
1 6-ounce package dried apricots
⅓ cup chopped pecans
1 slightly beaten egg white
Apricot Icing

In a large mixing bowl stir together 1½ cups of the flour and the yeast. In a saucepan heat apricot nectar, margarine or butter, sugar, and salt till warm (120° to 130°), stirring constantly. Add to flour mixture along with eggs. Beat with an electric mixer on low speed for 30 seconds, scraping bowl constantly. Beat on high speed for 3 minutes.

Reserve 4 or 5 dried apricots; snip remaining apricots. Using a spoon, stir the snipped apricots and pecans into the dough. Stir in as much of the remaining flour as you can.

Turn the dough out onto a lightly floured surface. Knead in enough remaining flour to make a moderately soft dough (3 to 5 minutes total). Shape into a ball. Place in a lightly greased bowl; turn once. Cover; let rise till double (about 1½ hours).

Punch dough down. Turn dough out onto a lightly floured surface. Cover and let rest for 10 minutes. Divide dough into 20 portions; shape into smooth balls. Arrange balls 2 inches apart on a greased baking sheet. Cover and let rise till almost double (30 to 45 minutes).

Brush dough with egg white. Bake in a 350° oven for 12 to 15 minutes or till golden. Cool on wire racks. Snip reserved apricots into 40 thin slivers. Using a spoon, top each bun with an X of Apricot Icing; decorate each X with 2 apricot slivers. Makes 20 rolls.

Apricot Icing: Combine 1 cup *sifted* powdered sugar and enough *apricot nectar* (about 1 tablespoon) to make an icing of drizzling consistency.

Make-ahead directions: Bake rolls as directed; cool thoroughly. Do not add Apricot Icing. Place in a freezer container or freezer bag and freeze for up to 8 months. To serve, thaw, covered, overnight in the refrigerator. Top with Apricot Icing and apricots.

Cost per serving: 25 cents
Nutrition information per bun: 196 cal., 7g fat, 32 mg chol., 4 g pro., 31 g carbo., 94 mg sodium, 2 g fiber. RDA: 11% iron, 18% vit. A, 17% thiamine, 14% riboflavin, 11% niacin.

Crunchy Parmesan Corn Bread

STUDDED WITH FENNEL AND SUN-DRIED tomatoes, this savory bread makes a great match for scrambled eggs—

1 cup boiling water
¼ cup bulgur
Yellow cornmeal
1 cup all-purpose flour
1 cup yellow cornmeal
⅓ cup grated Parmesan cheese
2 tablespoons sugar
1 tablespoon baking powder
½ teaspoon fennel seed
½ teaspoon dried basil, crushed
2 eggs
1 cup milk
¼ cup olive oil or cooking oil
⅓ cup sun-dried tomatoes (oil pack), drained and chopped, or diced pimiento, drained
⅓ cup sliced green onion

Pour boiling water over bulgur; let stand for 5 minutes. Drain. Meanwhile, grease an 8x4x2-inch or 9x5x3-inch loaf pan or a 6-cup soufflé dish. Sprinkle bottom and sides with cornmeal.

In a large mixing bowl stir together flour, the 1 cup cornmeal, Parmesan cheese, sugar, baking powder, fennel, and basil. Make a well in the center.

In another mixing bowl beat eggs slightly. Stir in milk and oil. Stir in bulgur. Add egg mixture all at once to dry mixture. Stir just till moistened. Fold in tomatoes or pimiento and onion.

Pour batter into pan. Bake in a 375° oven for 40 minutes. Cover loosely with foil; bake for 10 to 15 minutes or till golden. Remove from pan. Cool on a wire rack for 30 minutes. Makes 1 loaf (8 to 10 servings).

Cost per serving: 84 cents
Nutrition information per serving: 272 cal., 11 g fat, 59 mg chol., 8 g pro., 35 g carbo., 231 mg sodium, 2 g fiber. RDA: 22% calcium, 12% iron, 10% vit. C, 26% thiamine, 23% riboflavin, 15% niacin.

Applesauce-Rhubarb Muffins

PICK A SIZE OR MAKE ALL THREE— giant, mini, or regular muffins—

2 cups all-purpose flour
1 cup whole wheat flour
2 teaspoons baking powder
2 teaspoons ground cinnamon
½ teaspoon baking soda
½ teaspoon salt
2 eggs
1½ cups packed brown sugar
1½ cups applesauce
½ cup cooking oil
1½ cups chopped rhubarb
Crumbled sugar cubes or cinnamon sugar

In a large mixing bowl stir together all-purpose flour, whole wheat flour, baking powder, cinnamon, baking soda, and salt. Make a well in center; set aside. In a medium mixing bowl beat eggs; stir in brown sugar, applesauce, and cooking oil. Add egg mixture all at once to flour mixture. Stir just till moistened (the batter should be lumpy). Fold in rhubarb. Make desired size muffins.

Giant muffins: Lightly grease 3½-inch muffin cups or line with paper bake cups; fill ⅔ full. Sprinkle with sugar or cinnamon sugar. Bake in a 350° oven for 30 to 35 minutes or till tops are firm and golden. Remove from pans; serve warm. Makes 10.

Mini muffins: Cut recipe in half. Lightly grease 1¾-inch muffin cups or line with paper bake cups; fill ⅔ full. Sprinkle with sugar or cinnamon sugar. Bake in a 400° oven for 10 to 12 minutes or till golden. Remove from pans; serve warm. Makes about 28.

Regular muffins: Lightly grease 2¾-inch muffin cups or line with paper bake cups; fill ⅔ full. Sprinkle tops with sugar or cinnamon sugar. Bake in a 400° oven for 18 to 20 minutes or till tops are golden. Remove muffins from pans; serve warm. Makes about 24.

Make-ahead directions: Bake muffins as directed. Cool; place in a freezer container. Freeze for up to 2 months. To serve, thaw overnight in the refrigerator or wrap in foil and heat in a 300° oven about 20 minutes or till warm.

Cost per giant muffin: 18 cents

Nutrition information per giant muffin: 406 cal., 14 g fat, 43 mg chol., 6 g pro., 67 g carbo., 230 mg sodium, 3 g fiber. RDA: 12% calcium, 20% iron, 23% thiamine, 17% riboflavin, 15% niacin.

Spiced Pita Crisps with Creamy Strawberry Spread

2 large pita bread rounds or four 7- to 8-inch flour tortillas
2 tablespoons sugar
½ teaspoon ground cinnamon
¼ teaspoon ground nutmeg
1 to 2 tablespoons margarine or butter, melted
1 8-ounce container soft-style cream cheese with strawberry or pineapple
1 teaspoon finely shredded orange peel
1 tablespoon orange juice

Cut each pita round into 6 wedges. Cut wedges in half crosswise to make single layers. Combine sugar, cinnamon, and nutmeg. Arrange wedges in a single layer on a baking sheet. Brush with melted margarine; sprinkle with spice mixture. Bake in a 350° oven for 10 to 15 minutes or till crisp and golden.

Meanwhile, stir together the cream cheese, orange peel, and orange juice. Serve with crisps. Makes 24 wedges.

Make-ahead directions: Bake the crisps a day ahead; cover and store in a cool, dry place. Cover and chill spread for up to 24 hours.

Cost per serving: 11 cents

Nutrition information per wedge with 2 teaspoons spread: 47 cal., 3 g fat, 8 mg chol., 1 g pro., 4 g carbo., 43 mg sodium, 0 g fiber.

Tea Sandwiches

Assorted breads, such as toasted mini bagels, pumpernickel or rye party bread slices, 6-inch flour tortillas, halved small pita bread rounds, crispy rye crackers, 5-inch Armenian cracker bread (lahvosh)
and/or Pineapple-Carrot Tea Bread (see recipe, page 56)
Assorted fillings, such as Honey-Vegetable Vinaigrette, Salmon and Lemon-Caper Cream, and/or Chicken-Cashew Curry (see recipes, page 56)
Margarine, butter, mayonnaise, and/or salad dressing.

If using lahvosh, dampen on both sides by holding under gently running warm water. Place bread between damp clean towels. Let stand at room temperature for 1 hour or till soft. Meanwhile, make desired fillings. Spread bread with margarine, butter, mayonnaise, or salad dressing (omit for vinaigrette filling). Top with desired fillings. For tortillas and softened lahvosh, roll up jelly-roll style; slice into ¾-inch-thick pinwheels.

Make-ahead directions: Prepare Chicken-Cashew Curry and Lemon-Caper Cream the day before serving. Cover and chill overnight.

Honey-Vegetable Vinaigrette: In a medium mixing bowl stir together 1 tablespoon *salad oil*, 1 tablespoon *vinegar*, 1 tablespoon *honey*, and 1 teaspoon *course-grain brown mustard*. Add 1½ cups chopped *Chinese cabbage* and ½ cup shredded *carrot*; toss gently to coat. Immediately top pita rounds, bagels, or party breads with thinly sliced *tomato or cucumber, lettuce leaves, and/or watercress*. Top with *2 tablespoons* cabbage mixture. Makes 1½ cups filling or 12 servings.

Cost per serving on pita bread rounds: 24 cents

Nutrition information per serving on pita bread rounds: 125 cal., 2 g fat, 0 mg chol., 4 g pro., 23 g carbo., 225 mg sodium, 1 g fiber. RDA: 17% vit. A, 17% thiamine, 10% niacin.

continued on page 56

continued from page 55

Salmon and Lemon-Caper Cream: In a small mixing bowl stir together ⅓ cup *mayonnaise* or *salad dressing,* 1 tablespoon drained *capers,* ½ teaspoon finely shredded *lemon peel,* ½ teaspoon *Dijon-style mustard,* and ⅛ teaspoon *white pepper.* Line bread with *curly endive or lettuce leaves.* Using 8 ounces total, arrange thinly sliced *smoked salmon (lox style) or smoked turkey* on lettuce. Top with *1 teaspoon* mayonnaise mixture. If desired, garnish with fresh dill. Serve at once. Makes ⅓ cup or 18 servings.

Cost per serving on bagel: 81 cents

Nutrition information per serving on bagel: 91 cal., 5 g fat, 8 mg chol., 4 g pro., 8 g carbo., 198 mg sodium, 0 g fiber.

Chicken-Cashew Curry: In a bowl stir together ½ cup *plain yogurt* and 2 tablespoons *soft-style cream cheese.* Stir in 2 tablespoons snipped *chives* or thinly sliced *green onions,* 1 teaspoon *curry powder,* and ¼ teaspoon *salt.* Stir in 1½ cups finely chopped, cooked *chicken or turkey* (8 ounces) and ¼ cup chopped *cashews or almonds.* Line bread with *curly endive or lettuce.* Spread with *2 tablespoons* filling. Top with *snipped chives* or thinly sliced *green onion.* Makes 1½ cups filling or 12 servings.

Cost per filled tortilla: 84 cents

Nutrition information per filled tortilla: 159 cal., 1 g fat, 19 mg chol., 9 g pro., 19 g carbo., 74 mg sodium, 1 g fiber. RDA: 11% iron, 11% riboflavin, 19% niacin.

Tea Sandwich Suggestions

Filling	Bread	Garnish
Honey-Vegetable Vinaigrette	*Pita bread*	*Cucumber and tomato*
♦ ♦ ♦	♦ ♦ ♦	♦ ♦ ♦
Salmon and Lemon-Caper Cream	*Halved mini bagel*	*Endive and dill*
♦ ♦ ♦	♦ ♦ ♦	♦ ♦ ♦
Chicken-Cashew Curry	*Pita or flour tortilla*	*Lettuce and chives*
♦ ♦ ♦	♦ ♦ ♦	♦ ♦ ♦
Cream cheese and ham	*Pineapple-Carrot Tea Bread*	*Mandarin orange and watercress*

Pineapple-Carrot Tea Bread

SPREAD BUTTER OR CREAM CHEESE ONTO slices of this go-with-anything bread. Or, crown them with different toppings, such as ham, watercress, and orange sections, as pictured on opposite page—

> 2¼ cups all-purpose flour
> 1 package active dry yeast
> 1 8-ounce can crushed pineapple (juice pack)
> ¼ cup sugar
> ¼ cup margarine or butter
> ½ teaspoon salt
> 1 egg
> 1 teaspoon vanilla
> ½ cup shredded carrot

Lightly grease an 8x4x2-inch loaf pan; set aside. In a large mixing bowl stir together ¾ *cup* of the flour and the yeast; set aside.

Drain pineapple, reserving ⅓ *cup* of the juice. In a saucepan heat and stir reserved pineapple juice, sugar, margarine or butter, and salt just till warm (120° to 130°) and margarine is almost melted. Add to flour mixture. Add egg and vanilla. Beat with an electric mixer on low to medium speed for 30 seconds, scraping bowl occasionally. Beat on high speed for 3 minutes. Stir in pineapple and carrot. Using a spoon, stir in remaining flour (batter will be sticky).

Spoon batter into prepared pan. Cover and let rise in a warm place till almost double (45 to 60 minutes). Bake in a 375° oven for 35 to 40 minutes or till golden, covering with foil the last 10 minutes if necessary. Remove bread from pan. Cool on a wire rack. Makes 1 loaf (16 servings).

Make-ahead directions: Bake bread as directed. Cool; wrap in freezer wrap. Freeze for up to 1 month.

Cost per slice: 7 cents

Nutrition information per slice: 116 cal., 4 g fat, 13 mg chol., 2 g pro., 18 g carbo., 106 mg sodium, 1 g fiber. RDA: 17% vit. A, 14% thiamine, 10% riboflavin.

Party Menu Ideas

Tea Sandwiches
♦ ♦ ♦
Pineapple-Carrot Tea Bread
♦ ♦ ♦
Pear Buttermilk Scones
♦ ♦ ♦
Chocolate Truffle Tarts
♦ ♦ ♦
Gingerbread Lemon Terrine
with Raspberry or Kiwi Sauce
♦ ♦ ♦
Sherry Almond Sponge Cake
♦ ♦ ♦
Assorted Teas

Pear Buttermilk Scones

A WHISPER OF SPICE ACCENTS THESE
British-style biscuits—

1¾ cups all-purpose flour
⅛ cup sugar
2 teaspoons baking powder
¼ teaspoon baking soda
¼ teaspoon salt
¼ teaspoon ground cardamom, nutmeg, or
allspice
⅛ cup margarine or butter
2 eggs
¼ cup buttermilk
½ cup chopped, peeled pear, drained
Powdered sugar
Whipped cream (optional)
Strawberries (optional)
Strawberry preserves (optional)

continued on page 58

Tea Sandwiches: Chicken-Cashew Curry on tortillas or
Pitas; Salmon and Lemon-Caper Cream on mini bagels;
Honey-Vegetble Vinaigrette on pita halves; Pineapple-
Carrot Tea Bread with ham ◆

continued from page 57

In a large mixing bowl stir together flour; sugar; baking powder; baking soda; salt; and cardamom, nutmeg, or allspice. Using a pastry blender, cut in margarine till mixture resembles coarse crumbs. Make a well in the center.

In a small mixing bowl beat eggs slightly; stir in buttermilk. Add the buttermilk mixture all at once to the flour mixture. Using a fork, stir just till moistened. Fold in pear.

Turn dough out onto a floured surface. Quickly knead dough by gently folding and pressing for 10 to 12 strokes or till nearly smooth. Pat or lightly roll the dough to ½-inch thickness. Cut dough into shapes with a 2½-inch-round biscuit cutter, dipping cutter into flour between cuts.

Place dough rounds 1 inch apart on an ungreased baking sheet. Bake in a 375° oven for 10 to 12 minutes or till golden. Cool on the baking sheet for 5 minutes, then transfer scones to a wire rack. Sift powdered sugar over tops. Serve warm with whipped cream, strawberries, and preserves, if desired. Makes 12 to 14 scones.

Cost per scone: 6 cents

Nutrition information per serving: 147 cal., 6 g fat, 36 mg chol., 3 g pro., 20 g carbo., 185 mg sodium, 1 g fiber. RDA: 10% vit. A, 13% thiamine, 11% riboflavin.

Gingerbread Lemon Terrine

TO MAKE THE CHAIN OF HEARTS IN THE kiwi sauce, as pictured on page 59, drop a few drops of raspberry sauce into the kiwi sauce on the plate, then draw a knife blade through it—

Gingerbread Pound Cake
(see recipe, page 59)
¾ cup sugar
1 envelope unflavored gelatin
¾ cup cold water
1 teaspoon finely shredded lemon peel
½ teaspoon finely shredded orange peel
¼ cup lemon juice
Few drops yellow food coloring (optional)
1 cup whipping cream
Kiwi Sauce (see recipe, right)
Raspberry Sauce (see recipe, right)

Prepare Gingerbread Pound Cake. When cake is cool, prepare filling. In a medium saucepan stir together sugar and gelatin. Stir in cold water, lemon peel, orange peel, and lemon juice. Heat and stir over low heat just till gelatin is dissolved; stir in food coloring. Set pan in an ice water bath; stir mixture constantly for 5 to 8 minutes or till of the consistency of corn syrup. Remove from water; set aside.

In a medium mixing bowl beat cream till soft peaks form. Fold *one-fourth* of the whipped cream into cooled gelatin mixture. Fold all of the mixture into remaining whipped cream. Chill about 20 minutes or till the mixture mounds when spooned.

To assemble, trim crusts from cooled gingerbread cake. Using a serrated knife, slice cake horizontally into 4 slices. Cut 1 slice in half lengthwise. Line a 9x5x3-inch loaf dish with plastic wrap. Place 1 of the whole slices on the bottom of the dish. Place the 2 half slices along each long side of dish. Spoon in *half* of the lemon filling.

Top with another whole slice of gingerbread, cutting to fit (see how-to photo, *opposite*). Spoon in remaining lemon filling. Top with remaining slice

of gingerbread, cutting to fit. Cover tightly and chill for at least 4 hours or till firm enough to slice.

Meanwhile, prepare the sauces; cover and chill. To serve, unmold the terrine onto a platter. Slice to serve. Spoon some of the Kiwi Sauce and Raspberry Sauce onto each plate. Lay a slice of the terrine atop sauces. Makes 12 servings.

Kiwi Sauce: In a blender container or food processor bowl combine 6 peeled *kiwi fruit* and 2 tablespoons *sugar*. Cover and blend or process till smooth. If desired, strain through a sieve to remove seeds. Cover and chill till serving time. Makes 1 cup sauce.

Raspberry Sauce: In a blender container or food processor bowl combine 1½ cups *frozen loose-pack red raspberries*, thawed slightly, and 2 tablespoons *sugar*. Cover and blend or process till smooth. If desired, strain through a sieve to remove the seeds. Cover and chill till serving time. Makes ¾ cup sauce.

Make-ahead directions: Bake and freeze the cake as directed. The day before serving, thaw the covered cake; make the lemon filling and the two sauces. Assemble the terrine; cover and chill overnight.

Cost per serving: 57 cents

Nutrition information per serving: 444 cal., 24 g fat, 130 mg chol., 5 g pro., 55 g carbo., 200 mg sodium, 2 g fiber. RDA: 10% calcium, 14% iron, 32% vit. A, 74% vit. C, 16% thiamine, 18% riboflavin, 10% niacin.

Gingerbread Pound Cake

USE THIS SPICY CAKE TO MAKE THE TERrine or slice and serve it on its own—

1 cup margarine or butter
4 eggs
2 cups all-purpose flour
1 teaspoon baking powder
1 teaspoon ground ginger
1 teaspoon ground cinnamon
¾ cup packed brown sugar
¼ cup molasses

Let margarine or butter and eggs stand at room temperature for 30 minutes. In a large mixing bowl stir together flour, baking powder, ginger, and cinnamon; set aside.

In another large mixing bowl beat margarine or butter with an electric mixer on medium speed for 30 seconds. Gradually add brown sugar, about *2 tablespoons* at a time, beating on medium to high speed about 6 minutes total or till very light and fluffy. Add eggs, one at a time, beating for 1 minute after each addition, scraping the sides of the bowl often. Beat in molasses. Gradually add

Gingerbread Lemon Terrine, Chocolate Truffle Tarts◆

After spooning in half of the lemon filling, top with a whole slice of Gingerbread Pound Cake.

flour mixture to butter mixture, beating on low speed just till combined.

Pour batter into a greased and floured 9x5x3-inch loaf pan. Bake in a 325° oven for 55 to 65 minutes or till a toothpick inserted near the center comes out clean. Cool on rack for 10 minutes. Remove cake from pan. Cool thoroughly on a wire rack. Makes 12 servings.

Make-ahead directions: Bake cake as directed. Cool thoroughly and wrap in freezer wrap or foil. Freeze the cake for up to 6 months.

Cost per serving: 11 cents

Nutrition information per serving: 307 cal., 18 g fat, 112 mg chol., 4 g pro., 33 g carbo., 207 mg sodium, 1 g fiber. RDA: 14% iron, 22% vit. A, 15% thiamine, 15% riboflavin.

Chocolate Truffle Tarts

DIVIDE THE FILLING AND FLAVOR EACH portion with a different liqueur—

½ of an 11-ounce package piecrust mix or
1 stick piecrust mix
¼ cup finely chopped pecans or hazelnuts
2 tablespoons sugar
4 ounces semisweet chocolate
¼ cup whipping cream
3 tablespoons butter or margarine
1 beaten egg yolk
2 tablespoons desired liqueur or
whipping cream
⅓ cup white baking pieces with cocoa
butter, melted (optional)
Fresh fruits (such as raspberries or
cherries), fruit preserves, nuts, or edible
flowers (such as violas)

Prepare piecrust mix according to package directions, *except* add the ¼ cup nuts and the sugar to dry mix. Shape into twenty-four ¾-inch balls. Press onto bottom and up sides of 24 ungreased 1¾-inch muffin cups. Bake in a 450° oven for 6 to 8 minutes or till edges begin to brown. Cool in pans on a wire rack. Remove from pans.

For filling, in a heavy saucepan combine chocolate, ¼ cup whipping cream, and butter or margarine. Cook and stir over low heat till chocolate is melted. Gradually stir about *half* of the hot mixture into the egg yolk. Return all of the mixture to the saucepan. Cook and stir just till mixture starts to bubble. Remove from heat.

Stir in liqueur. Transfer chocolate mixture to a small bowl; chill for 1½ to 2 hours or till mixture is cool and smooth, stirring occasionally. (The butter may separate but will blend in when the mixture is stirred.)

Beat the chilled chocolate mixture with an electric mixer on medium speed about 2 minutes or till light and fluffy. If desired, spoon the chocolate mixture into a decorating bag fitted with a large star tip (about ½ inch opening). Pipe or spoon mixture into baked tart shells. Cover and chill for up to 24 hours.

Before serving, let stand at room temperature for 15 to 20 minutes. If desired, drizzle with white chocolate and top with fruits, preserves, nuts, or edible flowers. Makes 24 tarts.

Make-ahead directions: Pipe the filling into the tart shells up to 24 hours ahead. Cover and chill till serving time. Decorate as desired.

Cost per tart using kahlua: 17 cents
Nutrition information per tart: 110 cal., 8 g fat, 16 mg chol., 1 g pro., 10 g carbo., 63 mg sodium, 0 g fiber.

Sherry-Almond Sponge Cake

FOR A GARNISH THAT SAYS SPRING, LOOK for edible flowers at your local greenhouse and some larger supermarkets—

4 egg yolks
⅓ cup dry or cream sherry
⅔ cup sugar
⅔ cup all-purpose flour
¼ cup ground toasted almonds
4 egg whites
½ teaspoon cream of tartar
⅓ cup sugar
1 cup whipping cream
1 tablespoon sugar
1 tablespoon dry or cream sherry
½ cup strawberry or raspberry preserves
2 tablespoons coarsely chopped toasted
almonds

In a small mixing bowl beat egg yolks with an electric mixer on high speed about 5 minutes or till thick and lemon colored. Add the ⅓ cup sherry. Beat on low speed till combined. Gradually beat in the ⅔ cup sugar. Increase speed to medium; beat till mixture thickens slightly and doubles in volume (about 5 minutes total). Sprinkle ⅓ cup of the flour over yolk mixture; gently fold in till combined. Repeat with remaining flour. Gently fold in ground almonds. Set aside.

Thoroughly wash beaters. In a large mixer bowl beat egg whites and cream of tartar on medium speed till soft peaks form (tips curl). Gradually add the ⅓ cup sugar, beating on high speed till stiff peaks form (tips stand straight). Fold about *1 cup* of the egg white mixture into the yolk mixture.

Gently fold the yolk mixture into the remaining white mixture.

Pour batter into 2 ungreased 8-inch round cake pans. Bake in a 325° oven about 25 minutes or till cake springs back when touched near center. Invert pans onto wire racks to cool.

In a chilled medium mixing bowl combine whipping cream, the 1 tablespoon sugar, and the 1 tablespoon sherry; beat till soft peaks form. Remove cooled cake from pans. Spread strawberry or raspberry preserves between cake layers. Spread whipped cream on top and sides of cake. Pat almonds onto sides. Cover and chill till serving time, up to 4 hours. Makes 12 servings.

Make-ahead directions: Bake cake as directed. Cool layers thoroughly and wrap each in freezer wrap or foil. Freeze for up to 6 months. To serve, thaw, covered, overnight in the refrigerator. Assemble as directed.

Cost per serving: 28 cents
Nutrition information per serving:
252 cal., 11 g fat, 98 mg chol., 4 g pro.,
33 g carbo., 30 mg sodium, 1 g fiber.
RDA: 15% vit. A, 14% riboflavin.

Calculating Recipe Costs

The costs for the recipes on pages 48-61 are based on prices in a Des Moines, Iowa, supermarket during September 1991. When possible, prices were selected from nationally available brands. The price of herbs and spices and optional ingredients are not included for any recipe. When alternate ingredients are given, the first alternate is priced, unless otherwise stated. For spring produce, we've made some seasonal price adjustments.

Sherry-Almond Sponge Cake◆

Prize Tested Recipes®

Portuguese-Style Turkey Steaks

MARILOU'S FAMILY LOVES THESE CUMIN-spiced turkey steaks with vegetable-olive sauce—

4 6-ounce turkey breast tenderloin
steaks (1½ pounds total)
2 tablespoons all-purpose flour
1 teaspoon ground cumin
1 teaspoon paprika
½ teaspoon pepper
¼ teaspoon salt
2 to 3 tablespoons olive oil or cooking oil
½ cup chopped red or green sweet pepper
¼ cup chopped celery
¼ cup sliced green onion
1 clove garlic, minced
¼ cup sliced pitted ripe olives
¼ cup sliced pimiento-stuffed olives
½ cup dry red wine
½ teaspoon cornstarch

Rinse turkey; pat dry. Place *each* breast half between 2 pieces of plastic wrap. Pound with a meat mallet to ¼ inch thickness. In a shallow dish combine flour, cumin, paprika, pepper, and salt. Dip turkey pieces into flour mixture, turning to coat.

In a large skillet cook turkey, 2 steaks at a time, in *2 tablespoons* of the hot oil over medium heat about 6 minutes or till no longer pink, turning once. Remove; keep warm. Repeat with remaining pieces, adding oil if necessary.

In same skillet cook and stir sweet pepper, celery, onion, and garlic over

medium heat for 7 to 8 minutes or till almost tender. Stir in olives. Stir together wine and cornstarch. Add to skillet. Cook and stir till bubbly. Cook and stir 1 minute more. Serve sauce over turkey. Makes 4 main-dish servings.

Nutrition information per serving: 290 cal., 13 g fat, 74 mg chol., 33 g pro.,

◆ Portuguese-Style Turkey Steaks

6 g carbo., 1 g fiber, 278 mg sodium. RDA: 17% iron, 22 % vit. C, 11% thiamine, 14% riboflavin, 52% niacin.
$200 WINNER
Marilou Robinson, Portland, Oreg.

◆ Hot Mexican Potato Salad

◆ Midwestern Baked Chili

Midwestern Baked Chili

THESE INDIVIDUAL CHILI CASSEROLES win on great taste. For sodium watchers, use tomato sauce with no added salt and rinse the cannellini beans with water to reduce the sodium by about 500 mg per serving—

1 pound ground raw turkey
1 cup chopped celery
¾ cup chopped onion
½ cup chopped green pepper
½ cup chopped peeled eggplant or winter squash (such as butternut)
2 teaspoons chili powder
½ teaspoon black pepper
½ teaspoon ground cumin
½ teaspoon crushed red pepper
1 15-ounce can tomato sauce
1 15-ounce can chili beans with chili gravy
1 15-ounce can cannellini beans or butter beans, drained
2 8½-ounce packages corn muffin mix
1 cup shredded cheddar cheese (4 ounces)
Dairy sour cream (optional)

In a skillet cook turkey, celery, onion, green pepper, and eggplant or squash till turkey is no longer pink. Add chili powder, black pepper, cumin, and red pepper. Cook and stir 2 minutes. Stir in tomato sauce and drained beans. Heat through; set aside.

Meanwhile, prepare corn muffin mix according to package directions. Spoon muffin batter into eight greased 12- to 16-ounce individual casseroles. Spoon chili mixture over batter. Bake, uncovered, in a 350° oven for 20 minutes. Sprinkle with cheese; bake 10 minutes more. Top with sour cream, if desired. Makes 8 main-dish servings.

Nutrition information per serving: 511 cal., 20 g fat, 75 mg chol., 24 g pro., 68 g carbo., 5 g fiber, 1,248 mg sodium. RDA: 21% iron, 21 % vit. A, 28 % vit. C, 23% thiamine, 23% riboflavin, 24% niacin.

$100 WINNER
Lisa Wroble, Plymouth, Mich.

Hot Mexican Potato Salad

MAKE THIS SALAD MILD TO SPICY depending on the picante dressing—

1 pound whole tiny new potatoes, quartered
¼ cup water
¼ cup picante sauce
1 to 2 tablespoons lime juice
1 tablespoon olive oil or salad oil
¼ teaspoon salt
⅛ teaspoon pepper
1 large tomato, seeded and chopped
½ cup sliced pitted ripe olives

continued on page 64

continued from page 63
¼ cup sliced green onion
1 tablespoon snipped cilantro or parsley

In a 2-quart microwave-safe casserole micro-cook potatoes and water, covered, on 100% power (high) for 9 to 11 minutes or till potatoes are tender, stirring once. Drain.

Meanwhile, in a small microwave-safe bowl combine picante sauce, lime juice, oil, salt, and pepper. Cook, uncovered, on high for 45 to 60 seconds or till heated through.

Add sauce to cooked potatoes. Stir in chopped tomato, olives, onion, and cilantro or parsley; toss to coat. Makes 4 side-dish servings.

Nutrition information per serving: 176 cal., 7 g fat, 0 mg chol., 3 g pro., 30 g carbo., 331 mg sodium, 3 g fiber. RDA: 52% vit. C, 16% thiamine, 15% niacin.

$200 WINNER
J. Hill, Sacramento, Calif.

Scalloped Potatoes and Spinach

RUTH TOTES THIS WINNING POTATO DISH to potluck dinners, then reheats it in the microwave—

5 medium potatoes, peeled and sliced ¼ inch thick (5 cups)
¼ cup water
⅛ teaspoon salt
⅓ cup chopped onion
3 tablespoons margarine or butter
3 tablespoons all-purpose flour
2 cups milk
¾ cup shredded cheddar cheese (3 ounces)
½ of a 10-ounce package frozen chopped spinach, thawed and well drained

1 tablespoon chopped pimiento
Paprika

In a 2-quart microwave-safe casserole micro-cook the sliced potatoes, water, and salt, covered, on 100% power (high) for 8 to 10 minutes or till potatoes are just tender, stirring twice. Drain; remove from casserole and set aside.

In same casserole cook onion in margarine or butter, covered, on high for 2 to 3 minutes or till tender. Stir in flour. Add milk all at once; stir to combine. Cook, uncovered, on high about 6 minutes or till thickened and bubbly, stirring every minute till sauce starts to thicken, then every 30 seconds. Add cheese; stir till melted. Stir in the cooked potatoes, spinach, and pimiento. Cook, covered, on high for 1 to 2 minutes or just till

Scalloped Potatoes and Spinach ◆

heated through (do not boil). Sprinkle with paprika. Makes 8 servings.

Nutrition information per serving: 209 cal., 9 g fat, 16 mg chol., 7g pro., 25 g carbo., 1 g fiber, 200 mg sodium. RDA: 23% calcium, 33% vit. A, 19% vit. C, 14% thiamine, 16% riboflavin, 10% niacin.

$100 WINNER
Ruth A. Thomson,
Southern Pines, N.C.

May

Chicken

Best Recipes from Coast to Coast

Prize Tested Recipes®

Pork and Pear Stir-Fry, Chicken Salad with

Tahini Sauce, Mocha Truffle Cookies, Cherry-Chocolate Cookies

Chicken
Best Recipes from Coast to Coast

Northwestern Chicken Salad

BY CHANGING THE FRUIT, VEGETABLE, and vinaigrette, you can taste the flavors of different regions of the country. Try the California or Honolulu versions another time—

Raspberry Vinaigrette (see recipe, page 70)
2 boneless, skinless chicken breast halves
(about 8 ounces)
8 to 10 asparagus spears
Lettuce leaves
4 cups shredded mixed greens (such as iceberg or Boston)
2 tablespoons chopped sweet onion (such as Walla Walla or red)
6 to 8 whole strawberries
1 pear, cored and sliced
8 to 10 whole pecan halves, toasted (optional)

Prepare Raspberry Vinaigrette; reserve *half* for dressing. Rinse chicken; pat dry. In a medium bowl combine remaining vinaigrette and chicken. Cover; marinate for 30 minutes in the refrigerator. Drain; reserve marinade.

Northwestern Chicken Salad ◆
Citrus Chicken ◆

Grill chicken on an uncovered grill directly over *medium-high* coals for 8 minutes. Turn and brush with reserved marinade. Continue grilling for 7 to 10 minutes or till no longer pink. (*Or*, place chicken on an unheated rack of a broiler pan. Broil 4 to 5 inches from heat about 9 minutes or till no longer pink, turning once and brushing with reserved marinade.) Discard any remaining marinade.

Meanwhile, in a medium saucepan cook asparagus, uncovered, in a small amount of boiling water for 6 to 8 minutes or till crisp-tender.

To serve, slice each chicken breast crosswise into 6 to 8 pieces. Line two plates with lettuce leaves. Divide shredded greens between plates. Top with chicken, asparagus, onion, strawberries, and pear. Serve with Raspberry Vinaigrette; sprinkle with pecans, if desired. Makes 2 servings.

Nutrition information per serving: 379 cal., 20 g fat, 59 mg chol., 26 g pro., 27 g carbo., 131 mg sodium, 5 g fiber.

California Chicken Salad: Prepare Cilantro Vinaigrette (see recipe, *page 71*). Reserve *half* of the vinaigrette for dressing. Marinate and grill or broil chicken as directed.

Prepare salad as directed above for Northwestern Chicken Salad *except* substitute 1 cup *yellow and/or green wax beans* for the asparagus; and 1 *carambola* (star fruit), sliced, and 1 *mango*, seeded, peeled, and sliced for the strawberries and pear.

In a saucepan cook the beans, uncovered, in a small amount of boiling water about 15 minutes or till crisp-tender. Serve as directed for Northwestern Chicken Salad, arranging the sliced chicken, beans, carambola, and mango

atop greens. Serve with reserved vinaigrette dressing. Sprinkle each serving with *chopped peanuts or sesame seed*, if desired.

Honolulu Chicken Salad: Prepare Papaya Vinaigrette (see recipe, *page 70*). Reserve *half* of the vinaigrette for dressing. Marinate and grill or broil chicken as directed.

Prepare salad as directed for Northwestern Chicken Salad *except* substitute 1 cup *pea pods* for the asparagus and 1 cup cubed *fresh* or *canned pineapple* and 1 *kiwi fruit*, sliced for the strawberries and pear.

In a small saucepan cook the pea pods, uncovered, in a small amount of boiling water about 2 minutes or till crisp-tender.

Serve as directed for Northwestern Chicken Salad, arranging sliced chicken,

pea pods, pineapple, and kiwi fruit atop greens. Serve with reserved vinaigrette dressing and sprinkle each serving with *toasted coconut*, if desired.

Citrus Chicken

2 boneless, skinless chicken breast halves (about 8 ounces)
1 teaspoon grated orange peel
½ cup orange juice
2 tablespoons balsamic vinegar or white wine vinegar
1½ teaspoons cornstarch
1 teaspoon honey
½ teaspoon instant chicken bouillon granules
Dash white pepper
1 cup sliced fresh shiitake or button mushrooms
1 tablespoon margarine or butter
4 ounces tomato linguine and/or plain linguine, cooked
Snipped chives (optional)
Orange slices, halved (optional)

Rinse chicken; pat dry with paper towels. Place each breast half between 2 pieces of plastic wrap. Working from center to edges, pound with the flat side of a meat mallet to ⅛-inch thickness. Remove plastic wrap.

In a small bowl stir together the orange peel, orange juice, vinegar, cornstarch, honey, bouillon granules, and pepper. Set aside.

In a large skillet cook mushrooms in hot margarine till tender; remove from skillet. In the same skillet cook chicken over medium-high heat for 4 minutes or till no longer pink, turning once. Remove chicken; cover to keep warm.

continued on page 68

Northwestern-
Chicken Salad

Greens with grilled chicken and fruit—a salad enjoyed anywhere. Vary the produce and dressing for a regional change of taste.

Citrus Chicken

For an easy 20-minute dinner, chicken comes to the rescue. Here, a sweet-and-sour glaze flavors the white meat fillets.

Tex-Mex Chicken Tostadas

Spiced ground chicken and crispy baked tostada shells jazz up a quick family favorite.

continued from page 67
Return mushrooms to skillet. Stir in juice mixture. Cook and stir till bubbly. Cook and stir 2 minutes more. To serve, divide hot linguine between two dinner plates. Place one breast half atop linguine. Spoon mushroom sauce over each. Sprinkle with chives and garnish with orange slices, if desired. Serves 2.

Nutrition information per serving: 485 cal., 10 g fat, 59 mg chol., 31 g pro., 68 g carbo., 342 mg sodium, 1 g fiber.

Tex-Mex Chicken Tostadas
SAVE A PREPARATION STEP BY BUYING cheese that's already shredded—

4 8-inch flour tortillas
1 pound ground raw chicken or turkey
1 teaspoon chili powder
1 8-ounce bottle medium or hot salsa
1 15-ounce can black beans or pinto beans
2 tablespoons diced pimiento
1 cup chopped lettuce
¼ cup thinly sliced radishes
¼ cup shredded cheddar cheese
1 2¼-ounce can sliced pitted ripe olives
Dairy sour cream (optional)
2 tablespoons thinly sliced green onion

For tostada shells, place tortillas in a single layer on the middle oven rack. Bake in a 350° oven about 6 minutes, turning halfway through baking time or till golden and crisp. (If tortillas bubble during baking, puncture bubble with a fork.) Set aside and cover to keep warm.

Meanwhile, in a medium skillet cook and stir chicken and chili powder over medium heat till chicken is no longer pink. Stir in salsa. Set aside; keep warm.

Drain beans, reserving liquid. In a small saucepan stir beans over low heat till heated through. With a potato masher or fork, mash beans adding reserved bean liquid till of spreadable consistency. Heat through.

◆ Tex-Mex Chicken Tostadas

To assemble, place a warm tortilla on each dinner plate. Spread with a thin layer of beans. Top with some of the chicken mixture, pimiento, lettuce, radishes, cheese, ripe olives, sour cream, if desired, and green onion. Garnish with *avocado* slices, if desired. Serves 4.

Nutrition information per serving: 355 cal., 13 g fat, 62 mg chol., 28 g pro., 38 g carbo., 730 mg sodium, 6 g fiber.

Pacific Rim Stir-Fry

California ingredients and Thai flavors— basil. tumeric. and red pepper—mesh in this quick-serve dish.

Pacific Rim Stir-Fry ◆

Pacific Rim Stir-Fry

THIS COLORFUL, MILDLY SPICY STIR-FRY is served over boiled rice sticks (thin, flat Chinese noodles). Look for them in the Oriental or noodle section of your supermarket or in Asian markets—

> 3 ounces rice sticks (also called rice noodles) or thin vermicelli, broken
> 12 ounces boneless, skinless chicken thighs or breasts
> ½ cup chicken broth
> 2 tablespoons soy sauce
> 2 tablespoons snipped fresh basil or 2 teaspoons dried basil, crushed
> 2 teaspoons cornstarch
> 1 teaspoon chili oil or ½ teaspoon crushed red pepper
> ½ teaspoon ground turmeric
> 1 tablespoon cooking oil
> 2 medium carrots, cut into julienne strips
> 2 cups broccoli flowerets
> 1 red or green sweet pepper, cut into 1-inch strips (½ cup)
> ¼ cup cashew halves or peanuts

In a saucepan cook rice sticks in boiling water for 3 minutes. (Or, cook vermicelli according to package directions.) Drain. Set aside; keep warm.

Meanwhile, cut chicken into thin, bite-size strips. For sauce, combine broth, soy sauce, basil, cornstarch, chili oil, and turmeric; set aside.

Add oil to wok. Preheat over medium-high heat (add more oil if necessary during cooking). Stir-fry carrots in hot oil for 1 minute. Add broccoli. Stir-fry for 2 minutes more; add sweet pepper. Stir-fry for 1½ to 2 minutes more. Remove vegetables. Stir-fry chicken 2 to 3 minutes or till no longer pink. Push chicken from center. Stir sauce; add to center of wok. Cook and stir till bubbly. Return vegetables to wok. Stir to coat. Cook and stir 2 minutes more or till heated through. Serve immediately over hot rice sticks or vermicelli. Top with nuts. Makes 4 servings.

Nutrition information per serving: 309 cal., 11 g fat, 45 mg chol., 21 g pro., 31 g carbo., 697 mg sodium, 1 g fiber.

Papaya Vinaigrette

USE THIS DRESSING FOR THE HONOLULU chicken salad—

¼ cup papaya or apricot nectar
2 tablespoons salad oil
2 tablespoons white wine vinegar
1 teaspoon sesame oil
½ to 1 teaspoon dried basil, crushed
½ teaspoon ground ginger
¼ teaspoon dry mustard

In a jar combine all ingredients. Cover; shake well. Refrigerate up to 2 weeks. Shake before serving. Makes ½ cup.

Nutrition information per tablespoon: 40 cal., 4 g fat, 0 mg chol., 0 g pro., 1 g carbo., 1 mg sodium, 0 g fiber.

Raspberry Vinaigrette

PREPARE THIS VINAIGRETTE FOR THE Northwestern Chicken Salad—

¼ cup pear nectar
2 tablespoons salad oil
2 tablespoons raspberry vinegar or white wine vinegar
½ to 1 teaspoon dried basil, crushed
1 teaspoon Dijon-style mustard
1 teaspoon sesame oil
⅛ teaspoon pepper

In a screw-top jar combine all ingredients. Cover; shake well. Store in refrigerator for up to 2 weeks. Shake before serving. Makes ½ cup.

◆ All-American Barbecued Chicken,
Minnesota Wild Rice Stuffed Chicken

Cilantro Vinaigrette

¼ cup papaya or apricot nectar
2 tablespoons olive oil or salad oil
*2 tablespoons rice wine vinegar or white
wine vinegar*
1 teaspoon sesame oil
*3 tablespoons fresh snipped cilantro or ½ to
1 teaspoon dried cilantro, crushed*
½ teaspoon ground ginger
⅛ to ¼ teaspoon ground red pepper

In a screw-top jar combine all ingredients. Cover; shake well. Store in refrigerator for up to 2 weeks. Shake before serving. Makes ½ cup.

All-American Barbecued Chicken

*1 2½- to 3-pound broiler-fryer chicken,
quartered*
*Classic, Texas-Style, or Ohio-Style
Barbecue Sauce*

Rinse chicken. Pat dry. Break wing, hip, and drumstick joints so pieces lie flat. Twist wing tips under back. Grill chicken, skin side down, on an uncovered grill directly over *medium* coals for 20 minutes. Turn chicken; grill 15 to 20 minutes more or till no longer pink. Brush with sauce during last 10 minutes of grilling. Heat remaining sauce till bubbly; pass with chicken. Serves 4 to 6.

Classic Barbecue Sauce: In a saucepan cook ½ cup finely chopped *onion* in 1 tablespoon *cooking oil* till onion is tender. Stir in 1 cup *catsup*, ½ cup *water*, ¼ cup *vinegar*, 2 to 3 tablespoons *brown sugar*, 2 tablespoons *Worcestershire sauce*, and 2 dashes *bottled hot pepper sauce*. Bring to boiling; reduce heat. Simmer,

uncovered, about 15 minutes or to desired consistency. Makes 1½ cups.

Texas-Style Barbecue Sauce: In a saucepan melt 1 tablespoon *margarine or butter*. Add ½ cup finely chopped *onion*; 2 cloves *garlic*, minced; 1 teaspoon *chili powder*; and ¼ teaspoon ground *sage*. Cook and stir till onion is tender. Stir in ½ cup *catsup*, 2 tablespoons *water*, 2 tablespoons *vinegar*, 1 tablespoon *sugar*, 1 tablespoon *lemon juice*, 1 tablespoon Worcestershire *sauce*, ½ teaspoon *salt*, ½ teaspoon *bottled hot pepper sauce*, and ¼ teaspoon cracked *black pepper*. Bring to boiling; reduce heat. Simmer, uncovered, about 5 minutes, stirring occasionally. Makes about 1 cup sauce.

Ohio-Style Barbecue Sauce: In a saucepan combine ½ cup *chili sauce*, ½ cup *catsup*, ⅓ cup *maple or maple-flavored syrup*, ¼ cup *vinegar*, 2 teaspoons *dry mustard*, and ¼ to ½ teaspoon *ground red pepper*. Bring to boiling, stirring occasionally. Simmer, uncovered, about 15 minutes. Makes about 1⅛ cups sauce.

Nutrition information per serving with Classic Barbecue Sauce: 401 cal., 19 g fat, 99 mg chol., 32 g pro., 27 g carbo., 881 mg sodium, 0 g fiber.

Minnesota Wild Rice Stuffed Chicken

*1 6-ounce package long grain and
wild rice mix*
*2 medium cooking apples,
cored and chopped*
3 cups sliced fresh mushrooms
1 cup shredded carrot
½ cup thinly sliced green onion
½ teaspoon pepper
1 4-pound broiler-fryer chicken
2 to 3 tablespoons apple jelly, melted

Cook rice according to package directions, except add apple, mushrooms, carrot, onion, and pepper to rice before cooking.

Meanwhile, rinse chicken; pat dry. Spoon some stuffing loosely into the neck cavity; pull neck skin to back and fasten with a small skewer. Lightly spoon stuffing into body cavity. Twist the wing tips under the back and tie legs to tail.

Place stuffed bird, breast side up, on a rack in a shallow roasting pan. Insert meat thermometer into the center of one
continued on page 72

- Buffalo Wings
- Crispy Chicken Bites

continued from page 71
of the inside thigh muscles. The bulb should not touch the bone. Roast, uncovered, in a 375° oven 1¾ to 2¼ hours or till chicken is no longer pink and drumstick moves easily in the socket. Brush chicken with melted jelly once or twice during the last 10 minutes of roasting. Transfer bird to a large platter. Spoon dressing around bird. Garnish with apple, if desired. Serves 8.

Nutrition information per serving: 344 cal., 14 g fat, 79 mg chol., 28 g pro., 27 g carbo., 473 mg sodium, 1 g fiber.

Crispy Chicken Bites

Dip these nibbles into one of three sauces: cherry, Cajun style, or mole.

Buffalo Wings

Buffalo, New York, takes credit for these fiery appetizers. To cool the flame, serve with Blue Cheese Dip.

Buffalo Wings

IF YOU LIKE BUFFALO WINGS WITH extra heat, use the upper range of the hot pepper sauce—

12 chicken wings (about 2 pounds)
2 tablespoons margarine or butter, melted
2 to 3 tablespoons bottled hot pepper sauce
1 teaspoon paprika
Salt and pepper (optional)
Blue Cheese Dip
Celery sticks (optional)

Preheat broiler. Meanwhile, rinse chicken wings; pat dry with paper towels. Cut off and discard tips of chicken wings. Cut wings at joints to form 24 pieces. Place chicken pieces in a shallow, nonmetal pan.

For sauce, in a small mixing bowl stir together the melted margarine or butter, bottled hot pepper sauce, and paprika. Pour mixture over chicken wings, stirring to coat. Cover chicken and let stand at room temperature for 30 minutes.

Drain chicken, reserving sauce. Place the chicken pieces on the unheated rack of a broiler pan. Sprinkle the chicken with salt and pepper, if desired. Brush with some of the reserved sauce.

Broil chicken 4 to 5 inches from the heat about 10 minutes or till light brown. Turn the chicken pieces; brush again with the reserved sauce. Broil for 10 to 15 minutes more or till the chicken is tender and no longer pink. Serve with Blue Cheese Dip and celery sticks, if desired. Makes 12 appetizer servings.

Blue Cheese Dip: In a blender container or a food processor bowl combine ½ cup *dairy sour cream,* ½ cup *mayonnaise* or *salad dressing,* ½ cup crumbled *blue cheese,* 1 clove *garlic,* minced, and 1 tablespoon *white wine vinegar or white* vinegar. Cover and blend or process dip till smooth. Store dip, covered, in the refrigerator for up to 2 weeks. If desired, top dip with additional crumbled blue cheese before serving. Makes 1¼ cups.

Nutrition information per 2 chicken wing pieces and 2 tablespoons dip: 225 cal., 19 g fat, 40 mg chol., 10 g pro., 0 g carbo.,197 mg sodium, 0 g fiber. RDA: 13% niacin.

Crispy Chicken Bites

NEED A QUICK-SERVE, PARTY APPETIZER? These cracker-coated, bite-size nuggets bake in less than 15 minutes—

*1 pound skinless, boneless chicken thighs or
skinless, boneless chicken breasts
¼ cup all-purpose flour
1 teaspoon dried parsley flakes
½ teaspoon poultry seasoning
⅛ teaspoon salt
Dash pepper
1 beaten egg
2 tablespoons milk
30 whole wheat or regular rich round
crackers, finely crushed (1¼ cups)
Lemon wedges (optional)
Michigan Cherry, Cajun, or Southwestern
Mole Dipping Sauce
(see recipes, right)*

Rinse chicken. Pat dry with paper towels. Cut the chicken thighs or breasts into 1-inch pieces. In a plastic bag combine the flour, dried parsley, poultry seasoning, salt, and pepper. Add the chicken pieces, a few at a time, to the seasoned flour mixture. Close the bag and shake to coat chicken pieces well. Set the chicken aside.

In a small mixing bowl combine the beaten egg and the milk. In another small bowl place the finely crushed crackers. Dip the flour-coated chicken pieces, one quarter of the pieces at a time, into the egg-and-milk mixture. Roll the chicken pieces in the crushed crackers. Place the coated chicken pieces in a single layer on a large ungreased baking sheet.

Bake in a 400° oven for 10 to 12 minutes or till chicken pieces are no longer pink. If desired, garnish with lemon wedges. Serve with dipping sauce. Makes 8 appetizer servings.

Nutrition information per 2 pieces: 95 cal., 4 g fat, 33 mg chol., 4 g pro., 11 g carbo., 139 mg sodium.

Michigan Cherry Dipping Sauce

THIS SAUCE IS QUICK TO MAKE WITH jelly, lemon juice, and spice—

*1 12-ounce jar cherry jelly
2 tablespoons lemon juice
⅛ teaspoon ground mace
Dash ground cloves*

In a saucepan combine all ingredients. Cook and stir over medium heat till heated through. Serve with Crispy Chicken Bites. Makes about 1 cup.

Nutrition information per tablespoon: 50 cal., 0 g fat, 0 mg chol., 0 g pro., 13 g carbo., 3 mg sodium, 0 g fiber.

Cajun Dipping Sauce

HOT PEPPER SAUCE ADDS EXTRA HOTNESS to the tomatoes—

*1 14½-ounce can Cajun-style
stewed tomatoes
2 teaspoons cornstarch
¼ teaspoon bottled hot pepper sauce*

In a blender container place the stewed tomatoes. Cover and blend till nearly smooth.

In a medium saucepan combine blended tomatoes and cornstarch. Cook and stir till bubbly. Cook and stir 2 minutes more. Stir in bottled hot pepper sauce. Serve with Crispy Chicken Bites. Makes 1½ cups.

Nutrition information per tablespoon: 5 cal., 0 g fat, 0 mg chol., 0 g pro., 1 g carbo., 55 mg sodium, 0 g fiber.

Southwestern Mole Dipping Sauce

YOU CAN FIND CANNED MOLE POWDER in the Mexican foods section of your supermarket or in Mexican markets—

*¼ cup mole poblano powder
¾ cup water*

In a saucepan combine mole powder and water. Bring to boiling; reduce heat. Simmer, uncovered, for 10 to 15 minutes or to desired consistency. Serve with Crispy Chicken Bites. Makes ⅔ cup.

Nutrition information per tablespoon: 18 cal., 1 g fat, 0 mg chol., 1 g pro., 2 g carbo., 33 mg sodium, 1 g fiber.

Country Captain

◆ Country Captain

Country Captain

The state of Georgia takes credit for this southern classic. Currants, tomatoes, curry, and mace make up the robust sauce—

1 2½- to 3-pound broiler-fryer chicken, cut up and skinned
1 14½-ounce can chunky-style stewed tomatoes
¼ cup snipped parsley
¼ cup currants or raisins
1 tablespoon curry powder
½ teaspoon instant chicken bouillon granules
½ teaspoon ground mace or nutmeg
¼ teaspoon sugar
1 tablespoon cornstarch
1 tablespoon cold water
Hot cooked rice
1 tablespoons toasted slivered almonds (optional)

Rinse chicken; pat dry. In a large skillet stir together *undrained* tomatoes, parsley, currants, curry powder, bouillon granules, mace, and sugar. Place chicken in skillet. Spoon sauce over chicken. Bring mixture to boiling; reduce heat.

Cover; simmer for 35 to 45 minutes or till chicken is no longer pink. Remove chicken from skillet; keep warm.

For sauce, skim fat from mixture in skillet. In a small bowl stir together cornstarch and cold water; add to skillet. Cook and stir till thickened and bubbly. Cook and stir 2 minutes more. Serve over rice. Sprinkle with almonds, if desired. Makes 6 servings.

Nutrition information per serving: 346 cal., 8 g fat, 72 mg chol., 27 g pro., 41 g carbo., 403 mg sodium, 2 g fiber.

Southwestern-Style Burgers

FOR A FUN PRESENTATION, SERVE with blanched cactus pads. (To cook cactus, boil in water 30 to 60 seconds)—

1 beaten egg
¼ cup crushed nacho-flavored or plain tortilla chips (1 ounce)
3 tablespoons finely chopped green pepper
¾ teaspoon chili powder
¼ teaspoon salt
¼ teaspoon pepper
1 pound ground raw chicken
1 avocado, halved, seeded, peeled, and sliced
4 ounces sliced Monterey Jack cheese with jalapeño peppers
4 kaiser rolls or hamburger buns, split
Lettuce leaves
Salsa
Cactus pads (optional)

In a medium mixing bowl combine egg, tortilla chips, green pepper, chili powder, salt, and pepper. Add ground chicken and mix well. Shape into four ¾-inch-thick patties.

Southwestern-Style Burgers

These burgers are flavored with jalapeño-studded Jack cheese, chili powder, and salsa.

To grill, on an uncovered grill place patties directly over *medium-hot* coals; cook for 15 to 18 minutes or till no longer pink, turning once. Top each patty with avocado slices and cheese. Grill 1 to 2 minutes more or till cheese is melted. Toast rolls on grill, if desired.

To broil patties, preheat broiler. Place patties on an unheated rack of a broiler pan. Broil 3 to 4 inches from heat for 6 minutes. Turn patties; broil 6 to 8 minutes more or till patties are no longer pink. Toast rolls under broiler, if desired. Top burgers with avocado and cheese. Broil 1 to 2 minutes or till cheese is melted.

To serve, place one lettuce leaf on bottom half of bun. Top with cooked burger and salsa. Makes 4 servings.

Hawaiian Chicken Burgers: Prepare meat mixture as above, *except* substitute ¼ cup *fine dry seasoned bread crumbs* for tortilla chips; 3 tablespoons chopped *water chestnuts* for green pepper; and ¾ teaspoon ground *ginger* for chili powder.

Grill or broil patties as above, *except* brush with ¼ cup *bottled sweet and sour sauce* during last 5 minutes of cooking. If grilling, place *fresh or canned pineapple slices* on grill rack during the last 5 minutes of cooking, if desired. Toast rolls on grill or under broiler, if desired.

continued on page 76
Southwestern-Style Burgers ◆

◆ Wisconsin Cheese-Stuffed Chicken Rolls
continued from page 75

To serve burgers, sprinkle bottom half of each bun with some shredded *spinach*. Top with patties. Brush patties with sweet-and-sour sauce and top with pineapple slices, if desired. Serves 4.

Nutrition information for one serving Southwestern-Style Burgers: 424 cal., 23 g fat, 133 mg chol., 29 g pro., 26 g carbo., 674 mg sodium, 2 g fiber.

Wisconsin Cheese-Stuffed Chicken Rolls

WISCONSIN PRODUCES MORE CHEESE than any other state—

*2 tablespoons sun-dried tomatoes
(not oil pack)
4 medium boneless, skinless chicken breast
halves (about 12 ounces total)
2 tablespoons all-purpose flour*

Wisconsin Cheese-Stuffed Chicken Rolls

Cheddar cheese, tomato bits, and herbs hide inside succulent chicken rolls.

*¼ teaspoon salt
⅛ teaspoon pepper
⅓ cup fine dry bread crumbs
2 tablespoons grated Parmesan cheese
½ teaspoon paprika
1 egg
4 ounces sharp cheddar cheese
½ to 1 teaspoon dried fines herbes or leaf
sage, crushed
1 tablespoon margarine or butter, melted*

In a small bowl place dried tomatoes. Add enough hot water to cover; soak for 10 minutes. Drain and pat dry. Finely chop. Set aside. Place each chicken breast half between clear plastic wrap and pound each with a meat mallet to ⅛-inch thickness. Remove plastic wrap.

In a small shallow bowl combine the flour, salt, and pepper. In another small, shallow bowl combine the bread crumbs, Parmesan cheese, and paprika. In another bowl slightly beat egg.

Cut cheddar cheese into four 3x1x½-inch pieces. Place a cheese stick on each

---

pounded chicken breast half. Sprinkle each half with some of the chopped dried tomatoes and dried herbs. Fold in the sides of each chicken breast and roll up tightly. Roll in flour mixture, egg, and then bread crumb mixture.

Arrange chicken rolls, seam sides down, in a shallow baking dish. (To make ahead, cover and chill for 1 to 4 hours.) Drizzle with melted margarine. Bake in a 350° oven for 20 to 25 minutes or till chicken is no longer pink. Makes 4 servings.

Nutrition information per serving: 318 cal., 17 g fat, 130 mg chol., 28 g pro., 12 g carbo., 587 mg sodium, 0 g fiber. RDA: 35% calcium, 10% iron, 23 % vit. A, 12% thiamine, 24% riboflavin, 50% niacin.

Maryland Fried Chicken

FOR THIS MARYLAND VERSION OF FRIED chicken, milk is added after partially cooking the chicken so it steams rather than fries—

*1 beaten egg
3 tablespoons milk
1 cup finely crushed crackers
(28 saltines)
1 teaspoon dried thyme, crushed
½ teaspoon paprika
⅛ teaspoon pepper
Meaty chicken pieces (2½- to 3-pounds)
2 to 3 tablespoons cooking oil
1 cup milk
Cream Gravy
Hot mashed potatoes (optional)*

In a small bowl combine the egg and the 3 tablespoons milk. In a shallow bowl combine the crackers, thyme, paprika, and pepper. Set aside.

Maryland Fried Chicken

Chicken lovers everywhere will enjoy old-fashioned Maryland Fried Chicken.

Rinse chicken pieces and pat dry with paper towels. Dip chicken pieces, one at a time, in egg mixture, then roll in cracker mixture.

In a large skillet heat oil. Add chicken to skillet, placing meatier pieces toward the center. Cook, uncovered, over medium heat for 10 to 15 minutes, turning occasionally to brown evenly. Drain fat. Add the 1 cup milk to skillet. Reduce heat to medium-low; cover tightly. Cook for 35 minutes. Uncover; cook for 10 minutes more or till chicken is tender and no longer pink. Prepare gravy, if desired. Makes 6 servings.

Cream Gravy: Transfer chicken to a serving platter; keep warm. Skim fat from drippings. Reserve 3 *tablespoons* drippings in skillet. In a screwtop jar combine ¾ cup *milk,* 3 tablespoons *all-purpose flour,* ¼ teaspoon *salt,* and ⅛ teaspoon *pepper;* shake till well combined. Add to skillet. Stir in ¾ cup additional *milk.* Cook over medium heat, stirring constantly, till thickened and bubbly. Cook and stir 1 minute more. (If desired, thin with additional milk.) Makes 1½ cups.

Nutrition information per serving with gravy: 393 cal., 19 g fat, 133 mg chol., 34 g pro., 18 g carbo., 402 mg sodium, 0 g fiber. RDA: 20% calcium, 15 % iron, 16 % vit. A.

Maryland Fried Chicken ◆

Prize Tested Recipes®

Pork and Pear Stir-Fry

PLUM PRESERVES GIVE THIS WINNING
stir-fry a delicious sweetness—

1½ cups fresh or frozen pea pods
(about 4 ounces)
1 pound pork tenderloin
½ cup plum preserves
3 tablespoons soy sauce
2 tablespoons lemon juice
1 tablespoon prepared horseradish
2 teaspoons cornstarch
½ teaspoon crushed red pepper
2 teaspoons grated gingerroot
1 tablespoon cooking oil
1 medium yellow or green sweet pepper,
cut into julienne strips
1 medium pear, cored and sliced
⅓ cup sliced water chestnuts
1 to 2 tablespoons sliced almonds, toasted
(optional)
Hot cooked rice

Thaw pea pods, if frozen. Cut pork
into thin bite-size strips. Set aside. For
sauce, in a bowl stir together preserves,
soy sauce, lemon juice, horseradish,
cornstarch, and red pepper. Set aside.

In a wok or large skillet stir-fry gingerroot in hot oil for 15 seconds over
medium-high heat. (Add more oil if necessary during cooking.) Add sweet pepper and pear; stir-fry for 1½ minutes
more. Remove vegetables from wok.
Add pork to wok; stir-fry for 2 to 3 minutes or till no longer pink. Push pork
from center of wok. Stir sauce; add to

◆ Pork and Pear Stir-Fry, *top*
◆ Chicken Salad with Tahini Sauce, *above*

wok. Cook and stir till bubbly. Add
water chestnuts. Return vegetables to
wok; stir to coat. Cook and stir about 2
minutes more. Top with pea pods; cover
and heat through. Sprinkle with
almonds, if desired. Serve with hot
cooked rice. Makes 4 servings.

Nutrition information per serving:
485 cal., 8 g fat, 81 mg chol., 30 g pro.,
72 g carbo., 3 g fiber, 883 mg sodium.
RDA: 29% iron, 69% vit. C.

$200 WINNER
Elaine Schultz, Miami, Fla.

Chicken Salad with Tahini Sauce

TAHINI (tuh-HEE-nee) IS A THICK PASTE made of ground sesame seed. Look for it in the foreign foods section of your grocery store or in Asian markets—

12 ounces boneless, skinless
chicken breast halves
6 to 10 green onions
2 small carrots
¼ cup tahini (sesame paste)
3 tablespoons soy sauce
3 tablespoons red wine vinegar
2 tablespoons salad oil
2 teaspoons sugar
½ to 1 teaspoon chili oil or ½ to 1 teaspoon
crushed red pepper flakes
1 clove garlic, minced
1 to 2 tablespoons brewed tea, cooled or
water (optional)
4 to 6 cups shredded bok choy, romaine, or
Chinese cabbage
2 to 3 tablespoons peanuts

Place the chicken on the unheated rack of a broiler pan. Broil 4 to 5 inches from the heat for 12 to 15 minutes or till tender and no longer pink, turning once. Cut chicken into thin, bite-size strips. Cut onions and carrots into julienne strips. In a large bowl combine the cooked chicken, onions, and carrots. Cover and chill till serving time.

For dressing, stir together the tahini, soy sauce, vinegar, salad oil, sugar, chili oil or red pepper flakes, and garlic. If necessary, thin with brewed tea or water. To serve, divide greens among 4 plates or place on a serving platter. Place chicken mixture atop greens. Top with dressing and sprinkle with peanuts. Makes 4 main-dish servings.

Nutrition information per serving: 316 cal., 21 g fat, 45 mg chol., 24 g pro., 11 g carbo., 3 g fiber, 874 mg sodium. RDA: 16% calcium, 21% iron, 127% vit. A, 63% vit. C, 21% thiamine, 13% riboflavin, 60% niacin.
$100 WINNER
Paul Michael Suino, Scottsdale, Ariz.

◆ Mocha Truffle Cookies

Mocha Truffle Cookies

THESE DOUBLE-CHOCOLATE COOKIES HAVE A soft trufflelike center, a crispy outside, and a delectable coffee flavor—

½ cup margarine or butter
½ cup semisweet chocolate pieces
1 tablespoon instant coffee crystals
¾ cup sugar

continued on page 80

Cherry-Chocolate Cookies

BETTY GIVES THE ALL-TIME FAVORITE, thumbprint cookies, the ultimate flavor twist by adding chocolate, orange, and cinnamon—

1 cup margarine or butter
¾ cup packed brown sugar
2 egg yolks
2 ounces semisweet chocolate, melted and cooled
1½ teaspoons finely shredded orange peel
1 teaspoon ground cinnamon
1 teaspoon vanilla
¼ teaspoon salt
2¼ cups all-purpose flour
1½ to 2 cups finely chopped pecans
2 egg whites
¾ cup cherry jelly or preserves

In large mixing bowl beat margarine or butter and brown sugar with an electric mixer on medium speed for 30 seconds. Add egg yolks, beating well. Blend in melted chocolate, orange peel, cinnamon, vanilla, and salt. Stir in flour.

Place pecans and egg whites in two separate small, shallow bowls. Slightly beat egg whites with a fork. Shape dough into 1-inch balls. Dip each ball into egg white; roll in pecans to coat. Place balls, 2 inches apart, on lightly greased baking sheets. Using your thumb, make slight indentation in top of each cookie.

Bake in a 350° oven about 12 minutes or till edges are firm. Cool cookies on a wire rack. Fill centers of cooled cookies with a small spoonful of jelly or preserves. Makes about 60 cookies.

Nutrition information per cookie: 88 cal., 5 g fat, 7 mg chol., 1 g pro., 10 g carbo., 0 fiber, 48 mg sodium.

$100 WINNER

Betty J. Nichols, Eugene, Oreg.

◆ Cherry-Chocolate Cookies

continued from page 79
¾ cup packed brown sugar
2 eggs
2 teaspoons vanilla
2 cups all-purpose flour
⅓ cup unsweetened cocoa powder
½ teaspoon baking powder
¼ teaspoon salt
1 cup semisweet chocolate pieces

Melt margarine and the ½ cup chocolate pieces over low heat. Remove from heat. Stir in coffee crystals; cool 5 minutes. Stir in sugars, eggs, and vanilla.

In a medium mixing bowl combine flour, cocoa powder, baking powder, and salt. Stir into coffee mixture. Stir in the 1 cup chocolate pieces. Drop dough by rounded tablespoons onto lightly greased cookie sheets. Bake in a 350° oven 10 minutes. Let cool 1 minute before removing from sheet. Makes 30 cookies.

Nutrition information per cookie: 143 cal., 6 g fat, 14 mg chol., 2 g pro., 22 g carbo., 0 g fiber, 65 mg sodium.

$200 WINNER

Donna Higgins, Halfway, Oreg.

June

8 Great Recipes
for Summer Cookouts

Prize Tested Recipes®

Seafood Enchiladas, Fish Fillets with Ginger-Dill Sauce,

Fried Strawberries with Honey Cream, Berry Meringue Pie

8 Great Recipes for Summer Cookouts

Backyard chefs share a passion for barbecue — the letters accompanying your entries in our Great American Barbecue Contest showed us just how much.

Peanut-Ginger Chicken with California Salsa ◆

Peanut-Ginger Chicken with California Salsa

12 chicken thighs (about 3 pounds),
skinned
½ cup hot water
½ cup creamy peanut butter
¼ cup chili sauce
¼ cup soy sauce
2 tablespoons salad oil
2 tablespoons vinegar
4 cloves garlic, minced
2 teaspoons grated gingerroot or ½ teaspoon
ground ginger
¼ teaspoon ground red pepper
1 cup chopped fresh fruit, such as peeled
peaches, nectarines, pears, or plums
1 cup chopped, seeded cucumber
2 tablespoons thinly sliced green onion
2 tablespoons snipped parsley or cilantro
1 tablespoon sugar

continued on page 84

continued from page 83

1 tablespoon salad oil
1 tablespoon vinegar
*Ti leaves (optional)**
Peach, nectarine, pear, or plum wedges

Rinse chicken; pat dry. Place chicken in a nonmetal bowl.

For marinade, in a small mixing bowl gradually stir hot water into peanut butter. (The mixture will stiffen at first.) Stir in chili sauce, soy sauce, the 2 tablespoons oil, the 2 tablespoons vinegar, garlic, gingerroot, and red pepper.

Place the chicken in a plastic bag set in a shallow bowl. Pour marinade over chicken. Seal the bag and turn to coat chicken thighs with marinade. Chill for 12 to 24 hours, turning the bag occasionally. For salsa, in a medium mixing bowl combine chopped fruit, cucumber, green onion, parsley or cilantro, sugar, 1 tablespoon oil, and 1 tablespoon vinegar. Cover and chill for 1 to 2 hours.

In a covered grill arrange *medium-hot* coals around a drip pan. Test for medium heat above the pan. (To test the heat of the coals, see the tip, *page 91*.) Remove chicken from marinade; discard marinade. Place chicken on the grill rack over the drip pan but not over the coals. Lower the grill hood. Grill chicken for 35 to 45 minutes or till no pink remains.

Serve chicken on ti leaves, if desired. Garnish with fruit. Spoon some salsa over; pass remaining. Makes 6 servings.

Nutrition information per serving: 342 cal., 21 g fat, 93 mg chol., 29 g pro., 10 g carbo., 550 mg sodium, 1 g fiber. RDA: 12% iron, 10% thiamine, 21% riboflavin, 56% niacin.

Note: If using ti leaves, be sure they are safe for contact with food. Wash them well.

Pacific Rim Grilled Pork Salad Josephine's eye catching entree blends grilled pork with ingredients from the eastern rim of the Pacific Ocean —soy sauce, ginger, hoisin sauce, rice wine vinegar, sesame, and enoki mushrooms.

Josephine B. Piro, Easton, Penn.

Pacific Rim Grilled Pork Salad

⅓ cup water
¼ cup dry sherry
¼ cup soy sauce
4 teaspoons grated gingerroot
3 cloves garlic, minced
1 1½-pound boneless pork loin roast, cut into ½-inch-thick slices
¼ cup hoisin sauce
2 tablespoons brown sugar
2 tablespoons salad oil
2 tablespoons rice wine vinegar or white wine vinegar
1 tablespoon toasted sesame oil
1 pound (12 cups) torn fresh spinach
6 thin red onion slices, separated into rings
1 tablespoon toasted sesame seed
1 pound plums, pitted and sliced (3 cups)
Fresh mushrooms, such as enoki or straw mushrooms (optional)

◆ Pacific Rim Grilled Pork Salad, *left*
◆ Grilled Tomatoes with Pesto

salad plates; arrange plum slices around edge. If desired, top each serving with enoki or straw mushrooms. Makes 6 main-dish servings.

Nutrition information per serving: 301 cal., 16 g fat, 51 mg chol., 20 g pro., 21 g carbo., 1,130 mg sodium, 4 g fiber. RDA: 12% calcium, 23% iron, 67% vit. A, 50% vit. C, 57% thiamine, 30% riboflavin, 31% niacin.

Grilled Tomatoes with Pesto

GRILL THESE TOMATOES ALONGSIDE A fast-cooking meat or after you've removed a larger or slower-cooking meat from the grill. Smoked almonds add to the very distinctive grill-smoke flavor. They can be found in the snack section of your supermarket—

3 whole medium tomatoes, cored and
halved crosswise, at room
temperature
2 tablespoons purchased pesto sauce
6 very thin onion slices
½ cup shredded Monterey Jack cheese
(2 ounces)
⅛ cup smoked almonds, chopped
2 tablespoons snipped parsley
Parsley sprigs (optional)

Using a spoon, hollow out the top ¼ inch of tomato halves. Top *each* tomato half with *1 teaspoon* of pesto sauce and an onion slice. Arrange tomatoes in 2 foil pie pans. In a covered grill arrange *medium-hot* coals around the edge of the grill. Test for *medium* heat in the center of the grill. (To test the heat of the coals, *continued on page 86*

For marinade, in a small bowl stir together water, sherry, soy sauce, ginger-root, and garlic. Reserve 2 tablespoons for the dressing. Place meat in a plastic bag set in a large bowl; pour remaining marinade over meat. Close bag and turn to coat meat. Chill for 1 hour.

Drain meat, discarding marinade. Grill meat, uncovered, directly over *medium-hot* coals for 10 to 12 minutes or till just a little pink remains in the center, turning once. (To test the heat of the coals, see the tip, *page 91.*)

For dressing, in a saucepan stir together reserved 2 tablespoons marinade, hoisin sauce, brown sugar, salad oil, and vinegar; heat to boiling. Stir in sesame oil. Remove from heat.

Thinly slice meat into bite-size strips. In a large salad bowl combine meat, spinach, onion slices, and sesame seed. Pour hot dressing over spinach mixture; toss gently to coat. Serve the mixture on

Grilled Tomatoes with Pesto Who says winning recipes have to be complicated? These hot tomatoes use only six ingredients. Ann's huge garden gave her the delicious inspiration. Ann L. Combs, New Hampton, N.H.

continued from page 85
see the tip, *page 91*.) Place the foil pans containing the tomatoes in the center of the grill rack, but not over the coals. Cover; grill for 10 to 15 minutes or till tomato halves are heated through.

Stir together cheese, almonds, and snipped parsley. Sprinkle over tomatoes. Cover and grill about 5 minutes more or till cheese is melted. Season to taste with salt and pepper. If desired, garnish with parsley before serving. Serves 6.

Nutrition information per serving: 133 cal., 10 g fat, 9 mg chol., 5 g pro., 7 g carbo., 98 mg sodium, 2 g fiber. RDA: 12% calcium, 10% vit. A, 27% vit. C, 10% riboflavin.

Peaches-and-Cream Tart

REBECCA MOE, A TOP WINNER, SUGGESTS baking the coconut macaroon crust early in the day (when it's cool)—

9 soft coconut macaroon cookies (half of a
13¾-ounce package)
1 cup (4 ounces) ground pecans
(see note, page 88)

"My tart shows off the beautiful fruits we grow in California," says Rebecca. "The rich macaroon crust and creamy filling make it a runaway favorite." Rebecca Moe, Carmichael, Calif.

3 tablespoons margarine or butter, melted
½ cup whipping cream
1 8-ounce package cream cheese, softened
⅛ cup sugar
2 teaspoons dark rum or orange juice
1 teaspoon vanilla
¼ teaspoon almond extract
2 to 4 medium peaches, peeled, pitted, and
thinly sliced (1½ to 3 cups)
2 tablespoons lemon juice
½ cup fresh raspberries
¼ cup apricot preserves
2 teaspoons honey

For crust, crumble macaroons (you should have about 2 cups). In a large mixing bowl stir together macaroon crumbs, pecans, and margarine or butter. Press mixture onto bottom and up sides of an 11-inch tart pan with a removable bottom or into a 12-inch pizza pan.

Bake in a 350° oven till golden, allowing 15 to 18 minutes for the tart pan or 12 to 15 minutes for the pizza pan. Cool on a wire rack.

For filling, chill a medium mixing bowl and beaters of an electric mixer. In the chilled bowl beat whipping cream with a mixer on medium speed till soft peaks form; set aside. In a small mixing bowl beat cream cheese and sugar with an electric mixer on medium speed till fluffy. Add rum or orange juice, vanilla, and almond extract; beat till smooth. Gently fold in whipped cream. Turn mixture into cooled crust; spread evenly. Cover and chill for 2 to 4 hours.

Before serving, toss peach slices with lemon juice. Arrange peaches and raspberries over filling. For glaze, in a small

continued on page 88
◆ Peaches-and-Cream Tart

continued from page 87

saucepan combine preserves and honey; heat and stir just till melted. Snip any large pieces of fruit in the glaze. Strain glaze, if desired. Carefully brush or spoon the glaze over the fruit.

If using a tart pan, gently remove sides; cut into wedges. Serves 10 to 12.

Nutrition information per serving: 384 cal., 28 g fat, 41 mg chol., 4 g pro., 33 g carbo., 119 mg sodium, 2 g fiber. RDA: 26% calcium, 11% thiamine.
Note: To grind pecans, blend nuts, ½ cup at a time, in blender till very finely chopped. Do not overprocess.

Tortilla-Black Bean Casserole

MERRY HOOVER USES LOW-FAT DAIRY products to make her prizewinning Tex-Mex favorite more healthful—

2 cups chopped onion
1½ cups chopped green pepper
1 14½-ounce can tomatoes, cut up
¾ cup picante sauce
2 cloves garlic, minced
2 teaspoons ground cumin
2 15-ounce cans black beans or red kidney beans, drained
12 6-inch corn tortillas
2 cups shredded low-fat Monterey Jack cheese (8 ounces)
2 medium tomatoes, sliced (optional)
2 cups shredded lettuce (optional)
Sliced green onion (optional)
Sliced pitted ripe olives (optional)
½ cup reduced-calorie dairy sour cream or plain yogurt (optional)

In a large skillet combine onion, green pepper, *undrained* tomatoes, picante sauce, garlic, and cumin. Bring

Tortilla-Black Bean Casserole This layered southwestern-style casserole is hearty enough to be a main dish, but it makes a delicious side dish, too. Merry says it disappears quickly at her cookouts. Merry Hoover, Long Beach, Calif.

to boiling; reduce heat. Simmer, uncovered, for 10 minutes. Stir in beans.

In a 13x9x2-inch baking dish spread *one-third* of the bean mixture over bottom. Top with *half* of the tortillas, overlapping as necessary, and *half* of the cheese. Add another *one-third* of the bean mixture, then remaining tortillas and bean mixture. Cover and bake in a 350° oven for 30 to 35 minutes or till heated through. Sprinkle with remaining cheese. Let stand 10 minutes.

If desired, top with tomato slices, lettuce, green onion, and olives. Cut into squares to serve. If desired, serve with sour cream or yogurt. Makes 10 to 12 side-dish servings or 6 to 8 main-dish servings.

Nutrition information per side-dish serving: 232 cal., 6 g fat, 14 mg chol., 16 g pro., 35 g carbo., 586 mg sodium, 7 g fiber. RDA: 14% calcium, 18% iron, 45% vit. C, 15% thiamine.

◆Tortilla Black Bean Casserole, *left*

◆ Pecan Rice and Feta Salad

Cook rice according to package directions, using 1 teaspoon *salt* as directed; cool slightly. In a mixing bowl combine cheese, peppers, onion, nuts, and pimiento; add cooled rice.

For dressing, stir together oil, vinegar, and pepper; add to rice mixture. Toss gently to coat. Cover; chill for up to 24 hours. If desired, serve over lettuce. Makes 8 side-dish servings.

Nutrition information per serving: 231 cal., 13 g fat, 12 mg chol., 6 g pro., 24 g carbo., 160 mg sodium, 1 g fiber. RDA: 10% calcium, 13% iron, 33% vit. C, 21% thiamine, 12% riboflavin.

Pecan Rice and Feta Salad

WITH A FLAVOR REMINISCENT OF PECANS, the rice in this refreshing salad grows only in Louisiana, but it's available in supermarkets in the rice section—

1 7-ounce package wild pecan
long-grain rice
4 ounces feta cheese, crumbled
½ cup chopped green pepper
½ cup chopped yellow sweet pepper
½ cup chopped onion
⅓ cup pine nuts or chopped
pecans, toasted
1 2-ounce jar diced pimiento, drained
¼ cup olive oil or salad oil
2 tablespoons tarragon white wine vinegar
or 2 tablespoons white wine vinegar plus ⅛
to ¼ teaspoon dried
tarragon, crushed
⅛ teaspoon pepper
Lettuce leaves (optional)

Pecan Rice and Feta Salad
Colorful peppers brighten this nutty,
tarragon-flavored salad. Stacey serves
it with grilled kabobs.   Stacey Swiantek,
Snyder, N.Y.

Tropical Fiesta Steak

FOR AN EASY GO-ALONG, CRINKLE-CUT some potato slices, season and brush with olive oil, then grill alongside the meat for 7 to 9 minutes per side—

⅓ cup frozen orange juice concentrate,
thawed
3 tablespoons cooking oil
3 tablespoons honey
1 tablespoon sliced green onion
2 teaspoons spicy brown or Dijon-style
mustard
1 teaspoon snipped fresh mint or ¼
teaspoon dried mint, crushed
Few drops bottled hot pepper sauce
1 1½-pound boneless beef sirloin steak (cut
1 to 1½ inches thick)
½ cup chopped red sweet pepper
½ cup chopped red apple
½ cup chopped pear
½ cup chopped, peeled peach

continued on page 90

continued from page 89

¼ cup chopped celery
2 tablespoons sliced green onion
2 teaspoons lemon juice
Pineapple-Mustard Sauce (optional)
Romaine leaves (optional)

For marinade, in a small bowl stir together orange juice concentrate, cooking oil, honey, the 1 tablespoon green onion, mustard, mint, and hot pepper sauce. Set aside *¼ cup* of the mixture for the relish; cover and chill till needed.

Place the steak in a plastic bag set in a shallow bowl. Pour the remaining marinade over meat. Seal the bag and turn to coat meat with marinade. Chill for 12 to 24 hours, turning the bag occasionally.

For relish, in a medium mixing bowl combine reserved ¼ cup marinade, red sweet pepper, apple, pear, peach, celery, the 2 tablespoons green onion, and lemon juice. Cover and refrigerate till serving time, up to 24 hours. If desired, make Pineapple-Mustard Sauce; chill.

Remove the steak from the plastic bag, reserving marinade. Grill steak, uncovered, directly over *medium-hot* coals to desired doneness, allowing 12 to 15 minutes for medium doneness on a 1-inch-thick steak or 18 to 22 minutes for medium doneness on a 1½-inch-thick steak. (To test the heat of the coals, see the tip, *opposite*) During cooking, turn meat once; brush occasionally with marinade. Season to taste with salt and pepper.

To serve, slice the steak into thin strips; arrange on romaine leaves, if desired. Serve with fruit relish and Pineapple-Mustard Sauce, if desired. Makes 6 servings.

Tropical Fiesta Steak
The first time Gloria created this summery steak, she served it for her son's surprise birthday party. It turned out to be as big a hit with our tasters as it was with hers.   Gloria Piantek, Nashville, Tenn.

Pineapple-Mustard Sauce: In a small mixing bowl stir together one 8-ounce carton *pineapple-yogurt*, 2 tablespoons milk, and 1 teaspoon *spicy brown mustard* or *Dijon-style mustard*; cover and chill till serving time, for up to 24 hours.

Nutrition information per serving: 287 cal., 12 g fat, 65 mg chol., 23 g pro., 22 g carbo., 77 mg sodium, 1 g fiber. RDA: 19% iron, 172% vit. C, 14% thiamine, 19% riboflavin, 23% niacin.

Lime and Lemon Ice Cream

MARCIE RICHARDSON BUYS FRESH lemons and limes when prices are low, then freezes the juice in ice-cube trays—

8 cups whole milk
3 cups sugar
2 cups whipping cream
⅔ cup lemon juice

⅓ *cup lime juice*
½ *teaspoon lemon extract*
Lemon slices (optional)
Lime slices (optional)

In a very large mixing bowl combine milk, sugar, whipping cream, lemon juice, lime juice, and lemon extract; stir to dissolve sugar. (The mixture may appear slightly curdled.)

Freeze in a 5-quart ice-cream freezer and ripen ice cream according to the manufacturer's directions. If desired, garnish with lemon and lime slices. Makes 4 quarts (24 servings).

Nutrition information per ³/₄*-cup serving*: 211 cal., 10 g fat, 38 mg chol., 3 g pro., 29 g carbo., 48 mg sodium, 0 g fiber. RDA: 14% calcium, 15% vit. A, 12% riboflavin.

Lime and Lemon Ice Cream
Soothe the fire from a spicy barbecue with refreshing spoonfuls of this luscious lemon-lime ice cream.

Marcie Richardson, Salt Lake City, Utah

Checking the Coals

To find out if your coals are the right temperature, first check whether you'll be cooking the food directly over the coals or indirectly (over a drip pan). Then, test the coals at the height the food will be cooking.

Hold your hand, palm side down, above the coals. Start counting the seconds. When your hand gets too hot, withdraw it. The number of seconds you count will tell you the coal temperature.

2 seconds.........*hot*
3 seconds.........*medium-hot*
4 seconds.........*medium*
5 seconds.........*medium-low*
6 seconds.........*low*

For direct cooking, the coals should match the temperatures above. For indirect cooking, the coals must be one level hotter to attain the correct heat over the drip pan. For example, to cook chicken indirectly on the grill rack at *medium* heat, the coals around the drip pan must be *medium-hot*.

Prize Tested Recipes®

◆ Seafood Enchiladas

down, in a greased 12x7½x2-inch microwave-safe baking dish. Stir milk into reserved soup mixture; pour over enchiladas. Cook, covered, on high for 12 to 14 minutes. Sprinkle with remaining cheese. Let stand 10 minutes. Garnish with *cilantro*, if desired. Makes 4 servings.

Nutrition information per serving: 510 cal., 24 g fat, 30 g pro., 1,272 mg sodium.

$200 WINNER
Jamie Lou Voss, San Diego, Calif.

Fish Fillets with Ginger-Dill Sauce

THIS GINGER-AND-SHRIMP DILL SAUCE complements any variety of fish—

⅓ cup mayonnaise or salad dressing
2 tablespoons dairy sour cream
½ teaspoon minced dried onion
¼ teaspoon ground ginger
1 teaspoon snipped fresh dillweed or ¼ teaspoon dried dillweed
¼ cup peeled, cooked small shrimp (fresh-cooked or canned)
1 pound fresh or frozen fish fillets, thawed (such as cod, sole, or flounder)
1 tablespoon margarine or butter
Lemon wedges (optional)
Fresh dill sprigs (optional)

In a small bowl stir together mayonnaise or salad dressing, sour cream,

Seafood Enchiladas

SERVE THESE WINNING ENCHILADAS with homemade or purchased salsa—

1 10¾-ounce can lower-sodium condensed cream of chicken soup
½ cup chopped onion
Several dashes bottled hot pepper sauce
Dash ground nutmeg
Dash pepper
1 10-ounce package frozen chopped spinach, thawed and drained
1 8-ounce package frozen crab-flavored, salad-style fish, chopped

1¾ cups shredded Monterey Jack cheese (7 ounces)
8 5- to 6-inch corn tortillas
1 cup milk

In a mixing bowl stir together soup, onion, hot pepper sauce, nutmeg, and pepper. In another bowl stir together *half* of the soup mixture, spinach, fish, and *1 cup* of the cheese; set aside.

Wrap tortillas in paper towels; microcook on 100% power (high) for 30 to 60 seconds. Place ⅓ *cup* fish mixture on each tortilla; roll up. Place, seam side minced onion, ginger, dillweed, and dash *salt*. Stir in shrimp; set aside. Place fillets in a 12x7½x2-inch microwave-safe baking dish. Dot with margarine or butter. Cover with waxed paper.

Micro-cook on 100% power (high) for 5 to 7 minutes or till fish just begins to flake easily, turning dish once. Spoon sauce atop fish. Cover; cook on high for 1½ to 2 minutes more or till sauce is heated through. Serve with lemon wedges and garnish with fresh dill sprigs, if desired. Makes 4 servings.

Nutrition information per serving: 269 cal., 20 g fat, 73 mg chol., 21 g pro., 1 g carbo., 252 mg sodium, 0 g fiber. RDA: 10% vit. A, 15% niacin.

$100 WINNER

Harriette Peterson, Alvin, Tex.

Fried Strawberries with Honey Cream

WHILE VISITING SCOTLAND, BETTIE sampled fried strawberries with a velvety cream cheese sauce. After returning home, she created this version—

4 cups fresh strawberries
Shortening or cooking oil for deep frying
1 cup all-purpose flour
1 tablespoon sugar
2 beaten eggs
½ cup dry white wine
2 tablespoons cooking oil
½ cup sugar
Honey Cream

Wash strawberries; remove stems. Pat dry with paper towels. Set aside. In a large, deep saucepan or deep fryer heat 2 inches melted shortening to 375°.

For batter, in a medium bowl combine the flour and the 1 tablespoon

sugar. Make a well in the center. Combine eggs, wine, and the 2 tablespoons oil; add to flour mixture. Beat with a rotary beater or wire whisk till smooth. Dip strawberries, a few at a time, into batter. Fry strawberries, a few at a time, in hot shortening for 1 to 2 minutes or till golden. Remove with a

Fish-Fillets with Ginger-Dill Sauce, *above* ◆
Fried Strawberries with Honey Cream, *left* ◆

slotted spoon; drain on paper towels. While still warm, roll in the remaining ½ cup sugar, if desired. Cool slightly. Serve warm with Honey Cream. Serves 8.

Honey Cream: In a medium bowl stir together ½ of an 8-ounce package *cream cheese,* softened; ¼ cup *dairy sour cream*; 2 tablespoons *sugar*; 2 tablespoons *honey*; and several drops *almond extract.* Cover and refrigerate leftover sauce up to 1 week. Makes 1 cup.

Nutrition information for 4 strawberries and 2 tablespoons sauce: 338 cal., 18 g fat, 72 mg chol., 5 g pro., 38 g carbo., 64 mg sodium, 2 g fiber. RDA: 13% vit. A, 71% vit. C.

$200 WINNER

Bettie Brown, Casa Grande, Ariz.

pecans; reserve for garnish. Coarsely chop remaining chocolate and finely chop remaining pecans. Combine and set aside.

Beat egg white mixture with an electric mixer on medium speed till soft peaks form. Add sugar, *1 tablespoon* at a time, beating on high speed till very stiff peaks form.

In a medium mixing bowl combine the coarsely chopped chocolate-and-pecan mixture and the crushed crackers. Fold cracker mixture into egg whites. Spread meringue into a greased 9-inch pie plate, building up sides slightly. Bake in a 350° oven about 25 minutes or till top is golden. Cool completely.

In a medium mixing bowl combine whipping cream, powdered sugar, and vanilla. Beat on low speed till soft peaks form. Fold in *1½ cups* of the sliced strawberries; spoon atop cooled meringue. Top with remaining strawberries and reserved chocolate-pecan mixture. Serve immediately or chill for up to 24 hours. Makes 8 servings.

Nutrition information per serving: 362 cal., 23 g fat, 41 mg chol., 4 g pro., 40 g carbo., 150 mg sodium, 2 g fiber. RDA: 17% vit. A, 36% vit. C.
$100 WINNER
Patricia A. Zeeb, El Cajon, Calif.

Berry Meringue Pie

STRAWBERRIES, CHOCOLATE, PECANS, and whipped cream fill this crisp meringue crust—

3 egg whites
1 teaspoon almond extract
½ teaspoon baking powder
¾ cup semisweet chocolate pieces
½ cup chopped pecans
¾ cup sugar
1 cup crushed rich round crackers
(about 23 crackers)
1 cup whipping cream
2 tablespoons sifted powdered sugar
½ teaspoon vanilla
2 cups sliced strawberries

In a large mixing bowl combine egg whites, almond extract, and baking powder. Let mixture stand at room temperature for 30 minutes.

Meanwhile, mix *2 tablespoons* of the chocolate pieces with *2 tablespoons* of the

July

Summer Fun
Outdoor Eats

Prize Tested Recipes®

Greek Tortellini Salad, Dill-Artichoke

Potato Salad, Honey Apple Ribs, Marvelous Mustard Ribs

Summer Fun Outdoor Eats

YAHOO! Head outside for some super-cool, summertime treats. Choose from 16 scrumptious ideas, all simple to make and exciting to eat. From totally awesome ice-cream dreams to dinner on the deck, these kid-pleasing mini recipes will get your family in the summer spirit. Besides, the mess is less outdoors.

Party-Size Banana Split

Gather the whole team to create this super-bowl sundae. Fill an extra-large bowl with bananas and scoops of ice cream. Drizzle with ice-cream toppings, then squirt on pressurized whipped cream. Top with nuts and maraschino cherries.

Sky-High Brownie Pie

CREATE YOUR OWN DESIGNER PIE USING a microwave brownie mix and your favorite flavors of ice cream or sherbet—

Nonstick spray coating
1 package microwave fudge brownie
   mix (refill size without frosting)
3 to 4 tablespoons ice cream topping (such
   as strawberry, pineapple, or chocolate)
1½ quarts sherbet or ice cream (any flavor)
1 cup fresh raspberries, blueberries, or
   sliced strawberries

Spray a 9-inch microwave-safe pie plate with nonstick spray coating. In a medium mixing bowl prepare the brownie-mix batter according to package directions. Spread evenly in the prepared pie plate. Micro-bake according to package directions. Transfer to a wire rack; cool completely.

Spread ice cream topping over brownie; freeze for 10 minutes. Let sit at room temperature for 10 minutes.

continued on page 98

◆ Sky-High Brownie Pie, *above*
Party-Size Banana Split, *right* ◆

continued from page 96

Quickly scoop sherbet or ice cream into crust. Freeze about 4 hours or till firm. Cover with freezer wrap; freeze up to 1 month. Let stand at room temperature 10 to 15 minutes. Top with berries. Cut into wedges. Serves 8.

Nutrition information per serving: 377 cal., 6 g fat, 11 mg chol., 4 g pro., 79 g carbo., 1 g fiber, 191 mg sodium. RDA: 10% calcium, 11% iron, 15% vit. C.

S'mores Sundae

1 The first step:
A big scoop of vanilla ice cream.

2 Pour on the chocolate syrup.
Are you hungry yet?

3 Add a spoonful of ooey,
gooey marshmallow creme.

4 Slip in two chocolate-covered
graham crackers; crumble another
one on top.

5 You'll definitely want s'more!

Ice Cream on a Stick

Cut a block of ice cream into rectangles. Place on a chilled baking sheet and freeze till firm. Add wooden sticks and freeze again. Spread with chocolate-fudge ice-cream coating and a variety of small candies.

◆ S'mores Sundae

◆ Ice Cream on a Stick

Zany-Zoo Mix

THE GOLDEN, HONEY-COATED POPCORN is as fun to make as it is to eat. Pop the popcorn, toss with a honey and cinnamon glaze, and bake—

6 cups popped popcorn
1 cup dry roasted peanuts
½ cup packed brown sugar
¼ cup margarine or butter
2 tablespoons honey
½ teaspoon ground cinnamon
1 10-ounce package bear-shaped graham snacks (4½ cups)
½ of a 5.4-ounce package (3 pouches) animal-shaped chewy fruit snacks

Place popcorn and peanuts in a buttered 15x10x1-inch baking pan. In a small saucepan combine brown sugar, margarine or butter, honey, and cinnamon. Cook and stir over low heat till boiling. Boil gently, uncovered, without stirring, for 4 minutes. Pour over popcorn and stir to coat.

Bake the coated popcorn mixture in a 300° oven for 20 minutes, stirring every 5 minutes. Transfer to a large mixing bowl; toss in bear-shaped graham snacks. Cool mixture completely. Add fruit snacks. Store in covered container. Makes about 10 cups.

Nutrition information per 1-cup serving: 327 cal., 13 g fat, 0 mg chol., 6 g pro., 49 g carbo., 1 g fiber, 288 mg sodium.

Zany Zoo Mix ◆

Wet-and-Wild Berry Slush

In a blender container combine 3 cups fresh strawberries, ½ of a 12-ounce can frozen cherry or orange juice concentrate, and a spoonful of sugar. While blending, add ice cubes through hole in lid till slushy. Grab a straw and start sippin'. Makes 4 servings.

State Fair Lemonade

For 1 glassful, slice a lemon in half; remove seeds. Squeeze juice from lemon halves into a large jar with a lid; drop in lemon halves. Add ¾ cup water and a couple spoonfuls of sugar. Cover jar; shake well. Remove lemon halves; serve lemonade over ice.

Peach 'n' Yogurt Smoothie

In a blender container combine 4 peeled and quartered ripe peaches, 8 ounces vanilla yogurt, ½ cup milk, a couple spoonfuls brown sugar, and a dash ground nutmeg. Blend till thick and smooth, adding ice cubes through the lid. Makes 4 servings.

Tortilla Fruit Cups

SO DELICIOUS, YOU CAN EVEN EAT THE dishes! Fill crispy-baked fruit cups with orange-glazed fresh fruit and serve as a snack or dessert—

4 6-inch flour tortillas
1 tablespoon margarine or butter, melted
1 teaspoon sugar
⅛ teaspoon ground cinnamon
or apple pie spice
¼ cup orange marmalade
3 cups assorted cut-up fresh fruit (such as plums, kiwi fruit, cantaloupe, and berries)
¼ cup chopped pecans (optional)

Wrap tortillas in foil and heat in a 350° oven for 5 to 10 minutes or till warm. Remove tortillas from foil and brush both sides of each tortilla lightly with margarine or butter. Place each tortilla in a 10-ounce custard cup, pleating as necessary to fit. Combine sugar and cinnamon or apple pie spice and sprinkle inside each tortilla. Bake in a 350° oven for 10 to 12 minutes or till crisp. Remove from cups; cool.

Meanwhile, in a small saucepan melt the orange marmalade over medium heat, stirring occasionally; cool to room temperature. Place fresh fruit in a large mixing bowl. Add the melted marmalade and gently toss to mix. Spoon fruit mixture into the tortilla cups. If desired, sprinkle with chopped pecans. Makes 4 servings.

Nutrition information per serving: 208 cal., 5 g fat, 0 mg chol., 3 g pro., 41 g carbo., 3 g fiber, 41 mg sodium.

Facing page
◆ Wet and Wild Berry Slush, *left,* State Fair Lemonade, *center,* Peach 'n' Yogurt Smoothie, *right*

Grilled Pizza

CRISPY-CRUST FANS WILL LOVE THIS cooked-over-the-coals pizza—

Assorted toppings such as thinly sliced zucchini or yellow summer squash, broccoli flowerets, pepperoni slices, cooked and peeled shrimp, and/or sliced mall tomatoes
1 10-ounce package refrigerated pizza dough
¾ cup pizza sauce or ⅓ cup pesto
1½ cups shredded mozzarella cheese

For toppings, if using zucchini, summer squash, or broccoli, blanch vegetables for 2 minutes in enough water to cover; drain and rinse immediately in cold water.

With your fingers, pat the pizza dough into a greased 12-inch pizza pan or two greased 8x1½-inch or 9x1½-inch round baking pans. Place pan(s) on the grill rack directly over *medium* coals. Grill, covered, for 5 minutes. Carefully remove the pan(s) from the grill.

Spread pizza sauce or pesto onto the grilled crust. Sprinkle with desired toppings; top with shredded cheese. Return

◆ Grilled Pizza

pizza to the grill rack. Grill, covered, about 10 minutes or till pizza is heated through and cheese is melted, checking occasionally to make sure the crust does not overbrown. Makes 6 main-dish servings.

Nutrition information per serving: 251 cal., 9 g fat, 47 mg chol., 16 g pro., 26 g carbo., 0 g fiber, 653 mg sodium. RDA: 25% calcium, 13% iron, 18% vit. A, 20% vit. C, 16% thiamine, 18% riboflavin, 16% niacin.

Turkey-Berry Club

Stir chopped nuts into soft style cream cheese; spread onto marble bread. Layer bread with deli turkey, sliced strawberries, and lettuce. Top with another slice of bread.

Peanut Butter Triple Decker

Sweeten peanut butter with honey; spread onto a toasted bagel half. Top with raisins, apple slices, and the other bagel half.

Peaanut Butter Triple Decker ◆

◆ Turkey-Berry Club

Hawaiian Hoagies

Slather a hoagie bun with mustard and sweet and sour sauce. Fill bun with deli ham, halved pineapple rings, and shredded cheese. Wrap in foil and grill till hot.

The Vegetarian

Mix equal parts of guacamole and sour cream and a dash of hot pepper sauce; spread inside a split pita. Stuff with cheese and veggies.

Hawaiian Hoagies ◆

◆ The Vegetarian

All-American Berries and Cream

BRING ON THE FLAG! LIVEN UP YOUR picnics with this colorful dessert—

½ cup apple jelly
1½ cups fresh blueberries
4 cups fresh strawberries, similar in size,
with stems removed
1 cup whipping cream
2 tablespoons sugar
½ teaspoon finely shredded orange peel
½ teaspoon vanilla
⅓ cup dairy sour cream

In a saucepan cook and stir apple jelly over medium heat till melted; cool. Toss blueberries with *half* of the jelly.

On a large rectangular platter or tray (about 13x9 inches) arrange blueberries in upper left-hand corner in a square. Place strawberries, stem side down, in horizontal rows (resembling a flag), leaving about 1 inch between each row for whipped cream filling. With a pastry brush, brush the strawberries with the remaining jelly.

For the whipped cream filling, in a chilled mixing bowl combine whipping cream, sugar, finely shredded orange peel, and vanilla. Beat with chilled beaters of an electric mixer on medium speed till soft peaks form (tips curl). Fold in sour cream. Place filling in a pastry bag fitted with a large, grooved tip.

Pipe the whipped cream filling in rows between the strawberries. Serve immediately or cover and chill for up to 2 hours. Makes 10 to 12 servings.

Nutrition information per serving: 179 cal., 11 g fat, 36 mg chol., 1 g pro., 21 g carbo., 2 g fiber, 17 mg sodium. RDA: 16% vit. A, 63% vit. C.

◆ All-American Berries and Cream

Banana Crunch Pops

THESE REFRESHING FROZEN POPS TAKE just minutes to make—

1 8-ounce carton yogurt (any flavor)
15 wooden sticks
3 bananas, peeled and cut into
5 pieces each
1½ cups granola, crisp rice cereal, or
Grape Nuts cereal

Place yogurt in a shallow dish. Insert a wooden stick into each banana piece. Roll banana pieces in the yogurt until the entire piece is covered. Place the cereal in a small, shallow dish. Roll the banana pieces in the cereal.

After coating with cereal, place banana pieces on a waxed-paper-lined baking sheet. Place in the freezer.

When frozen, wrap each in freezer wrap and label. Store in freezer. Let stand at room temperature for 10 minutes before serving. Makes 15 pops.

Nutrition information per pop: 90 cal., 2 g fat, 1 mg chol., 2 g pro., 16 g carbo., 1 g fiber, 20 mg sodium.

Banana Crunch Pops ◆

Greek Tortellini Salad

THIS POTLUCK-SIZE SALAD CAN BE MADE
several hours ahead—

2 9-ounce packages plain or tricolored
refrigerated cheese tortellini,
cooked and drained
2 red and/or green sweet peppers, cut into
thin strips (2 cups)
1 small red onion, thinly sliced
¼ cup sliced pitted ripe olives
½ cup rice wine vinegar or white vinegar
½ cup olive oil or salad oil
3 tablespoons snipped fresh mint or 1
tablespoon dried mint
3 tablespoons lemon juice
2 tablespoons dry sherry
1½ teaspoons seasoned salt
1 teaspoon garlic powder
1 teaspoon pepper
⅛ to ¼ teaspoon crushed red pepper
½ cup crumbled feta cheese

In a large bowl combine cooked pasta,
sweet peppers, onion, and olives. For
dressing, combine vinegar, oil, mint,
lemon juice, sherry, seasoned salt, garlic
powder, pepper, and crushed red pepper. Pour over salad; toss to coat. Cover;
chill 4 to 24 hours. Stir in feta cheese.
Use a slotted spoon to serve. Makes 12
to 14 side-dish servings.

Nutrition information per serving:
236 cal., 13 g fat, 27 mg chol., 8 g pro.,
24 g carbo., 415 mg sodium. RDA:
30% vit. C.

$200 WINNER

Tracy Yonker, Pittsboro, N.C.

Dill-Artichoke Potato Salad

DIANE UPDATES HER POTATO SALAD WITH
artichokes and dillweed—

3 pounds whole tiny new potatoes
1 cup mayonnaise or salad dressing
2 tablespoons red wine vinegar
2 tablespoons Dijon-style mustard
1 tablespoon lemon-pepper seasoning
1 tablespoon snipped fresh dill or 2 to 3
teaspoons dried dillweed, crushed
4 hard-cooked eggs, peeled and chopped
2 6-ounce jars marinated artichoke hearts,
drained and sliced
¾ cup chopped onion
2 tablespoons chopped dill pickle

◆ Greek Tortellini Salad, *top*
◆ Dill-Artichoke Potato Salad, *above*

Scrub potatoes with a vegetable brush under running water. In a Dutch oven cook unpeeled potatoes, covered, in boiling lightly salted water about 20 minutes or just till tender. Drain. Cool potatoes; cut into bite-size pieces.

In a very large bowl stir together mayonnaise or salad dressing, vinegar, mustard, lemon-pepper seasoning, and dill. Gently fold in cooked potatoes, eggs, artichoke hearts, onion, and chopped dill pickle. Cover and chill 4 to 24 hours. Stir gently before serving. Makes 16 side-dish servings.

Nutrition information per serving: 224 cal., 14 g fat, 61 mg chol., 4 g pro., 22 g carbo., 1 g fiber, 572 mg sodium. RDA: 13% iron, 27% vit. C, 10% niacin.

$100 WINNER
Diane Schendel, Modesto, Calif.

Honey Apple Ribs

WANT AN EASY, NEW BARBECUE SAUCE? Just add apple jelly, honey, catsup, sweet relish, and cinnamon to bottled barbecue sauce for finger-lickin' great flavor—

¾ cup bottled barbecue sauce
⅓ cup honey
⅓ cup apple jelly
¼ cup catsup
¼ cup water
¼ cup finely chopped celery
1 tablespoon brown sugar
2 teaspoons sweet pickle relish
1½ teaspoons prepared mustard
½ teaspoon ground cinnamon
3½ pounds pork loin back ribs, cut into 2- to 3-rib portions

In a medium saucepan combine barbecue sauce, honey, jelly, catsup, the ¼

cup water, celery, brown sugar, relish, mustard, and cinnamon. Cook and stir over medium heat till bubbly. Reduce heat. Simmer, uncovered, about 15 minutes, stirring frequently. Remove from heat; let cool.

Meanwhile, place ribs in a Dutch oven. Add water to cover. Bring to boiling. Reduce heat and simmer, covered, 45 minutes or till tender. Drain. Cool slightly. Place ribs in 3-quart baking dish; pour cooled sauce over ribs. Cover and chill several hours.

Before serving, remove ribs from sauce. Reserve sauce. Grill ribs directly over *medium* coals or broil 4 to 5 inches

◆ Honey Apple Ribs

from heat for 15 to 20 minutes, turning and brushing with sauce once. (Watch closely to prevent burning.) Heat any remaining sauce till bubbly; pass with ribs. Makes 5 servings.

Nutrition information per serving: 677 cal., 38 g fat, 150 mg chol., 37 g pro., 45 g carbo., 1 g fiber, 608 g sodium. RDA: 10% calcium, 22% iron, 48% thiamine, 40% riboflavin, 49% niacin.

$200 WINNER
Maria Pangelinan, Bakersfield, Calif.

Marvelous Mustard Ribs

FOR THESE TASTY RIBS, FIRST RUB A SPICE mixture over the ribs, then grill and baste with a mustard-and-honey sauce—

⅓ cup sugar
1 teaspoon pepper
2 teaspoons paprika
1 teaspoon curry powder
½ teaspoon salt
3½ to 4 pounds pork country-style ribs
1 cup packed brown sugar
⅔ cup white vinegar or
cider vinegar
½ cup chopped onion
⅓ cup spicy brown mustard
2 cloves garlic, minced
2 tablespoons honey
2 teaspoons liquid smoke
¼ teaspoon celery seed

In a small bowl combine the sugar, pepper, paprika, curry powder, and salt. Rub mixture over ribs, coating well. Place ribs in shallow pan. Cover and chill for 2 to 6 hours.

In a covered grill, arrange *medium* coals around a drip pan. Test for *medium-low* heat above pan. Place ribs, fat side up, on grill rack over drip pan but not over coals. Lower grill hood. Grill about 1¼ hours or till tender, turning once, and adding more coals as needed.

Meanwhile, for sauce, in a medium saucepan combine brown sugar, vinegar, onion, mustard, garlic, honey, liquid smoke, and celery seed. Bring to boiling; reduce heat. Cook, uncovered, for 25 to 30 minutes or till slightly thickened, stirring occasionally.

Brush sauce over ribs occasionally during last 10 to 15 minutes of grilling. Heat any remaining sauce till bubbly and pass with ribs. Makes 8 servings.

Nutrition information per serving: 513 cal., 24 g fat, 127 mg chol., 34 g pro., 42 g carbo., 0 g fiber, 370 mg sodium. RDA: 22% iron, 57% thiamine, 30% riboflavin, 42% niacin.
$100 WINNER
Mrs. Carolyn Funk,
Mount Pleasant, Pa.

◆ Marvelous Mustard Ribs

August

Garden Fresh Recipes

Easy Cooking for Lazy Summer Days

Prize Tested Recipes®

Golden Fruit Conserve, Western-Style Pepper Jelly,

Cucumber Buns, Warm Dilled Potato Salad

Garden Fresh Recipes

Easy Cooking for Lazy Summer Days

Within easy reach, the year's freshest foods await—ripe and ready for picking. Juicy tomatoes, peppers, plums, berries, and other garden treasures are all part of our easy-on-the-cook recipes. You'll find them in a sampling of summery dishes, from appetizers to desserts, on the following pages.

Ratatouille Pizza

BESIDES HAVING EVERY VOWEL IN THE alphabet, Italian ratatouille (raa taa TOO ee) also contains just about every vegetable from your garden, making it a tasty spread for this easy-to-hold snack—

1 small eggplant (12 ounces)
½ cup chopped onion
2 cloves garlic, minced
2 tablespoons olive oil or cooking oil
4 medium tomatoes, peeled,
seeded, and chopped (about 2 ⅔ cups)
1 tablespoon snipped fresh oregano
or thyme or 1 teaspoon dried oregano or
thyme, crushed
½ teaspoon sugar
¼ teaspoon salt
⅛ teaspoon pepper
1 16-ounce package Boboli (12-inch
Italian bread shell)
2 medium red and/or yellow tomatoes,
halved lengthwise and thinly sliced
1 small zucchini, thinly sliced (2 cups)
1 small crookneck squash,
thinly sliced (2 cups)
⅓ cup crumbled feta cheese
2 tablespoons sliced pitted ripe olives
½ cup shredded mozzarella cheese
(2 ounces)

Chop enough of the eggplant to make *1 cup.* Halve remaining eggplant lengthwise and thinly slice; set aside.

◆ Ratatouille Pizza

In a medium skillet cook onion and garlic in *1 tablespoon* of the oil till tender but not brown. Add chopped eggplant, chopped tomatoes, oregano or thyme, sugar, salt, and pepper. Cook, uncovered, over medium-low heat about 15 minutes or till liquid is evaporated and mixture is of spreading consistency, stirring occasionally during cooking.

Place the bread shell on a lightly greased baking sheet. Spread the warm tomato mixture onto bread. Arrange the tomato and eggplant slices around the outside edge. Arrange zucchini and crookneck squash slices in the center. Brush vegetables with the remaining 1 tablespoon oil. Sprinkle with feta cheese and olives. Sprinkle with shredded mozzarella cheese.

Bake, uncovered, in a 400° oven for 12 to 15 minutes or till vegetables are warm and cheese is melted. Transfer the bread to a serving platter. Cut into wedges to serve. Makes 12 appetizer servings.

Nutrition information per serving: 168 cal., 7 g fat, 7 mg chol., 7 g pro., 23 g carbo., 321 mg sodium, 2 g fiber. RDA: 12% calcium, 22% vit. C, 16% thiamine, 13% riboflavin, 11% niacin.

Thai Steak and Pasta Salad with Peanut-Pepper Dressing

YOU'LL FIND LEMONGRASS, A LEMON-flavored herb, in farmers' markets or Oriental food shops. Or, use cilantro—

4 ounces fine noodles or fusilli pasta, broken (2½ cups)
⅓ cup rice wine vinegar or vinegar
⅓ cup salad oil
3 tablespoons soy sauce
2 tablespoons peanut butter

1 tablespoon chopped fresh lemongrass or snipped fresh cilantro
2 cloves garlic, minced
¼ teaspoon crushed red pepper
1 pound boneless beef top sirloin steak, cut 1 inch thick
5 cups shredded Savoy or Chinese cabbage, spinach, romaine, and/or bok choy
½ cup shredded carrot
4 green onions, cut lengthwise into fourths and bias-sliced into 1-inch pieces
½ of a medium cucumber, sliced
1 medium yellow summer squash, cut into julienne strips
¼ cup chopped peanuts
Fresh red hot peppers (optional)

Cook noodles in boiling salted water according to package directions; drain, cover, and chill. For dressing, in a blender container or food processor

◆ Thai Steak and Pasta Salad with Peanut-Pepper Dressing

bowl combine vinegar, salad oil, soy sauce, peanut butter, lemongrass, garlic, and red pepper. Cover and blend or process till combined.

Trim excess fat from meat; place meat in a shallow dish. Add ⅓ cup dressing; turn once. Cover; marinate in refrigerator for 2 hours or let stand at room temperature for 30 minutes. Drain meat, discarding marinade. Place steak on the unheated rack of a broiler pan. Broil 3 inches from heat for 12 to 15 minutes for medium doneness, turning once. (Or, grill, uncovered, directly over *medium* coals for 12 to 15 minutes.) Cut meat into thin strips.

continued on page 112

continued from page 111

Meanwhile, in a mixing bowl combine noodles, cabbage, carrot, and green onions. Add about ¼ *cup* of the remaining dressing; toss to coat. Arrange the noodle mixture on 4 salad plates; top with warm meat, cucumber, and squash. Drizzle with remaining dressing; sprinkle with chopped peanuts. If desired, garnish each serving with fresh hot peppers. Makes 4 main-dish servings.

Nutrition information per serving: 478 cal., 24 g fat, 101 mg chol., 36 g pro., 33 g carbo., 536 mg sodium, 4 g fiber. RDA: 10% calcium, 36% iron, 65 % vit. A, 59% vit. C, 51% thiamine, 36% riboflavin, 57% niacin.

Double Apricot Margaritas

BLEND FRESH OR CANNED APRICOTS with apricot nectar for an icy double-fruit refresher—

1¼ cups halved, pitted, unpeeled apricots or one 16-ounce can unpeeled apricot halves (juice pack), drained
½ cup tequila
¼ cup sugar
¼ cup lime juice
¼ cup apricot nectar
20 to 24 ice cubes (about 3 cups)
Lime juice
Coarse salt

In a blender container combine apricot halves, tequila, sugar, ¼ cup lime juice, and apricot nectar. Cover and blend till smooth.

With the blender running, add the ice cubes, a few at a time, through the hole in the lid, blending till slushy.

Rub the rims of 8 to 10 glasses with lime juice. Invert glasses into a shallow dish of coarse salt. Shake off any excess salt. Pour in the margarita mixture. Makes 8 to 10 (4-ounce) servings.

Nutrition information per serving: 81 cal., 0 g fat, 0 mg chol., 1 g pro., 13 g carbo., 3 mg sodium, 1 g fiber. RDA: 15% vit. A., 11% vit. C.

Double Apricot Coolers (nonalcoholic): Prepare Margaritas as directed at left, *except* increase the apricot nectar to one 6-ounce can and omit the tequila.

Nutrition information per serving: 56 cal., 0 g fat, 0 mg chol., 1 g pro., 14 g carbo., 3 mg sodium, 1 g fiber. RDA: 17% vit. A., 11% vit. C.

Garden Fresh Dinner Menu

Double Apricot Margaritas

or Double Apricot Coolers

Vegetarian Pasta

Steamed Green Beans

Lemon-Pepper Breadsticks

Fresh Fruit with Cherry Cream

◆ ◆ ◆

Double Apricot Margaritas, Vegetarian Pasta, ◆ Steamed Green Beans, Lemon-Pepper Breadsticks, Fresh Fruit with Cherry Cream

Vegetarian Pasta

THE PASTA IN THIS SATISFYING ENTRÉE IS mafalda—a long, flat, ribbonlike pasta with ruffled edges—

8 ounces mafalda pasta or fettuccine,
broken in half
1 medium red, yellow, or green sweet
pepper, cut into thin
2-inch-long strips (1 cup)
1 medium leek or 4 green onions, sliced
1 cup cold evaporated milk
2 teaspoons all-purpose flour
2 teaspoons snipped fresh dill or ½ teaspoon
dried dillweed
¼ teaspoon salt
⅛ teaspoon white pepper
¾ cup shredded Havarti or Swiss cheese
(3 ounces)
1 small tomato, seeded and chopped
¼ cup toasted pecan halves
Grated Parmesan cheese (optional)
Fresh dill (optional)

In a large saucepan cook pasta, uncovered, in boiling salted water, allowing 10 minutes for mafalda or 8 minutes for fettuccine. Add pepper strips and leek or green onions; cook for 4 minutes more. Drain pasta and vegetables; return to pan.

Meanwhile, for sauce, in a saucepan use a fork to stir together cold milk, flour, dill, salt, and white pepper. Cook and stir over medium heat till thickened and bubbly. Cook and stir 1 minute more. Add Havarti cheese; stir till melted. Stir in tomato; heat through.

To serve, stir ½ cup of the sauce into pasta mixture; toss gently to coat. Serve remaining sauce over pasta. Top with pecans and grated Parmesan, if desired. Garnish with fresh dill, if desired. Makes 4 main-dish servings.

Preparing a Backyard Dinner

◆ About an hour and a half before dinner, mix up a batch of apricot margaritas or apricot coolers and relax on the patio before you head for the kitchen.

◆ An hour ahead of time, clean, cut, and measure all of the ingredients you'll be needing for dinner.

◆ Whip up the dessert topping; cover and refrigerate the topping until serving time.

◆ When you've finished the topping, heat the water for the pasta.

◆ Twist, brush, and pop the breadsticks into the oven.

◆ About 15 minutes before dinner, cook the beans and pasta and vegetables.

◆ Cook and stir the pasta sauce, then pour it over the pasta.

Microwave directions: Prepare as directed at left, *except*, for sauce, in a 4-cup glass measure stir together cold milk, flour, dill, salt, and white pepper. Cook, uncovered, on 100% power (high) 3 to 5 minutes or till thickened and bubbly, stirring every minute till sauce starts to thicken, then every 30 seconds. Cook, uncovered, for 30 seconds more. Add cheese; stir till melted. Stir in tomato. Cook, uncovered, on high 30 seconds or till heated through.

Nutrition information per serving: 466 cal., 19 g fat, 45 mg chol., 14 g pro., 58 g carbo., 311 mg sodium, 2 g fiber. RDA: 39% calcium, 20% iron, 14% vit. A, 42% vit. C, 47% thiamine, 65% riboflavin, 22% niacin.

Lemon-Pepper Breadsticks

KEEP REFRIGERATED BREADSTICKS ON hand so you can bake these easy attention-getters anytime—

½ teaspoon finely shredded lemon peel
1 tablespoon water
1 tablespoon lemon juice
¼ teaspoon salt
¼ to ½ teaspoon coarsely ground pepper
1 package (8) refrigerated breadsticks

In a small mixing bowl combine lemon peel, water, lemon juice, salt, and pepper. Arrange breadsticks on an ungreased baking sheet, twisting ends in opposite directions several times. Brush twists with lemon-pepper mixture. Bake according to package directions. Makes 8 breadsticks.

Nutrition information per breadstick: 101 cal., 2 g fat, 0 mg chol., 3 g pro., 17 g carbo., 297 mg sodium, 0 g fiber. RDA: 80% thiamine.

Fresh Fruit with Cherry Cream

ADDING VANILLA YOGURT TO WHIPPING cream cuts the fat and gives silky smoothness at the same time—

½ cup whipping cream
¼ cup vanilla yogurt
1 tablespoon sugar
1 tablespoon kirsch or cherry liqueur

4 cups mixed fresh fruit, such as sliced
nectarines or peaches, whole raspberries,
and/or halved and pitted sweet cherries

In a chilled mixing bowl combine
whipping cream, yogurt, sugar, and
liqueur. Beat with chilled beaters of an
electric mixer on medium speed till soft
peaks form. Cover; chill for up to 2
hours. To serve, dollop atop fruit. Serve
immediately. Makes 4 to 6 servings.

Nutrition information per serving:
230 cal., 12 g fat, 41 mg chol., 3 g pro.,
29 g carbo., 20 mg sodium, 4 g dietary
fiber. RDA: 24% vit. A, 29% vit. C,
10% riboflavin.

Cauliflower Toss with Pecan Dressing

YES, YOU CAN USE FROZEN OR CANNED
corn in this side-dish salad but, in the
midst of summer, why not take advan-
tage of sweet kernels right off the cob—

4 fresh ears of corn or 2 cups frozen or
canned sweet corn
⅓ cup chopped pecans
3 cloves garlic, minced
¼ cup almond oil or salad oil
¼ cup white wine vinegar
2 tablespoons snipped chives
2 tablespoons snipped parsley
1 teaspoon sugar
½ teaspoon salt
⅛ teaspoon pepper
3 cups small cauliflower flowerets
2 cups quartered cherry tomatoes
Leaves of greens, such as flowering kale,
leaf lettuce, spinach,
or romaine leaves (optional)

For fresh ears of corn, remove husks;
scrub with a stiff brush to remove silks.

Garden Fresh Salads

Cauliflower Toss with Pecan Dressing

♦ ♦ ♦

Grilled Chicken Salad with Plum
Vinaigrette

♦ ♦ ♦

New Style Potato Salad

Rinse. Cook, covered, in a small amount
of boiling salted water for 5 to 7 minutes
or till tender. (*Or,* micro-cook in a
microwave-safe baking dish with 2 tablespoons water on 100% power [high] for
9 to 11 minutes, rearranging once.)
Rinse under cold water. Using a sharp
knife, remove corn kernels from cobs
(see photograph, *above*). (*Or,* for frozen

♦ Cauliflower Toss with Pecan Dressing

Using a sharp knife, cut lengthwise down
the cob to remove kernels.

corn, cook according to package directions. For canned corn, drain and do not
cook.) You should have about 2 cups.

continued on page 116

continued from page 115

In a small saucepan cook pecans and garlic in *2 tablespoons* of the oil for 1 minute. Remove from heat; cool slightly. Remove pecans with a slotted spoon, reserving garlic mixture; drain pecans on paper towels.

For dressing, in a screw-top jar combine reserved garlic mixture, remaining oil, vinegar, chives, parsley, sugar, salt, and pepper. Cover; shake well to mix.

In a large mixing bowl combine corn, cauliflower flowerets, and tomatoes. Add dressing; toss gently to coat. Cover and chill for 4 to 24 hours. Stir in pecans. To serve, line a large serving bowl with desired salad greens; add chilled salad mixture. Makes 12 side-dish servings.

Nutrition information per serving: 103 cal., 7 g fat, 0 mg chol., 2 g pro., 10 g carbo., 98 mg sodium, 3 g fiber. RDA: 41% vit. C, 11% thiamine.

Grilled Chicken Salad with Plum Vinaigrette

FOR A RAINBOW OF COLOR, USE SEVERAL plum varieties—Kelsey, Queen Ann, Red Beaut, Santa Rosa, or Ace—

⅓ cup white wine vinegar
¼ cup bottled plum sauce, plum preserves, or sweet-and-sour sauce
3 tablespoons salad oil
¼ teaspoon ground coriander
¼ teaspoon coarsely ground black pepper
1 pound skinless, boneless chicken breasts, cut into 2x1-inch strips
4 medium plums
1 cup pea pods, halved crosswise
2 tablespoons water
6 cups torn mixed greens, such as romaine or red leaf lettuce

For vinaigrette, in a mixing bowl combine vinegar, plum sauce, oil, coriander, and pepper. Reserve *¼ cup* for brushing sauce; set aside remaining vinaigrette for salad dressing.

Soak sixteen 5- to 6-inch-long wooden skewers in hot water for 5 minutes. Thread chicken strips accordion-style onto 8 skewers. Cut each plum into 8 wedges; thread plum wedges onto remaining 8 skewers.

Grill skewered chicken, uncovered, directly over *medium-hot* coals for 8 to 10 minutes or till chicken is no longer pink, adding the skewered plums during the last 3 minutes and brushing occasionally with the ¼ cup plum vinaigrette.

◆ Grilled Chicken Salad with Plum Vinaigrette

Meanwhile, cook pea pods in the water in a 1-quart microwave-safe casserole, covered, on 100% power (high) for 2 to 2½ minutes or till just tender. Drain pea pods.

To serve, in a large bowl toss together pea pods and greens. Arrange pea pod mixture, chicken, and plums on 4 dinner plates. Serve with remaining plum vinaigrette. Makes 4 main-dish servings.

Broiling directions: Arrange skewered chicken on the unheated rack of a broiler pan. Broil 4 inches from the heat for 10 to 12 minutes, adding the skewered plums the last 3 minutes and brushing occasionally with the ¼ cup plum vinaigrette.

◆ New-Style Potato Salad

salad dressing, basil, capers, mustard, and sugar. Cover and chill dressing and vegetables till serving time.

To serve, on a lettuce-lined platter arrange beets, potatoes, peppers, and tomatoes. If desired, garnish with yellow cherry tomatoes. Top with dressing. Makes 6 side-dish servings.

Microwave directions: In a 1½-quart microwave-safe casserole combine beets, ¼ cup *water*, and 1 teaspoon *cooking oil*. Cook, covered, on 100% power (high) for 15 to 17 minutes or till tender.

Nutrition information per serving: 227 cal., 5 g fat, 6 mg chol., 6 g pro., 41 g carbo., 3 g fiber, 177 mg sodium. RDA: 12% calcium, 18% iron, 41% vit. A, 129% vit. C, 22% thiamine, 13% riboflavin, 18% niacin.

Nutrition information per serving: 300 cal., 15 g fat, 59 mg chol., 26 g pro., 21 g carbo., 101 mg sodium, 4 g fiber. RDA: 11% calcium, 23% iron, 54% vit. A, 79% vit. C, 18% thiamine, 21% riboflavin, 64% niacin.

New-Style Potato Salad

3 medium beets, trimmed
1¾ pounds whole tiny new potatoes
1 8-ounce carton plain yogurt
¼ cup milk
2 tablespoons mayonnaise or salad dressing
1 tablespoon snipped fresh basil or 1 teaspoon dried basil, crushed
1 tablespoon drained capers

1 tablespoon Dijon-style mustard
1 teaspoon sugar
Butterhead or Boston lettuce leaves
2 medium green, red, yellow, or orange sweet peppers, cut into strips
2 medium yellow or red tomatoes, sliced or cut into wedges
Yellow cherry tomatoes (optional)

In a large saucepan cook beets, covered, in boiling water for 40 to 50 minutes or till tender; drain. Cool slightly; slip off skins and slice.

Cut potatoes into quarters. In another large saucepan cook potatoes, covered, in enough lightly salted boiling water to cover, about 12 minutes or till tender; drain. Rinse with cold water; set aside.

For dressing, in a mixing bowl stir together yogurt, milk, mayonnaise or

Fennel-Lemon Roasted Vegetables

1 pound tiny new potatoes, halved, or 3 medium potatoes, cut into eighths
3 medium red, green, or yellow sweet peppers, cut up
2 medium chayote, pattypan or sunburst squash, or kohlrabi, peeled (if desired) and cut into 1-inch cubes
1 medium red onion, cut into wedges
2 fennel bulbs or 6 stalks celery, sliced ½ inch thick (3 cups)*
6 cloves garlic
1 teaspoon finely shredded lemon peel
¼ cup lemon juice
3 tablespoons olive oil or cooking oil
1 teaspoon sugar
½ teaspoon salt
¼ teaspoon pepper
⅓ cup sliced pitted ripe olives

continued on page 118

continued from page 117

In a greased 15x10x2-inch roasting pan combine potatoes; peppers; chayote, squash, or kohlrabi; onion; fennel or celery; and garlic. Combine lemon peel, lemon juice, oil, sugar, salt, and pepper; drizzle over vegetables.

Bake, uncovered, in a 450° oven about 40 minutes or till vegetables are tender, stirring twice. Transfer to a serving bowl; top with olives. Makes 8 to 10 side-dish servings.

Microwave directions: Prepare as above, *except* omit peppers at first. In a 2-quart microwave-safe casserole cook vegetable-lemon mixture on 100% power (high) for 25 to 28 minutes or till crisp-tender, stirring every 10 minutes. Stir in peppers. Cook, covered, on high for 5 to 10 minutes more or till tender, stirring twice.

*Note: If using the celery, stir ½ teaspoon crushed fennel seed into the lemon mixture.

Nutrition information per serving: 145 cal., 6 g fat, 0 mg chol., 3 g pro., 22 g carbo., 1 g fiber, 211 mg sodium. RDA: 11% iron, 13% vit. A, 99% vit. C, 10% thiamine, 10% niacin.

Garden Fresh Side Dishes

Fennel-Lemon Roasted Vegetables

◆ ◆ ◆

Vegetables with Macadamia Nut Butter

◆ ◆ ◆

Carrot Cups with Summer Sauce

Vegetables with Macadamia Nut Butter

SLATHER THE TOASTY NUT BUTTER ONTO any kind of vegetable. Just check the chart, page 125, for grilling directions—

◆ Fennel-Lemon Roasted Vegetables, *far left*
◆ Vegetables with Macadamia Nut Butter, *above*

¼ cup butter
2 tablespoons ground macadamia nuts
or almonds
2 tablespoons walnut, almond,
or olive oil
1 tablespoon snipped fresh cilantro
or parsley
2 pounds fresh vegetables, such as
asparagus, baby carrots, fennel, sweet
peppers, crookneck squash, leeks, eggplant,
tiny new potatoes, and/or zucchini

In a small saucepan combine butter, nuts, oil, and cilantro or parsley. Cook, uncovered, over medium heat for 5 to 6 minutes or till nuts are toasted, stirring occasionally.

Prepare and grill vegetables according to the chart on page 125, brushing them occasionally with nut butter. Sprinkle with salt and pepper to taste. Makes 8 side-dish servings.

Nutrition information per serving: 126 cal., 11 g fat, 15 mg chol., 2 g pro., 7 g carbo., 131 mg sodium, 1 g fiber. RDA: 10% vit. A, 17% vit. C.

Carrot Cups with Summer Sauce

WHIP UP THESE ELEGANT CUSTARDS AND sauces in a blender or food processor—

3 medium carrots, peeled and cut up
2 small parsnips, peeled and cut up
1 12-ounce can evaporated milk
(1½ cups)
4 eggs
½ teaspoon finely shredded orange peel
¼ teaspoon salt
⅛ teaspoon ground red pepper
¾ cup fresh spinach leaves
1 green onion
2 sprigs parsley
1 teaspoon snipped fresh rosemary or
¼ teaspoon dried rosemary, crushed
Dash salt
Fresh rosemary (optional)

In a covered saucepan cook carrots and parsnips in a small amount of boiling water for 25 to 30 minutes or till very tender; drain. In a blender container or food processor bowl combine cooked carrots and parsnips, *1 cup* of the evaporated milk, eggs, orange peel, the ¼ teaspoon salt, and red pepper. Cover and blend or process till smooth.

continued on page 120
Carrot Cups with Summer Sauce ◆

continued from page 119

Place six greased 6-ounce custard cups in a 12x7½x2-inch baking dish. Divide the blended carrot mixture among the cups. Place baking dish on the oven rack. Pour boiling water into the dish around the cups to a depth of 1 inch. Bake, uncovered, in a 325° oven 30 to 35 minutes or till a knife inserted near the centers comes out clean.

For rosemary sauce, in a blender container or food processor bowl combine remaining evaporated milk, spinach, green onion, parsley, rosemary, and the dash salt. Cover; blend or process till smooth. Transfer sauce to a saucepan; heat and stir for 3 to 5 minutes or till of desired consistency. Keep warm over low heat till serving time.

To serve, use a knife or a spatula to loosen edges of custards, slipping the point down the sides to let the air in (see how-to photo, *below*). Invert cups onto dinner plates. Spoon the rosemary sauce around each vegetable cup. If desired, garnish each serving with fresh rosemary. Makes 6 servings.

Nutrition inforrnation per serving: 180 cal., 9 g fat, 158 mg chol., 9 g pro., 18 g carbo, 245 mg sodium, 2 g fiber.

Loosen edges with a knife, slipping the point down the sides to let the air in.

RDA: 25% calcium, 127% vit. A, 18% vit. C, 31% riboflavin.

Garden Fresh Desserts

Tropical Cream in a Coconut Puff

♦ ♦ ♦

Almond Melon Tart

♦ ♦ ♦

Very Berry Cheesecake

Tropical Cream in a Coconut Puff

YOU CAN MAKE THE PUFF-STYLE CRUST ahead and freeze up to 2 months. Thaw at room temperature for 10 minutes—

½ cup ground coconut* or ¾ cup
flaked coconut
1 cup water
½ cup margarine or butter
1 cup all-purpose flour
4 eggs
½ cup sugar
3 tablespoons cornstarch
1⅓ cups milk
2 beaten eggs
½ cup vanilla yogurt
2 teaspoons finely shredded lime peel
¼ cup lime juice
1 teaspoon grated gingerroot or ¼ teaspoon
ground ginger
½ cup whipping cream
2 cups fresh fruit, such as sliced nectarines
or peaches, halved strawberries, sliced kiwi
fruit, raspberries, sliced plums, and/or
melon balls

continued on page 122
Tropical Cream in a Coconut Puff. ♦
Almond Melon Tart, Very Berry Cheesecake

continued from page 120

To grind flaked coconut, place it in a blender container. Cover and blend till ground.

In a medium saucepan combine coconut, water, and margarine or butter. Bring to boiling. Add flour all at once, stirring vigorously. Cook and stir till the mixture forms a ball that doesn't separate. Remove from heat. Cool for 5 minutes. Add the 4 eggs, *one* at a time, beating with a wooden spoon after each addition till smooth.

On a greased baking sheet pat *one-third* of the dough into a 7-inch circle about ¼ inch thick. Using a pastry bag fitted with a large star tip, pipe remaining dough around the edge of the circle (see how-to photo, *right*). (*Or,* spoon the dough around the edge.)

Bake, uncovered, in a 400° oven about 35 minutes or till golden and firm. (The dough will puff and spread as it bakes.) Cool on a wire rack. (The center will sink slightly.)

Meanwhile, for filling, in a saucepan stir together sugar and cornstarch; stir in milk. Cook and stir over medium heat till thickened and bubbly. Cook and stir for 2 minutes more. Remove from heat. Gradually stir about *half* of the hot mixture into the 2 beaten eggs.

Return the egg mixture to mixture in pan; cook and stir over medium-low heat till thickened but *do not boil.* Reduce heat. Cook and stir for 2 minutes more. Remove from heat. Stir in yogurt, peel, juice, and ginger. Pour into a bowl; cover surface with clear plastic wrap. Cool slightly. Chill, without stirring, till thickened.

In a chilled small mixer bowl use chilled beaters to beat cream on medium speed of an electric mixer till soft peaks form; fold into chilled mixture. Spoon into puff. Top with fruit. Serve immediately. Makes 12 servings.

*Note: You can purchase ground coconut at health food stores or grind flaked coconut in a blender.

Nutrition information per serving: 263 cal., 16 g fat, 122 mg chol., 6 g pro., 26 g carbo., 145 mg sodium, 1 g fiber. RDA: 26% vit. A, 23% vit. C, 10% thiamine, 20% riboflavin.

Using a pastry bag fitted with a large star tip, pipe remaining dough around the edge of the dough circle.

Almond-Melon Tart

HONEYDEW AND CANTALOUPE MAY BE the most familiar, but try other melons—Persian, casaba, Santa Claus, Juan Canary, Crenshaw, or Muscatine—atop this summery tart, too—

½ of an 11-ounce package piecrust mix (1 ⅓ cups)
1 8-ounce container dairy sour cream
Nonstick spray coating
1 egg

1 cup ground blanched almonds (4 ounces)
½ cup light corn syrup
Several drops almond extract
½ of an 8-ounce container soft-style cream cheese with pineapple (½ cup)
½ to ¾ pound fresh melon, peeled and seeded
½ of a medium mango or papaya, peeled and seeded
¼ cup apple jelly

For crust, in a small mixing bowl combine piecrust mix and ¼ cup of the sour cream; stir till moistened. Turn dough onto a generously floured surface; knead about 12 times or till dough is firm enough for easy handling. Spray nonstick coating onto an 11x8x1½-inch rectangular or a 10-inch round tart pan with a removable bottom. Press dough evenly onto the bottom and up the sides of the pan.

For filling, in a medium mixing bowl beat egg slightly. Stir in almonds, corn syrup, and almond extract. Pour into tart shell, spreading evenly. Bake, uncovered, in a 375° oven for 25 to 30 minutes or till crust is brown and filling is set. Cool in pan on a wire rack.

In a mixing bowl stir together remaining sour cream and cream cheese; spread atop almond mixture. Using a cheese slicer or a vegetable peeler, thinly slice the peeled melon and mango or papaya (see how-to photo, *right*).

Arrange the fruit slices atop the filling. Cover and chill for up to 2 hours.

Before serving, in a saucepan melt jelly over medium heat; brush onto melon and mango. Cut into squares or wedges. Serve immediately. Serves 8.

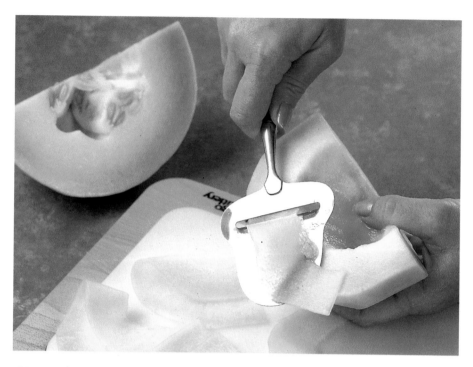

Using a cheese slicer, cut the peeled melon and mango or papaya into thin slices to decorate the top of the tart.

Nutrition information per serving:
424 cal., 26 g fat, 52 mg chol., 6 g pro., 42 g carbo., 229 mg sodium, 2 g fiber. RDA: 12% calcium, 13% iron, 16% vit. A, 27% vit. C, 11% thiamine, 19% riboflavin.

Very Berry Cheesecake

A RICH REWARD FOR PICKING YOUR WAY through the thorny brambles—

40 vanilla wafers
6 tablespoons margarine or butter, melted
2 8-ounce packages light cream cheese
(Neufchâtel) or regular
cream cheese, softened
¾ cup sugar
2 tablespoons all-purpose flour
2 teaspoons vanilla
1 cup cream-style cottage cheese
¼ cup blackberry or cherry brandy
or orange juice
3 eggs
3½ cups fresh red or gold raspberries,
blueberries, blackberries, boysenberries,
and/or chopped pitted cherries
1 tablespoon blackberry or cherry brandy
or orange juice
1 tablespoon sugar

For crust, finely crush wafers (you should have about 1½ cups). In a medium mixing bowl stir together vanilla wafers and margarine or butter; transfer to an 8-inch springform pan. Press the mixture onto the bottom and 1¾ inches up sides of pan. Set aside.

In a mixing bowl mix cream cheese, ¾ cup sugar, flour, and vanilla. Beat with an electric mixer on medium speed till combined. Set aside.

Place cottage cheese in a blender container or food processor bowl. Cover; blend or process till smooth. Stir into cream cheese mixture. Stir in the ¼ cup brandy or juice. Add eggs all at once; beat on low speed just till combined but *do not overbeat*.

Pour *half* of the cheese mixture into the crust-lined pan. Spread *1 cup* of the fruit atop. Top with remaining cheese mixture and *½ cup* of the fruit. Place in a shallow baking pan in a 375° oven. Bake, uncovered, for 40 to 45 minutes or till center appears nearly set when shaken.

Cool on a wire rack for 15 minutes; loosen sides. Cool completely on wire rack. Cover; chill till serving time.

For topping, in a medium mixing bowl combine remaining *2 cups* fruit, the 1 tablespoon brandy or juice, and the 1 tablespoon sugar. Cover and chill for up to 2 hours.

To serve, cut cheesecake into wedges. Top each serving with fruit topping. Makes 12 servings.

Nutrition information per serving:
303 cal., 17 g fat, 85 mg chol., 6 g pro., 30 g carbo., 244 mg sodium, 2 g fiber. RDA: 24% vit. A, 15% vit. C, 15% riboflavin.

◆ Cherry-Apricot Freezer Jam

Garden Fresh Preserves

Cherry-Apricot Freezer Jam

◆ ◆ ◆

Cherry-Apricot Freezer Jam

STASH A JAR OF THIS SPARKLING ROSY spread in the refrigerator for your family to enjoy right now, then freeze the rest for later. Months from today, you can still savor sweet spoonfuls of summer—

1 pound fully ripe apricots, halved and pitted (2 cups)
½ pound dark sweet cherries, pitted (1¼ cups)
4 cups sugar
2 tablespoons lemon juice
¼ teaspoon almond extract
¾ cup water
1 1¾-ounce package regular powdered fruit pectin

Wash apricot halves and cherries; drain thoroughly in a colander. Finely chop the fruit. (You should have a total of about *2½ cups* chopped fruit.) In a medium mixing bowl stir together the chopped fruit, sugar, lemon juice, and almond extract. Cover loosely and let the mixture stand for 10 minutes.

In a small saucepan stir together the water and powdered fruit pectin. Heat and stir over high heat till the mixture reaches a full rolling boil. Boil, uncovered, for 1 minute. Immediately pour the hot pectin mixture over the fruit mixture; stir constantly for 3 minutes.

Ladle the fruit mixture into hot, clean half-pint jars or freezer containers, leaving a half-inch headspace at the top of each container. Seal the containers tightly. Wipe the containers and the lids. Label each with the recipe name and date. Let the containers stand at room temperature about 24 hours or till the jam is set. Store for up to 3 weeks in the refrigerator or for up to 1 year in the freezer. Makes 6 half-pints.

Nutrition information per tablespoon: 35 cal., 0 g fat, 0 mg chol., 0 g pro., 9 g carbo., 0 g fiber, 1 mg sodium.

Timings for Grilled Vegetables

Vegetable	Preparation	Precooking time	Grilling time
Asparagus	Snap off and discard tough bases of stems. Precook, then tie asparagus in bundles with strips of cooked green onion tops.	3 to 4 minutes	3 to 5 minutes
Crookneck squash	Rinse, trim, and slice 1 inch thick.	Do not precook.	5 to 6 minutes
Eggplant	Cut off top and blossom ends. Cut eggplant crosswise into 1-inch-thick slices.	Do not precook.	8 minutes
Fennel	Snip off feathery leaves. Cut off stems.	Precook whole bulbs for 10 minutes. Cut bulbs into 6 to 8 wedges.	8 minutes
Fresh baby carrots	Cut off carrot tops. Wash and peel.	3 to 5 minutes	3 to 5 minutes
Leeks	Cut off green tops; trim bulb roots and remove 1 or 2 layers of white skin.	10 minutes or till tender. Halve lengthwise.	5 minutes
New potatoes	Halve potatoes.	10 minutes or till almost tender.	10 to 12 minutes
Sweet peppers	Remove stem. Quarter peppers. Remove seeds and membranes. Cut peppers into 1-inch-wide strips.	Do not precook.	8 to 10 minutes
Zucchini	Wash; cut off ends. Quarter lengthwise into long strips.	Do not precook.	5 to 6 minutes

Selecting Summer's Fresh Vegetables

When shopping, look for plump, crisp, tender vegetables. They should be heavy for their size, an indicator of moistness. They should also be free of shriveling, mold, mildew, cuts, or other blemishes. Savor their freshness by storing vegetables properly and serving them as soon as you can. Here are some pointers on selecting and storing the vegetables in this story.

Vegetable	How to Choose	How to Store
Asparagus	Pick firm, straight stalks with compact, closed tips. Avoid very thin or thick stalks.	Wrap the bases in wet paper towels and seal in a plastic bag for up to 4 days.
Beans	Choose long, straight pods that snap crisply when you bend them.	Wash and refrigerate in sealed plastic for up to 4 days.
Beets	Look for well-shaped, firm, small to medium beets with bright color and smooth skins. The leaves should be deep green and fresh looking. Avoid very large beets as they may be tough and less sweet.	Trim and refrigerate unwashed beets in an open container for up to 1 week. Refrigerate beet greens, wrapped in a paper towel and plastic, for up to 3 days.
Carrots	Select firm, straight, bright orange carrots that are not shriveled or cracked.	Refrigerate in a plastic bag for up to 2 weeks.
Cauliflower	Pick solid, heavy heads with bright green leaves.	Refrigerate in a plastic bag for up to 4 days.
Celery	Look for crisp ribs that are firm, unwilted, and unblemished. The leaves should be fresh and green, not yellow or droopy.	Refrigerate in a plastic bag for up to 2 weeks.
Chayote	Select small, unblemished vegetables.	Refrigerate in a plastic bag for up to 2 weeks.
Corn	Check for bright green husks that are well-filled with even rows of plump kernels.	Refrigerate in plastic for up to 2 days.
Cucumber	Find firm cucumbers without shriveled or soft spots. Smaller cucumbers will be more tender.	Refrigerate in a plastic bag for up to 2 weeks.
Eggplant	Choose plump, glossy, heavy eggplants. The caps should look fresh and tight and be free of mold.	Refrigerate in plastic for up to 2 days.

Vegetable	How to Choose	How to Store
Green onions	Look for crisp tops and clean white ends.	Wrap in plastic and refrigerate for up to 5 days.
Kohlrabi	Find small, young bulbs with healthy-looking stems and leaves.	Refrigerate in a plastic bag for up to 1 week.
Leeks	Select leeks with crisp, green outer leaves.	Refrigerate in a plastic bag for up to 5 days.
Lettuce and leafy greens	Pick heads or bunches with crisp, tender leaves.	Remove any damaged outer leaves. Wash and pat lettuce dry. Refrigerate in an airtight container for up to 5 days.
Mushrooms	Find firm, plump mushrooms with closed caps. Avoid those with spots.	Refrigerate unwashed mushrooms in a paper bag for up to 2 days.
Onions	Look for firm, short necks and papery outer skins.	Keep summer onions in a paper bag in the refrigerator for several weeks.
Parsnips	Pick firm, small to medium parsnips with fairly smooth skin and few rootlets.	Refrigerate in a plastic bag for up to 2 weeks.
Pea pods	Select crisp, bright green pods.	Refrigerate in a plastic bag for up to 3 days.
Peppers	Look for firm, glossy peppers.	Refrigerate in a plastic bag for up to 5 days.
Potatoes	Find firm, smooth potatoes with shallow eyes. Avoid those with sprouts.	Keep in a cool, humid, well-ventilated, dark place for several weeks.
Summer Squash (zucchini or crookneck)	Choose firm, glossy squash that are heavy for their size. Avoid those with hard or dull rinds.	Refrigerate in plastic for up to 4 days.

Selecting Fresh Summer Fruits

When picking fruits for these recipes, look for plumpness, tenderness, and bright color. The fruits should be heavy for their size and free from mold, mildew, bruises, cuts, or other blemishes. Below are directions for selecting and storing the fruits used in this story.

Fruit	How to Choose	How to Store
Apricots	Look for skin with a red blush.	Ripen firm fruit in a paper bag at room temperature until it yields to gentle pressure and is golden in color. Refrigerate ripe fruit for up to 2 days.
Berries	If picking your own, select berries that separate easily from their stems.	Refrigerate berries in a single layer, loosely covered, for up to 2 days.
Cherries	Select firm, brightly colored fruit.	Refrigerate in a plastic bag for up to 4 days.
Kiwi Fruit	Choose fruit that yields to gentle pressure.	Let fruit ripen at room temperature until the skin yields to gentle pressure, then refrigerate for up to 1 week.
Mangos	Look for fully colored fruit that smells fruity and feels fairly firm when pressed.	Let ripen at room temperature, then refrigerate for up to 5 days.
Melons	Pick fruit with a sweet aromatic scent, not a strong smell that could indicate overripeness. Melons should feel heavy for their size and should be well shaped. The blossom end should give to gentle pressure when ripe.	Let ripen at room temperature, then refrigerate for up to 4 days.
Nectarines and peaches	Look for fruit with a healthy golden yellow skin without tinges of green. Ripe fruit should yield slightly to gentle pressure.	Let ripen at room temperature in a paper bag, then refrigerate for up to 5 days.
Papaya	Choose fruit that is at least half yellow and feels somewhat soft when pressed. The skin should be smooth.	Let ripen at room temperature until yellow, then refrigerate in a plastic bag for up to 1 week.
Plums	Find firm, plump, well-shaped fresh plums. They should give slightly when gently pressed. The bloom (light gray cast) on the skin is natural protection and doesn't affect quality.	Let ripen at room temperature, then refrigerate for up to 5 days.
Tomatoes	Pick well-shaped, plump, firm tomatoes.	Let ripen in a brown paper bag with other ripening fruits, then use within 3 days. Store only ripe tomatoes in the refrigerator.

Freezer Fresh Vegetables—Freeze and Enjoy All Year

Here's a guide to help you freeze fresh garden vegetables all summer. Enjoy them up to eight to 12 months later.

Vegetable	Preparation	Blanching/Freezing
Asparagus	Allow 2½ to 4½ pounds per quart. Wash; scrape off scales. Break off woody bases where spears snap easily. Wash again. Sort by thickness. Leave whole or cut into 1-inch lengths.	Blanch medium spears 3 minutes. Cool quickly. Fill containers; shake down, leaving a ½-inch headspace.
Beans, green or wax	Allow 1½ to 2½ pounds per quart. Wash; remove ends and strings. Leave whole or snap or cut into 1-inch pieces.	Blanch 3 minutes; cool quickly. Fill containers; shake down, leaving a ½-inch headspace.
Broccoli	Allow about 1 pound per pint. Wash; remove outer leaves and tough parts of stalks. Wash again. Cut lengthwise into spears. Cut to fit containers.	Blanch 3 minutes in boiling water; cool quickly. Package, leaving no headspace.
Cauliflower	Allow 1 to 1½ pounds per pint. Wash; remove leaves and woody stems. Break into 1-inch pieces.	Blanch 3 minutes; cool quickly. Package, leaving no headspace.
Corn, whole kernel	Allow 4 to 5 pounds per quart. Remove husks; scrub with a vegetable brush to remove silks. Wash and drain. Do not cut corn off cobs.	Blanch 6 ears at a time for 4 minutes; cool quickly. Cut corn from cobs at two-thirds depth of kernels; do not scrape. Fill containers, shaking to pack lightly and leaving a 1/2-inch headspace.
Peas	Allow 2 to 2½ pounds per pint. Wash, shell, rinse, and drain.	Blanch 1½ minutes; chill quickly. Fill containers, shaking down and leaving 1/2-inch headspace.
Sweet peppers	Wash. Remove stems, seeds, and membrances. Cut into large pieces or leave whole.	Do not blanch. Spread peppers in a single layer on a baking sheet; freeze firm. Fill container, shaking to pack closely and leaving no headspace.
Winter squash and pumpkin	Allow 1½ to 3 pounds per quart. Peel and cut into 1-inch cubes.	Instead of blanching, simmer cubes in 1 to 2 inches of water about 15 minutes or till tender. Drain; place pan in ice water to cool quickly. Mash. Fill containers, shaking to pack lightly and leaving a ½-inch headspace.

Prize Tested Recipes®

Golden Fruit Conserve

SPREAD THIS AMBROSIAL MIX OF FRUIT and almonds atop biscuits or scones—

1¾ pounds nectarines (about 5)
1½ pounds apricots (about 15) or 1¼ pounds peaches (about 4)
1 cup light raisins
2 tablespoons lemon juice
5½ cups sugar
1 1¾-ounce package powdered fruit pectin
½ teaspoon margarine or butter
1 cup sliced almonds

Peel, pit, and coarsely chop nectarines and apricots or peaches separately; mash both fruits (should have 2¼ cups nectarine mixture and 2 cups apricot).

In an 8- or 10-quart kettle or Dutch oven combine the mashed fruit, raisins, and lemon juice. Place sugar into a bowl; set aside. Add the pectin and margarine to the fruit mixture; bring to a full rolling boil over high heat, stirring constantly with a wooden spoon. Add sugar quickly. Return to a full rolling boil, stirring constantly. Boil hard for 1 minute, stirring constantly. Remove from heat; skim off any foam with a metal spoon. Stir in the almonds.

Ladle mixture into hot, clean, half-pint canning jars, leaving a ¼-inch headspace. Wipe rims; adjust lids. Process in boiling-water bath for 15 minutes (start timing after water boils). Remove canning jars from water bath; cool on wire rack. Makes 8 half-pints.

Nutrition information per tablespoon: 49 cal., 1 g fat, 0 mg chol., 0 g pro., 12 g carbo.
$200 WINNER
Wilma J. DeGraffenreid, Marshall, Mo.

Western-Style Pepper Jelly

SPOON THIS SPUNKY JELLY ATOP CORN bread muffins or brush over chicken while roasting—

◆ Golden Fruit Conserve

2 medium cooking apples (such as Granny Smith or Jonathan), cored and coarsely chopped
1 medium green sweet pepper, seeded and coarsely chopped
6 to 8 jalapeño peppers, halved
1½ cups cider vinegar
5 cups sugar
¼ cup water
½ of a 6-ounce package liquid fruit pectin (1 foil pouch)

¼ cup finely chopped green sweet pepper
¼ cup finely chopped red sweet pepper
1 small banana pepper, finely chopped

In a 4- or 5-quart Dutch oven combine apples, the coarsely chopped green pepper, jalapeño peppers, vinegar, sugar, and water. Bring to boiling; reduce heat. Boil gently, uncovered, for 10 minutes. Strain mixture through a sieve, pressing with the back of a spoon to remove all liquid (should have *4 cups*). Discard pulp. Return liquid to Dutch oven; bring to boiling. Add pectin; return to boiling. Boil hard for 1 minute, stirring constantly. Remove from heat. Stir in the finely chopped red and green sweet peppers and the hot pepper.

Pour into hot, clean, half-pint canning jars, leaving a ¼-inch headspace. Wipe rims; adjust lids. Process in boiling-water bath for 5 minutes (start timing after water boils). Remove canning jars from water bath; cool on wire rack till set (jelly will take 2 to 3 days to set). Makes about 5 half-pints.

Note: Chopped pepper pieces will float to top on standing.

Nutrition information per tablespoon: 47 cal., 0 g fat, 0 mg chol., 0 g pro., 13 g carbo., 0 g fiber, 13 mg sodium.

$100 WINNER
Margaret Pache, Mesa, Ariz.

Cucumber Buns

3¼ to 3¾ cups all-purpose flour
1 package active dry yeast
2 tablespoons snipped fresh chives
or 1 tablespoon dried chives
1 teaspoon snipped fresh dill or
½ teaspoon dried dillweed

1 medium cucumber, peeled and
cut up (1½ cups)
½ cup dairy sour cream
¼ cup water
1 tablespoon sugar
1 teaspoon salt

In a large mixing bowl combine *1¼ cups* of the flour, yeast, chives, and dill.

In a food processor bowl, process the cucumber till smooth (should have ¾ cup). In a saucepan heat and stir cucumber puree, sour cream, water, sugar, and salt till warm (120° to 130°). (Mixture will look curdled.) Add to flour mixture. Beat with an electric mixer on low to medium speed for 30 seconds, scraping

continued on page 132

◆ Western-Style Pepper Jelly, *top*
◆ Cucumber Buns, *above*

continued from page 131

bowl. Beat on high speed for 3 minutes. Using a spoon, stir in as much of the remaining flour as you can.

Turn out onto a lightly floured surface. Knead in enough of the remaining flour to make a moderately stiff dough that is smooth and elastic (6 to 8 minutes total). Shape into a ball. Place in a lightly greased bowl; turn once. Cover; let rise till double (about 45 minutes). Punch down dough. Turn out onto a lightly floured surface. Cover; let rest for 10 minutes. Divide into 12 pieces. Shape each piece into a ball; arrange in a greased 13x9x2-inch baking pan, allowing space between each ball. Cover; let rise in a warm place till nearly double (about 30 minutes). Bake in a 350° oven for 20 to 25 minutes or till light brown. Serve warm or cool. Makes 12 rolls.

Nutrition information per roll: 133 cal., 2 g fat, 4 mg chol, 4 g pro, 24 g carbo., 1 g fiber, 184 mg sodium. RDA: 10% iron, 23% thiamine, 15% riboflavin.

$200 WINNER
Philip B. Mohr, Schaumburg, Ill.

◆ Warm Dilled Potato Salad

Warm Dilled Potato Salad

TOSS TOGETHER THIS WARM SALAD IN just 15 minutes—

*1 pound whole tiny new potatoes,
quartered
2 cups brussels sprouts (about 8 ounces),
halved or one 1 10-ounce package frozen
brussels sprouts, thawed and halved
1 cup cherry tomatoes, halved
2 tablespoons sliced green onion
¼ cup white wine vinegar
1 tablespoon olive oil or salad oil*

*1 teaspoon snipped fresh dill or
¼ teaspoon dried dillweed
½ teaspoon sugar
⅛ teaspoon salt*

In a large saucepan cook new potatoes and brussels sprouts, covered, in a small amount of boiling water about 12 minutes (if using thawed frozen sprouts, add them the last 5 minutes of cooking) or till potatoes are tender. Drain potatoes and sprouts and transfer to a medium serving bowl. Add cherry tomatoes and green onion.

Meanwhile, for dressing, in a screw-top jar combine vinegar, olive oil, dill, sugar, and salt. Cover and shake well. Add to potato mixture; toss to coat. Serve warm or cold. Makes 8 side-dish servings.

Nutrition information per serving: 87 cal., 2 g fat, 0 mg chol., 2 g pro., 17 g carbo., 1 g fiber, 46 mg sodium. RDA: 10% iron, 51% vit. C.

$100 WINNER
Lawrence Bellew, Oneonta, Ala.

September

Eat Smart on the Run

A food pro shares her quick, healthful recipes

Prize Tested Recipes®

Heart-Healthy Apple Coffee Cake, Graham-Streusel Coffee Cake, Artichoke and Basil Hero, Spicy Beef Pitas

Eat Smart on the Run
A food pro shares her quick, healthful recipes

OH, TO LIVE THE LIFE OF A GLAMOROUS food stylist—preparing beautiful, delectable foods for photography and, yes, tasting those *mouth-watering recipes*. Judy Vance, a food stylist in Chicago, lives such a life. By day, she skillfully makes picture-pretty foods. But when she's at home, like most working moms, Judy's biggest challenge is quickly getting a *nutritious meal* on the table for her family.

Because tiring photography sessions often keep Judy working late, planning dinner ahead tops her list of priorities. "Any working person needs to be organized; that's especially important if *homemade* meals really matter to you and your family," says Judy. So, whether it's making double-batch recipes or preparing foods before-hand, *planning saves time* for Judy.

Once tempted to run out for fast food after a long day at work, Judy now advocates serving home-cooked meals to her family instead. Cooking or planning ahead guarantees that the Vances' busy weekday dinners are more relaxed and enjoyable.

What are Judy's strategies for keeping on schedule? Sometimes she fixes an entire recipe and stashes it in the freezer for another day. Other times, she simply cuts up vegetables the night before. And often her husband, Jim, and son, Ryan, pitch in to help. Having them help out in the kitchen not only speeds up the

It may take Judy Vance hours to style picture-perfect food for photos. But when she makes family meals, nutrition and convenience are far more important.

process but also gives the family a chance to catch up on what has happened with each other during the day.

Two years ago, the Vances' streamlined cooking met a new challenge. Jim found out his blood cholesterol was alarmingly high at 317 mg/dl (200 mg/dl or below is considered optimal for healthy adults). So, on top of preparing quick meals, the family was faced with adding a healthful bent to their everyday meals. Even with her undergraduate degree in nutrition, Judy realized that she had a lot to learn about how to put the information into practice.

"Our diets were never that bad, but we obviously needed to make some changes," Judy says.

High-fat snacks turned out to be leading culprits in Jim's resulting high cholesterol. He now munches on fruits, lower fat yogurt and cheese, or pretzels instead of regular cheese or chocolate. His meat-centered diet was another stickler. "When you grow up on a ranch in Wyoming, as I did, eating a lot of meat is a way of life," Jim says. Today, the Vances cut the size of their meat portions, serve meatless dishes occasionally, and choose leaner cuts of meat, such as beef flank steak.

By attending a cholesterol-reducing program offered through a local hospital, Jim learned what specific changes he needed to make. Today, he proudly reports a blood cholesterol of 204 mg/dl. "After awhile, you lose your desire for fattier foods," Jim says.

"Changing our family diet became a game. How could I make a quick meal and cut down on the fat?"—Judy Vance

Orange-Tarragon Fish

SQUEEZING ON FRESH ORANGE JUICE IS A
simple way to flavor baked fish—

*4 fresh or frozen dressed trout or other
dressed fish (2¼ pounds total), such as lake
trout, sea trout, or pike
2 medium carrots,
cut into julienne strips (about 1 cup)
2 small oranges
1 tablespoon snipped fresh tarragon
or 1 teaspoon dried tarragon, crushed
Fresh tarragon (optional)
Purple kale (optional)
Cherry or pear tomatoes (optional)*

continued on page 136
Orange-Tarragon Fish ◆

September

continued from page 135

Thaw fish, if frozen. Bone fish; remove head and tails, if necessary. Spray a 15x10x1-inch baking pan with *nonstick spray coating.* Place fish, skin side down, in pan. Season with *salt* and *pepper,* if desired.

In a saucepan cook carrots, covered, in a small amount of boiling water for 2 to 3 minutes or till crisp-tender; drain. Slice *one* of the oranges into 8 slices. Halve slices; set aside.

Squeeze the juice from the remaining orange over *each* piece of fish. Top *each* serving with *some* of the carrots, *4* of the orange slices, and tarragon.

Bake fish, covered, in a 400° oven for 12 to 15 minutes or till fish flakes easily with a fork. To serve, place fish, skin side down, on dinner plate. Garnish with tarragon, kale, and tomatoes, if desired. Makes 4 servings.

Lemon-Dill Fish: Prepare fish as directed *except* substitute 1 medium *zucchinni,* thinly sliced, for carrots; 1 *lemon* for the oranges; and fresh snipped or dried *dill* for the tarragon.

In a saucepan cook zucchini, covered, in a small amount of boiling water for 2 minutes or till tender.

Cut lemon in half. Slice *half* of the lemon into thin slices. Halve slices; reserve for garnish. Squeeze the juice from the remaining lemon half over *each* serving. Top *each* with *some* of the cooked zucchini and dill. Bake as directed. Garnish with reserved lemon slices. Makes 4 servings.

Nutrition information per serving of Orange-Tarragon Fish: 319 cal., 8 g fat, 130 mg chol., 48 g pro., 12 g carbo., 3 g fiber, 81 mg sodium. RDA: 23% calcium.

Exercise is critical to keeping Jim's cholesterol in check.

How have these changes affected 8-year-old Ryan? He's now a fat sleuth. "Ryan makes comments about foods, like 'This is good for you.' Or, when we're grocery shopping, he reads the labels and comments about fat-free products," Judy says. Like any kid his age, he sometimes eats chips and cookies, but he often asks for nutritious foods, such as fruit.

Eating well is only part of the Vances' secret to good health. Exercise, Jim points out, is a must. The heart-healthy program taught him that while a low-fat diet aids in reducing cholesterol, exercise has been shown to increase HDL (the "good cholesterol"). Whether the family is walking, biking, or roller blading together, they have found that exercise combined with a new lifetime eating plan has paid off. Judy and Jim agree, "We get sick less often and feel better, too."

Judy's fat-cutting tips

◆ Limit fatty meats, like sausage or processed meats. An occasional splurge, such as a few times a month, won't hurt, but don't consume fatty meats every day.

◆ Toss vegetables, instead of meat, into spaghetti sauce. For example, sauté zucchini, yellow squash, onions, and red sweet peppers in a small amount of broth and add low-sodium pasta sauce. Heat through and serve over whole wheat pasta. Sprinkle with a dusting of grated Parmesan cheese.

◆ Use very little fat in cooking. Instead, use nonstick pans, spray coating, or a small amount of broth or water to sauté or "fry" vegetables or meat.

◆ Substitute, substitute. Whenever possible, use lower-fat versions of ingredients (such as lower-fat mayonnaise or lower-fat cheeses) to prepare recipes.

◆ Look for ways to cut fat when preparing packaged mixes. For example, when preparing a cake mix, Judy replaces the oil called for with the same amount of plain low-fat yogurt. Our Test Kitchen found this really works! Or, simply cut back on the amount of fat. Use half the amount of butter called for in a packaged mix.

◆ Keep cut-up, cleaned, and ready-to-eat snacks of carrots and celery in the refrigerator to avoid any high-fat temptations.

◆ Season your foods with flavor-rich fresh or dried herbs instead of heavy sauces, salt, or fats. Judy grows all types of herbs in her garden in the summer and in a sunny window in the winter to use in cooking.

Judy's timesaving tips

◆ Organize and file recipes that you want to try. This simplifies meal planning and eliminates last-minute searches for recipe ideas.

◆ Make a big pot of soup on Sunday. Serve half, and freeze or refrigerate the remainder for later.

◆ Cook enough meat for more than one meal, and use the rest later. For example, roast chicken or pork makes quick-fix sandwiches.

◆ Cut up or chop vegetables for stir-fries or soups when you have time. Refrigerate them in plastic bags for use during the week.

Beef-and-Noodle Stir-Fry

THE GRILLED FLANK STEAK SAVED FROM last night's meal featuring Lemony Flank Steak adds a delicious lemon flavor to Judy's pasta stir-fry—

4 ounces fettuccine
1 cup beef broth
2 tablespoons soy sauce
1 tablespoon cornstarch
1 teaspoon grated gingerroot
Dash pepper
1 teaspoon sesame oil
1 medium summer squash, halved
lengthwise and sliced
⅛ inch thick (1¼ cups)

continued on page 138
Beef-and-Noodle Stir-Fry ◆

continued from page 137
1 small green pepper,
cut into bite-size pieces
¼ cup sliced green onion
1 clove garlic, minced
8 ounces (about ½ recipe) leftover Lemony
Grilled Flank Steak (see recipe, page 140)
or 8 ounces cooked beef, thinly sliced
into bite-size pieces
1 cup quartered cherry tomatoes
Snipped fresh cilantro or parsley

Cook fettuccine according to package directions; drain. Set aside.

Meanwhile, for sauce, in a small bowl stir together beef broth, soy sauce, cornstarch, gingerroot, and pepper. Set aside.

In a large nonstick skillet heat ½ *teaspoon* of the sesame oil till hot. Stir-fry the squash, green pepper, onion, and garlic in hot oil about 3 minutes or till squash is crisp-tender. Remove vegetables from skillet.

Add remaining oil to skillet. Stir-fry meat in hot oil till heated through. Push meat from center of skillet. Stir soy sauce mixture; add to center of skillet. Cook and stir till thickened and bubbly. Cook and stir 1 minute more. Add cooked pasta, vegetables, and tomatoes to skillet. Stir to coat with sauce. Cook and lightly stir till heated through. Sprinkle with cilantro before serving. Makes 3 or 4 main-dish servings.

Nutrition information per serving: 320 cal., 12 g fat, 41 mg chol., 21 g pro., 33 g carbo., 2 g fiber, 789 mg sodium. RDA: 26% iron, 44% vit. C.

Potato-Bean Soup

A MEATLESS MAIN DISH THAT RELIES mainly on vegetables for the protein—

½ cup sliced celery
2 medium carrots, shredded
1 clove garlic, minced
2 teaspoons margarine, melted
4 cups chicken broth*
3 medium potatoes,
peeled and cut up (3 cups)
2 tablespoons snipped fresh dill or 2
teaspoons dried dillweed
1 15-ounce can cannellini beans or great
northern beans, drained
½ cup lower-calorie dairy sour cream or
plain nonfat yogurt
1 tablespoon all-purpose flour
⅛ teaspoon pepper

In a large saucepan cook and stir celery, carrots, and garlic in hot margarine over medium heat for 4 minutes or till tender. Carefully stir in broth, potatoes, and dill. Heat to boiling; reduce heat. Simmer, covered, for 20 to 25 minutes or till potatoes are tender. With the back of a spoon, lightly mash about *half* of the potatoes in the broth. Add the drained beans to the potato mixture.

In a small bowl stir together sour cream or yogurt, flour, pepper, and salt to taste, if desired; stir into potato mixture. Cook and stir till thickened and bubbly. Cook and stir 1 minute more. Makes 4 to 6 main-dish servings.

*Note: If you need to watch your sodium intake, use lower-sodium chicken broth and save about 150 mg sodium per serving.

Nutrition information per serving: 280 cal., 6 g fat, 4 mg chol., 16 g pro., 48 g carbo., 5 g fiber, 1,035 mg sodium.

All types of soups are mainstays in Judy's quick menu plans because they are nutritious. Two of the Vances' favorites: Potato-Bean Soup and Spinach and Lentil Soup.

Spinach and Lentil Soup

1 cup dry lentils
5 cups water
1 medium onion, chopped
1 cup chopped celery
1 cup sliced carrot
2 teaspoons instant
chicken bouillon granules
2 cloves garlic, minced
½ teaspoon grated lemon peel
⅛ teaspoon ground red pepper
1 cup cubed fully cooked ham*
2 cups chopped fresh spinach

Rinse and drain lentils. In a large saucepan combine lentils, water, onion, celery, carrot, bouillon granules, garlic, lemon peel, and red pepper. Bring to boiling; reduce heat. Cover and simmer for 45 minutes.

Add ham; simmer, uncovered, 15 minutes. Stir in spinach and serve. Makes 4 to 6 main-dish servings.

*Note: If you need to watch your sodium intake, use lower-sodium ham and save about 130 mg sodium per serving of soup.

Nutrition information per serving: 273 cal., 4 g fat, 21 mg chol., 23 g pro., 38 g carbo., 10 g fiber, 1,034 mg sodium.

Potato-Bean Soup . Spinach and Lentil Soup ◆

Menu
Lemony Flank Steak
Apple-and-Sweet-Pepper Slaw
Grilled vegetables

Lemony Flank Steak

A SIMPLE MARINADE TURNS LEAN FLANK steak into a special, but fast, meal. After grilling, set aside half of the steak to use in Beef-and-Noodle Stir-Fry (see recipe, *page 137*)—

*1 1½-pound beef flank steak or
boneless beef top sirloin steak
1 teaspoon grated lemon peel
½ cup lemon juice
2 tablespoons sugar
2 tablespoons soy sauce
1½ teaspoons snipped fresh oregano or ½
teaspoon dried oregano, crushed
⅛ teaspoon pepper
Assorted grilled vegetables (optional)*

Score meat by making shallow cuts at 1-inch intervals diagonally across the steak in a diamond pattern; repeat on other side of meat. Place meat in a plastic bag set into a shallow dish.

For marinade, in a 1-cup glass measure stir together lemon peel, lemon juice, sugar, soy sauce, oregano, and pepper. Pour marinade over meat; close bag. Marinate in refrigerator for 2 hours or overnight.

Drain meat, reserving marinade. Grill steak on an uncovered grill directly over *medium* coals for 12 to 14 minutes for

Lemony Flank Steak. Apple-and-Sweet-Pepper Slaw◆

medium doneness, turning once during cooking and brushing with reserved marinade. Discard any remaining marinade. Wrap and refrigerate or freeze *half* of the steak for another meal.

To serve remaining steak, thinly slice meat across the grain. Makes two meals, 3 servings each.

Nutrition information per serving: 177 cal., 8 g fat, 53 mg chol., 22 g pro., 3 g carbo., 0 g fiber, 238 mg sodium. RDA: 14% iron, 12% riboflavin, 28% niacin.

Apple-and-Sweet-Pepper Slaw

NO FAT IS FOUND IN THIS SLAW WHEN it's made with nonfat yogurt, mayonnaise, or salad dressing—

⅓ cup plain nonfat yogurt or nonfat
mayonnaise or salad dressing
¼ of a 0.4-ounce package buttermilk ranch
salad dressing mix (about 1 teaspoon)
1 teaspoon honey
2 cups shredded red and/or green cabbage
1 small red or green sweet pepper, cut into
thin strips (about ½ cup)
1 carrot, shredded
¼ cup thinly sliced celery
1 small apple, chopped

For dressing, in a small bowl stir together the yogurt or mayonnaise, dressing mix, and honey till blended. Thin with a little water if necessary. Cover; refrigerate till ready to serve.

In a large bowl combine cabbage, sweet pepper, carrot, celery, and apple. To serve, pour chilled dressing over cabbage mixture. Toss to coat. Makes 3 or 4 side-dish servings.

Nutrition information per serving: 70 cal., 0 g fat, 1 mg chol., 2 g pro., 16 g carbo., 3 g fiber, 109 mg sodium.

Menu

Skillet Chicken Paella
Orange and Beet Spinach Salad
Pound Cake with Raspberries

Skillet Chicken Paella

*1¼ pounds skinless, boneless chicken
breasts, cut into bite-size strips
1 tablespoon olive oil or cooking oil
1 medium onion, chopped
2 cloves garlic, minced
2¼ cups chicken broth
1 cup uncooked long grain rice
1 teaspoon dried oregano, crushed
½ teaspoon paprika
¼ teaspoon salt
¼ teaspoon pepper
⅛ teaspoon ground saffron
or ground turmeric
1 14½-ounce can stewed
tomatoes, cut up
1 medium red sweet pepper, cut into strips
¾ cup frozen peas*

Rinse chicken; pat dry with paper
towels. In a 10-inch skillet cook chicken
strips, *half* at a time, in hot oil for 2 to 3
minutes or till no longer pink. Remove
chicken from skillet.

Add onion and garlic to skillet; cook
till tender but not brown. Remove skillet
from heat. Add broth, *uncooked* rice,
oregano, paprika, salt, pepper, and saffron

Skillet Chicken Paella, Orange and Beet Spinach ◆
Salad, Pound Cake with Raspberries

or turmeric. Bring the mixture to boiling. Reduce heat. Simmer, covered, about 15 minutes.

Add *undrained* tomatoes, sweet pepper, and frozen peas to skillet. Cover and simmer about 5 minutes more or till rice is tender. Stir in cooked chicken. Cook and stir about 1 minute more or till heated through. Makes 6 main-dish servings.

Nutrition information per serving: 297 cal., 6 g fat, 50 mg chol., 24 g pro., 36 g carbo., 2 g fiber, 642 mg sodium. RDA: 22% iron, 10% vit. A, 41% vit. C.

Orange and Beet Spinach Salad

*2 small fresh beets or one 8-ounce can
beets, drained and cut into julienne strips
6 cups torn fresh spinach,
leaf lettuce, or romaine
3 oranges, peeled and thinly sliced
½ of a medium cucumber, thinly sliced
½ cup bottled lower-calorie salad dressing,
such as herb vinaigrette or Italian*

If using fresh beets, remove tops and wash beets. In a medium saucepan cook whole, unpeeled fresh beets, uncovered, in a small amount of lightly salted boiling water for 35 minutes or till tender. Transfer to a small bowl. Cover; chill till ready to serve. Cut into julienne strips. Divide greens among 6 salad plates. Top *each* serving with *some* of the beets, orange, and cucumber. Serve with dressing. Makes 6 servings.

Nutrition information per serving: 61 cal., 3 g fat, 0 mg chol., 2 g pro., 9 g carbo., 3 g fiber, 274 mg sodium. RDA: 11% iron, 48% vit. A, 56% vit. C.

Pound Cake with Raspberries

*½ cup seedless raspberry jam
1 10¾-ounce loaf nonfat pound cake
1 8-ounce carton raspberry
lower-fat yogurt
¾ cup fresh raspberries*

In a small saucepan heat jam just till melted. Cut cake into cubes. Divide cubes among 6 dessert dishes. Top *each* serving with warmed jam, yogurt, and berries. Serve at once. Serves 6.

Nutrition information per serving: 245 cal., 0 g fat, 2 mg chol., 5 g pro., 56 g carbo., 1 g fiber, 204 mg sodium.

Heart-Healthy Apple Coffee Cake

WITH ONLY 5 GRAMS OF FAT, KATHLEEN'S coffee cake can be served with no regrets—

*Nonstick spray coating
⅔ cup all-purpose flour
½ cup whole wheat flour
1 teaspoon baking soda
1 teaspoon ground cinnamon
¼ teaspoon salt
1½ cups peeled, cored, and finely chopped
apple (2 large), such as Jonathan or
Granny Smith
¼ cup frozen egg product, thawed
¾ cup sugar
¼ cup chopped walnuts or pecans
¼ cup applesauce
¼ cup packed brown sugar
1 tablespoon all-purpose flour
1 tablespoon whole wheat flour
½ teaspoon ground cinnamon
1 tablespoon margarine
¼ cup chopped walnuts or pecans*

Spray a 9-inch round baking pan with nonstick coating; set aside. In a medium bowl combine the ⅔ cup all-purpose flour, ½ cup whole wheat flour, baking soda, the 1 teaspoon cinnamon, and salt; set aside.

In a large mixing bowl toss together the chopped apple and egg product. Stir in the ¾ cup sugar, the first ¼ cup nuts, and applesauce. Add flour mixture and stir just till combined. Pour batter into prepared pan.

For topping, stir together the brown sugar, the remaining all-purpose flour, whole wheat flour, and cinnamon. Cut in margarine till crumbly. Stir in remaining ¼ cup chopped nuts. Sprinkle topping over batter in pan. Bake in a 350° oven for 30 to 35 minutes or till a toothpick inserted near the center comes out clean. Cool in pan for 10 minutes. Remove from pan and serve warm. Makes 10 servings.

Nutrition information per serving: 199 cal., 5 g fat, 0 mg chol., 4 g pro., 37 g carbo., 2 g fiber, 163 mg sodium. RDA: 12% thiamine.

$200 WINNER

Kathleen Fishman, Scottsdale, Ariz.

◆ Heart-Healthy Apple Coffee Cake

- ◆ Graham-Streusel Coffee Cake *left*
- ◆ Artichoke and Basil Hero, *above*

Graham-Streusel Coffee Cake

A GRAHAM-CRACKER-AND-NUT STREUSEL swirls inside this cake mix fix-up—

1½ cups graham cracker crumbs
(about 21 crackers)
¾ cup chopped pecans or walnuts
¾ cup packed brown sugar
1½ teaspoons ground cinnamon
⅔ cup margarine or butter, melted
1 package 2-layer-size yellow or
white cake mix
1 cup water
¼ cup cooking oil
3 eggs
Powdered Sugar Icing

For streusel, in a medium mixing bowl combine graham cracker crumbs, chopped pecans or walnuts, brown sugar, and cinnamon. Stir in the melted margarine or butter. Set aside.

In a large mixing bowl combine cake mix, water, cooking oil, and eggs. Beat on low speed with an electric mixer just till moistened. Beat on medium speed for 1½ minutes. Pour *half* of the batter into a greased 13x9x2-inch baking pan. Sprinkle with *half* of the streusel mixture. Carefully spread remaining batter over streusel; sprinkle with remaining streusel. Bake in 350° oven for 35 to 40 minutes or till a toothpick inserted near center comes out clean. Cool slightly; drizzle with Powdered Sugar Icing. Serve warm. Makes 12 to 16 servings.

Powdered Sugar Icing: In a small mixing bowl stir together 1 cup sifted *powdered sugar,* 1 teaspoon *vanilla,* and enough *water* to make an icing of drizzling consistency.

Nutrition information per serving: 508 cal., 25 g fat, 53 mg chol., 4 g pro., 68 g carbo., 1 g fiber, 478 mg sodium. RDA: 14% calcium, 14% iron, 19% vit. A, 16% thiamine, 17% riboflavin.
$100 WINNER
Martha Myers, Ash Grove, Mo.

Artichoke and Basil Hero

A CHEESE SANDWICH NEVER TASTED so good! Fresh basil, spinach, tomato, and artichoke hearts make up this ace sandwich—

1 cup fresh basil (leaves only)
⅓ cup olive oil or salad oil
2 tablespoons grated Parmesan cheese
1 tablespoon capers, drained
1 tablespoon white wine vinegar
2 teaspoons Dijon-style mustard

continued on page 146

◆ Spicy Beef Pitas

continued from page 145

1 clove garlic, quartered
1 16-ounce loaf unsliced French bread
1 14-ounce can artichoke hearts,
drained and sliced
4 ounces sliced provolone cheese
1 medium tomato, thinly sliced
2 cups torn fresh spinach

In a blender container or food processor bowl combine the basil, oil, Parmesan cheese, capers, vinegar, mustard, and garlic. Cover; blend or process till nearly smooth. Set aside.

Cut bread in half lengthwise. Hollow out each half, leaving a 1-inch shell. (Save bread crumbs for another use.) Spread the basil mixture over *each* bread half. On the bottom half, layer artichoke hearts, provolone cheese, tomato, and spinach. Cover with bread top. Cut sandwich crosswise into 6 to 8 pieces. Makes 6 to 8 servings.

Nutrition information per serving: 413 cal., 21 g fat, 15 mg chol., 14 g pro., 43 g carbo., 2 g fiber, 738 mg sodium. RDA: 37% calcium, 22% iron, 24% vit. A, 18% vit. C.
$200 WINNER
Ellen Nishimura, Fair Oaks, Calif.

Spicy Beef Pitas

YOU'LL LOVE WHAT KIM'S ZESTY PICANTE marinade does for deli roast beef—

1 pound thinly sliced cooked beef
½ cup picante sauce
⅓ cup red wine vinegar
¼ cup olive oil or cooking oil
1 tablespoon snipped fresh cilantro or parsley
⅛ teaspoon garlic powder
⅛ teaspoon cracked black pepper
4 large pita bread rounds, halved
1 medium tomato, chopped
1 medium avocado, sliced
¼ cup crumbled feta cheese (1 ounce)

Place sliced beef in a plastic bag set inside a bowl. For marinade, in a medium bowl combine the picante sauce, vinegar, oil, cilantro or parsley, garlic powder, and pepper. Pour marinade over beef. Seal bag; marinate in the refrigerator for 4 to 24 hours, turning bag occasionally. To serve, drain and discard marinade. Fill each pita bread half with beef. Top beef with tomato, avocado, and cheese. Makes 8 servings.

Nutrition information per serving: 399 cal., 32 g fat, 55 mg chol., 16 g pro., 14 g carbo, 1 g fiber, 364 mg sodium. RDA: 15% iron, 15% vit. C, 15% thiamine, 16% riboflavin.
$100 WINNER
Kim Magana, Scottsbluff, Nebr.

October

The Simple Pleasures
of Home Baking

Prize Tested Recipes®

Cranberry-Pear Pie, Chocolate and Pear Bread Pudding,

Quick Veggie Chili con Queso, Fruit-and-Nut Chili

The Simple Pleasures of
Home Baking

Ah-h-h—the pleasures of baking from scratch. The fun starts when you roll up your sleeves and dust your hands with flour. It peaks when you bite into that still-warm loaf of bread or a fresh-from-the-oven cookie. With our collection of fall baking favorites, you'll follow in Grandma's baking footsteps, taking a few shortcuts along the way. It blends the best of the old with the convenience of today.

Whole Wheat Sourdough Bread

BAKING WITH WATER HELPS THE BREAD form an old-world-style crust—

1½ cups Whole Wheat Sourdough Starter
(see recipe, page 150)
3¾ to 4¼ cups all-purpose flour
1 package active dry yeast
1½ cups warm water (120° to 130°)
3 tablespoons brown sugar
3 tablespoons olive oil or cooking oil
1½ teaspoons salt
2 cups whole wheat flour
1 tablespoon cornmeal

Bring sourdough starter to room temperature. In a large mixing bowl combine *2 cups* of the all-purpose flour and the yeast; set aside.

In a medium mixing bowl stir together the warm water, brown sugar, oil, and salt; add to flour mixture. Add sourdough starter. Beat with an electric mixer on low to medium speed for 30 seconds, scraping sides of bowl. Beat on high speed for 3 minutes. Using a spoon, stir in the whole wheat flour and as much of the remaining all-purpose flour as you can.

On a lightly floured surface, knead in enough of the remaining all-purpose flour to make a stiff dough that is

continued on page 150
Whole Wheat Sourdough Bread. ◆
Sourdough Breadsticks

October

148

Micowave Hints for Rising

You can cut the waiting for dough by letting it rise in your microwave oven. First, check your manual to see if proofing is recommended. Or, use this test:

◆ Place 2 tablespoons cold stick margarine in a custard cup in the center of the oven. (Use only stick margarine, not corn oil spread.)

◆ Cook, uncovered, on 10% power (low) 4 minutes.

◆ If the stick margarine completely melts in less than 4 minutes, you cannot proof bread dough in your oven.

◆ If the stick margarine is not completely melted in 4 minutes, you can proof bread in your microwave oven.

Here's how:

◆ While preparing and kneading the dough, heat 3 cups water in a 4-cup glass measure on 100% power (high) for 6 ½ to 8 ½ minutes or till boiling.

◆ Move the measure to the back of the microwave oven.

◆ Place kneaded dough in a lightly greased microwave-safe bowl; turn once. Cover with waxed paper; place in microwave oven with glass measure containing hot water.

◆ Heat dough and water on 10% power (low) for 13 to 15 minutes or till dough has nearly doubled.

◆ Continue as your recipe directs.

To knead, fold the dough and push down with the heel of your hand.

continued from page 148
smooth and elastic (8 to 10 minutes total) (see how-to photo, *above*). Shape dough into a ball. Place dough in a greased bowl; turn once to grease the surface. Cover; let rise in a warm place till double (about 45 to 60 minutes).

Punch dough down. Turn out onto a lightly floured surface. Divide in half. Cover and let rest for 10 minutes.

On a lightly floured surface, shape dough into 2 long loaves, each about 12x4 inches wide. Lightly grease 1 or 2 large baking sheets; sprinkle with cornmeal. Place loaves on sheet(s). Cover with a warm damp cloth. Let rise in a warm place till double (20 to 30 minutes). (*Or*, let dough rise, covered, in the refrigerator for 12 hours.)

Place a pan of warm water on the lowest rack of oven. Preheat oven to 375°. Use a serrated knife to make 4 or 5 diagonal slashes about ½ inch deep across the tops of the loaves. Place baking sheet(s) with bread on rack above pan of water. Bake, uncovered, 40 to 45 minutes or till bread sounds hollow when tapped. If necessary, cover with foil the last 15 minutes to keep the bread from overbrowning. Remove bread from baking sheet(s). Cool on a wire rack. Makes 2 loaves (48 slices).

Nutrition information per slice: 68 cal., 1 g fat, 0 mg chol., 2 g pro., 13 g carbo., 1 g fiber, 68 mg sodium. RDA: 10% thiamine.

Bulgur Sourdough Bread: In a small saucepan bring 1 cup *water* to boiling. Add ½ cup *bulgar*. Remove from heat. Let stand, covered, 5 minutes. Drain well. Prepare bread as directed, *except* add bulgur with the whole wheat flour.

Whole Wheat Sourdough Starter

ALTHOUGH MANY SOURDOUGH STARTERS call for all-purpose flour, this version calls for whole wheat. Use it to add a nuttier flavor to any recipe calling for sourdough starter—

1 package active dry yeast
2½ cups warm water (105° to 115°)
2 cups whole wheat or all-purpose flour
1 tablespoon brown sugar

In a large mixing bowl dissolve the yeast in ½ cup of the warm water. Stir in the remaining water, flour, and brown sugar. Stir the mixture till smooth.

Cover the mixing bowl with several thicknesses of 100% cotton cheesecloth. Let stand at room temperature (75° to 85°) for 5 to 10 days or till the mixture has a sour, fermented aroma, stirring 2 or 3 times every day. (The fermentation time will depend upon the room temperature. A warmer room speeds the fermentation process.)

When the mixture has fermented, transfer the starter to a 1-quart jar. Cover it with the cheesecloth and refrig-

Storing Sourdough Starter

By feeding your sourdough starter regularly, you can keep it on hand indefinitely to add tang to your baked favorites. If you do not use your sourdough starter for a period of 10 days, stir in 1 teaspoon *brown sugar*. Add more brown sugar every 10 days until you use the starter.

You may notice that your starter becomes thicker over time. You will not need to adjust your recipes to compensate for the extra thickness; however, you may find yourself needing the lesser amount of flour when a range is given in yeast bread recipes.

After you use your sourdough starter, replenish as necessary with *whole wheat or all-purpose flour, warm water,* and *brown sugar,* following these amounts:

Amount starter used	Amount flour to add	Amount warm water to add	Amount brown sugar to add
½ cup	⅓ cup	⅓ cup	½ tsp.
1 cup	¾ cup	¾ cup	1 tsp.
1½ cups	1 cup	1 cup	1½ tsp.

Cover with cheesecloth. Let stand at room temperature till bubbly (1 day). Refrigerate, covered, for later use. Bring desired amount to room temperature.

Twist and stretch each dough strip into a 12-inch stick, then shape into spirals or zigzags.

erate until you're ready to use the starter. (*Do not cover the jar with a tight-fitting lid.*) Bring the starter to room temperature before using. To maintain and replenish the starter, see the tip, *above.* Makes about 2 cups.

Sourdough Breadsticks
STRAIGHTEN UP THESE STICKS OR TWIST and shape 'em into swirls—

*½ cup Whole Wheat Sourdough Starter
(see recipe, opposite)
2½ to 3 cups all-purpose flour
1 package active dry yeast
½ cup milk*

*¼ cup margarine or butter
2 tablespoons sugar
½ teaspoon salt
1 egg
1 beaten egg white
1 tablespoon water
Toppings such as sesame seed, poppy seed, coarse salt, or grated Parmesan cheese*

Bring sourdough starter to room temperature. In a medium mixing bowl stir together *1 cup* of the flour and the yeast.

In a medium saucepan combine milk, margarine, sugar, and salt. Heat and stir the mixture over medium heat just till warm (120° to 130°) and the margarine is almost melted. Add the warm liquid to the flour mixture. Add sourdough starter and the 1 egg.

Beat with an electric mixer on low to medium speed for 30 seconds, scraping the sides of the bowl occasionally during mixing. Beat on high speed for 3 minutes. Using a spoon, stir in as much of the remaining flour as you can.

On a lightly floured surface, knead in enough of the remaining flour to make a stiff dough that is smooth and elastic (8 to 10 minutes total). Shape into a ball. Place dough in a lightly greased bowl; turn once to grease the surface. Cover and let rise in a warm place till double (45 to 60 minutes).

Punch dough down. Turn out onto a lightly floured surface. Divide in half. Cover and let rest 10 minutes.

On a lightly floured surface, roll each half into a 10x6-inch rectangle. Cut each rectangle into twelve 10x½-inch strips. Twist and stretch each strip into a 12-inch breadstick. If desired, coil into spirals or make zigzags (see how-to photo, *above*). Place 2 inches apart on greased baking sheets. Cover the dough and let it rise in a warm place till nearly double (about 30 minutes).

continued on page 152

continued from page 151

Combine egg white and water; brush onto sticks. Sprinkle with toppings. Bake, uncovered, in a 375° oven 10 to 12 minutes or till done. Cool on a wire rack. Makes 24.

Nutrition information per breadstick: 86 cal., 3 g fat, 9 mg chol., 2 g pro., 13 g carbo., 1 g fiber, 75 mg sodium.

Parmesan-Herb Sourdough Bread-sticks: Prepare breadsticks as directed, *except* add ⅓ cup grated *Parmesan cheese;* ¾ teaspoon *dried, crushed basil or oregano;* and ¼ teaspoon *garlic powder.*

Cheddar Batter Bread

1 tablespoon cornmeal
2 cups all-purpose flour
1 package quick-rising active dry yeast
¼ teaspoon onion powder
¼ teaspoon pepper
1 cup milk
2 tablespoons sugar
2 tablespoons margarine or butter
¼ teaspoon salt
1 egg
¾ cup shredded cheddar or Monterey Jack cheese with jalapeño peppers (3 ounces)
½ cup cornmeal

Grease an 8x4x2-inch loaf pan; sprinkle with the 1 tablespoon cornmeal. Set aside. In a large mixing bowl stir together *1½ cups* of the flour, the yeast, onion powder, and pepper; set aside.

In a small saucepan combine milk, sugar, margarine, and salt; heat and stir over medium heat just till mixture is warm (120° to 130°) and margarine is almost melted. Add the warm milk mixture to the flour mixture. Add the egg.

Beat with an electric mixer on low to medium speed for 30 seconds, scraping bowl. Beat on high for 3 minutes. Stir in cheese and the ½ cup cornmeal. Stir in remaining flour. (The batter will be soft and sticky.)

Turn batter into the prepared pan. Cover and let rise in a warm place till nearly double (about 20 minutes). Bake, uncovered, in a 350° oven for 40 minutes. If necessary, cover with foil the last 15 minutes of baking to prevent over-browning. Remove bread from pan. Cool on a wire rack. Makes 1 loaf (16 slices).

Nutrition information per slice: 123 cal., 4 g fat, 20 mg chol., 4 g pro., 17 g carbo., 1 g fiber, 95 mg sodium. RDA: 15% thiamine, 14% riboflavin.

The batter for Cheddar Batter Bread will be soft and sticky.

◆ Cheddar Batter Bread, *top*

Shortbread Cookies

CUT THE ROLLED-OUT DOUGH INTO FANciful autumn leaf shapes or make traditional Scottish-style shortbread—formed into a circle and cut into wedges—

1¼ *cups all-purpose flour*
3 tablespoons sugar
½ cup butter
Milk (optional)
Coarse sugar (optional)

In a medium mixing bowl stir together flour and sugar. Using a pastry blender or fork, cut in butter till mixture resembles fine crumbs and starts to cling. Form the mixture into a ball. Knead the dough in the bowl about 1 minute or till smooth.

On a lightly floured surface, roll dough to ¼ inch thickness. Using desired cutters or a knife, cut into shapes that are 2 to 2½ inches in diameter, rerolling and cutting trimmings as necessary (see how-to photo, *right*). If desired, brush cutouts with milk and sprinkle with coarse sugar. Arrange on an ungreased cookie sheet.

Bake in a 325° oven for 14 to 16 minutes or till bottoms just start to brown. Remove from cookie sheet. Cool on a wire rack. Makes 12 to 14 cookies.

Nutrition information per cookie: 123 cal., 8 g fat, 21 mg chol., 1 g pro., 12 g carbo., 78 mg sodium, 0 g fiber.

Ginger Shortbread: Prepare cookies as directed, *except* stir ¼ cup finely chopped *crystallized ginger* and ¼ teaspoon *ground ginger* into the flour.

Orange-Poppy-Seed Shortbread: Prepare cookies as directed, *except* stir 2 teaspoons *poppy seed* and 1 teaspoon finely shredded *orange peel* into the flour.

Shortbread Cookies

Fall's gentle shower of leaves inspires buttery leaf-shaped cookies that evoke memories of warm and cozy kitchens.

Shortbread Wedges: Prepare cookie dough as directed. On an ungreased cookie sheet pat or roll dough into an 8-inch circle. Using your fingers, press to make a rounded edge. Cut circle into 16 pie-shaped wedges, leaving wedges in the circle on the cookie sheet. If desired,

Leaf-shaped cookie cutters are available at specialty cookware stores or where cake decorating supplies are available.

continued on page 154

◆ Shortbread Cookies, *top*

October

153

continued from page 153
brush dough with milk and sprinkle with sugar. Bake in a 325° oven for 20 to 25 minutes or till bottom just starts to brown and center is set. Cut circle into wedges again while warm. Cool on the cookie sheet for 5 minutes. Remove from cookie sheet. Cool on a wire rack. Makes 16 wedges.

Apple-Cranberry Deep-Dish Pie

COOKIE CUTTERS MAKE EASY WORK OF the top crust; just cut and randomly overlap pastry pieces atop fruit—

¼ cup sugar
3 tablespoons all-purpose flour
1 teaspoon apple pie spice or ¼ teaspoon ground nutmeg
1 teaspoon finely shredded orange peel
1½ cups canned whole cranberry sauce
7 cups peeled and thinly sliced cooking apples, such as Golden Delicious or Jonathan (about 2¼ pounds)
Single-Crust Pastry (see recipe, right)
1 egg yolk
1 tablespoon water
1 tablespoon sugar
Vanilla ice cream (optional)

In a bowl combine the ¼ cup sugar, flour, apple pie spice, and orange peel. Stir in cranberry sauce. Add apples; toss to coat fruit. Transfer to a 10-inch deep-dish pie plate or a 1½-quart casserole.

On a lightly floured surface, flatten pastry dough. Roll dough from center to edges, forming a 14-inch circle. Using cookie cutters, cut desired shapes from pastry, rerolling and cutting trimmings as necessary. Arrange cutouts atop fruit mixture (see how-to photo, *right*).

In a small bowl stir together egg yolk and water; brush onto pastry cutouts. Sprinkle with 1 tablespoon sugar. To prevent overbrowning, cover edge of pie with foil. Place on a baking sheet. Bake in a 375° oven for 25 minutes. Remove foil. Bake for 25 to 30 minutes more or till top is golden, apples are tender, and filling is bubbly. Use a spoon to serve warm or cool with vanilla ice cream, if desired. Makes 8 servings.

Nutrition information per serving: 312 cal., 8 g fat, 27 mg chol., 3 g pro., 61 g carbo., 3 g fiber, 83 mg sodium. RDA: 12% vit. C, 18% thiamine.

Pear-Persimmon Deep-Dish Pie: Prepare pie as directed, *except* increase sugar to ½ cup. Substitute 7 cups sliced, peeled *pears (Bosc, Bartlett, or Anjou)* for the apples and 2 cups chopped, peeled *persimmons* for the cranberry sauce. Serve as directed.

Single-Crust Pastry

USE THIS BASIC PASTRY FOR THE DEEP-dish pie, the dumplings, and any of your recipes that call for one piecrust—

1¼ cups all-purpose flour
¼ teaspoon salt
⅓ cup shortening
3 to 4 tablespoons cold water

In a mixing bowl stir together flour and salt. Using a pastry blender, cut in shortening till pieces are the size of small peas. Sprinkle *1 tablespoon* of the water over part of the mixture; gently toss with a fork. Push to the side of the bowl. Repeat, using *1 tablespoon* water at a time, till all is moistened. Form dough into a ball. Roll out as directed in recipe.

Overlap just the edges of the cutouts, so they bake evenly.

Apple-Cranberry Deep-Dish Pie

Take a spoon and dig deep, through layers of flaky pastry to the sweet and juicy fruit underneath. Top each serving of still-warm pie with a generous scoop of ice cream, then watch the ice cream puddle into rich, creamy pools.

Apple-Cranberry Deep-Dish Pie ◆

Brandied Apricot-Pear Dumplings

SUBSTITUTE PEAR OR APRICOT NECTAR for the brandy, if you prefer a nonalcoholic version—

2 tablespoons snipped dried apricots
2 tablespoons soft-style cream cheese
4 small pears
Single-Crust Pastry (see recipe, page 154)
4 whole cloves (optional)
1 egg white
1 tablespoon water
1 tablespoon sugar
1¼ cups pear or apricot nectar
¼ cup dark corn syrup
¼ cup apricot brandy or brandy or pear or apricot nectar
Light cream (optional)

For filling, in a mixing bowl combine apricots and cream cheese. Peel and core pears (see how-to photo, *right*). Spoon the filling into the center of each pear.

On a lightly floured surface, flatten pastry dough. Roll dough from center to edges, forming a 13-inch circle. Trim to form a 12-inch square. Using a fluted pastry wheel or knife, cut dough into fourteen 12x¾-inch strips.

Pat pears with paper towels. Using one of the pastry strips and starting ½ inch above the base of a pear (do not cover bottom of pear), wrap pastry strip around pear. Moisten end of strip and seal to the end of a second pastry strip. Complete wrapping pear with another pastry strip to cover the hole and filling. Moisten end to seal. Repeat, using 3 pastry strips on each remaining pear.

With a knife, cut leaf shapes (similar to diamonds) from remaining 2 pastry strips; mark veins on leaves. Attach leaves to tops of pears, moistening as

Brandied Apricot-Pear Dumplings ◆

Brandied Apricot-Pear Dumplings

The dowdy dumpling goes dramatic. Do it by simply wrapping ribbons of pastry around stuffed pears.

necessary to attach. Top pears with whole cloves for stems, if desired. In a small bowl stir together egg white and water; brush onto pastry. Sprinkle with the sugar.

Using a spatula, transfer pears to a shallow baking dish. Stir together pear or apricot nectar, corn syrup, and

Insert an apple corer or vegetable peeler firmly into the stem end of the pear. Twist and pull to remove the core.

brandy or nectar; pour around pears in dish. Bake, uncovered, in a 400° oven for 45 to 50 minutes or till golden. Serve warm with light cream, if desired. Makes 4 servings.

Nutrition information per serving:
522 cal., 18 g fat, 8 mg chol., 6 g pro.,
78 g carbo., 5 g fiber, 195 mg sodium.
RDA: 21% iron, 16% vit. C, 28% thiamine, 23% riboflavin, 17% niacin.

Brandied Date-Apple Dumplings:
Prepare dumplings as directed, *except*
substitute 4 medium peeled, cored *cook-*
ing apples (such as Golden Delicious or
Jonathan) for the pears and use chopped
pitted dates for the dried apricots.
Substitute *apple cider or juice* for the pear
or apricot nectar and *apple brandy* for
the apricot or pear brandy.

Creamy, Fudgy, and Nutty Brownies

THIS BROWNIE-LOVER'S DREAM COMES
from the pages of Better Homes
and Gardens® *Spectacular Desserts*
cookbook—

4 squares (4 ounces) unsweetened
chocolate, chopped
½ cup margarine or butter
1 cup all-purpose flour
½ cup chopped walnuts or
pecans, toasted
¼ teaspoon baking powder
1½ cups sugar
3 eggs
1 teaspoon vanilla
3 ounces semisweet or bittersweet
chocolate, chopped
2 3-ounce packages cream cheese
1 egg
¼ cup sugar
1 tablespoon milk
½ teaspoon vanilla
2 squares (2 ounces) semisweet
chocolate (optional)
1 teaspoon shortening (optional)
Fresh raspberries (optional)

◆ Creamy, Fudgy, and Nutty Brownies

Creamy, Fudgy, and
Nutty Brownies

Lace these sinfully rich morsels with a
satiny drizzle of chocolate. Or, serve
them as your mom did, with a glass of
milk after school.

Carefully spread the chocolate-cream-cheese
mixture over the hot brownies.

In a small saucepan melt unsweetened
chocolate and the margarine or butter
over low heat, stirring occasionally.
Remove from heat; cool.

Grease and lightly flour an 8x8x2-
inch baking pan; set aside. In a medium
mixing bowl stir together flour, walnuts
or pecans, and baking powder; set aside.

In a large mixing bowl stir together
the cooled melted chocolate mixture and
the 1½ cups sugar. Add the 3 eggs and 1
teaspoon vanilla. Using a wooden spoon,

continued on page 159

Honey-Nut Cheesecake

Layer upon layer of buttery phyllo

creates a delicate, translucent crust

and the crispy topping for this

Greek inspired dessert.

continued from page 157
lightly beat mixture *just till combined.* (Do not overbeat or brownies will rise during baking, then fall and crack.) Stir in the flour mixture. Pour the batter into the prepared pan; spread to edges. Bake in a 350° oven for 40 minutes.

Meanwhile, for topping, in a small saucepan melt the 3 ounces semisweet or bittersweet chocolate over low heat, stirring occasionally; cool slightly. In a medium mixing bowl beat cream cheese with electric mixer on medium speed about 30 seconds or till softened. Add the melted semisweet or bittersweet chocolate, 1 egg, ¼ cup sugar, milk, and ½ teaspoon vanilla. Beat till combined.

Carefully spread topping evenly over hot brownies (see how-to photo, *page 157*). Bake in the 350° oven about 10 minutes more or till topping is set. Cool in pan on a wire rack. Cover; chill at least 2 hours.

To serve, cut brownies into triangles or bars. (To cut into triangles, first cut into rectangles, then cut in half diagonally.) If desired, in a small saucepan melt 2 squares semisweet chocolate and shortening; drizzle over brownies and onto plate. Garnish with raspberries, if desired. Cover and refrigerate to store. Makes 12 to 16 servings.

◆ Honey-Nut Cheesecake

Nutrition information per serving: 398 cal., 25 g fat, 87 mg chol., 6 g pro., 44 g carbo., 160 mg sodium, 0 g fiber. RDA: 13% iron, 24% vit. A, 10% thiamine, 16% riboflavin.

Honey-Nut Cheesecake

COVER THE SHEETS OF PHYLLO WITH A damp cloth until you're ready to use them to prevent drying and cracking—

¾ cup ground hazelnuts, pecans, or
walnuts* (3 ounces)
8 sheets frozen phyllo dough (about
17x12-inch rectangles), thawed
¼ cup margarine or
butter, melted
2 tablespoons sugar
2 8-ounce packages cream cheese
1 cup mascarpone or
ricotta cheese (8 ounces)
⅔ cup honey
2 tablespoons all-purpose flour
3 eggs
¼ cup milk

For crust, generously grease the bottom and sides of a 9-inch springform pan. Sprinkle ¼ cup of the ground nuts evenly over the bottom of the pan. Set aside.

Unfold phyllo. Cover phyllo with a slightly damp cloth, removing sheets as needed. Brush *one* phyllo sheet with some of the melted margarine or butter. Top with another sheet of phyllo, overlapping to create a 17x14-inch rectangle; brush with margarine. Repeat with remaining phyllo and margarine to make 8 layers in a 17x14-inch rectangle.

Using kitchen shears, trim phyllo to a 14-inch circle, reserving trimmings. Ease into the prepared pan, creasing as neces-

Gently ease the layers of phyllo into the springform pan, creasing and folding as necessary.

sary and being careful not to tear dough (see how-to photo, *above*). Trim even with top of pan, reserving trimmings.

Combine remaining nuts and sugar; reserve *1 tablespoon* for topping. Sprinkle remaining nut mixture over phyllo in pan. Cut reserved phyllo trimmings into ½- to 1-inch pieces; place on a greased baking sheet.

Bake crust and trimmings in a 425° oven till golden, allowing 4 to 6 minutes for trimmings and 6 to 8 minutes for crust. Cool slightly on a wire rack. Reduce oven temperature to 350°.

For filling, in a large mixing bowl combine cream cheese, mascarpone or ricotta cheese, honey, and flour; beat on low speed of electric mixer till smooth. Add eggs all at once; beat on low speed just till mixed. *Do not overbeat.* Stir in milk just till combined.

Pour filling into phyllo crust. Bake, uncovered, in a 350° oven for 50 to 55 minutes or till the center appears nearly set when shaken. If necessary, to prevent overbrowning, carefully cover the crust with foil the last 20 minutes.

continued on page 160

continued from page 159

Cool cheesecake in pan on a wire rack for 5 to 10 minutes. Loosen sides of pan. Cover and chill for at least 4 hours. Store trimmings in a tightly covered container in a cool, dry place.

Before serving, remove sides of pan. Top cheesecake with phyllo trimmings and reserved sugar-nut mixture. Makes 12 to 16 servings.

Nutrition information per serving: 314 cal., 23 g fat, 72 mg chol., 6 g pro., 23 g carbo., 1 g fiber, 171 mg sodium. RDA: 24% vit. A, 11% riboflavin.

Cappuccino Cheesecake: Prepare cheesecake as directed, *except* substitute ¾ cup *orange marmalade* for the honey and dissolve 1 tablespoon *instant coffee crystals* in the milk.

Lemon Curd Cheesecake: Prepare cheesecake as directed, *except* substitute *lemon curd* for the honey.

*Note: To grind nuts, blend or process nuts, ½ cup at a time, in your blender or food processor. Cover and blend till very finely chopped, but be careful not to overprocess or the nuts will form a paste.

Old-Fashioned Popovers ◆

Old-Fashioned Popovers

Just like magic, these light and crisp buns go poof! Break one open and you'll discover why — there's nothing but hot air inside.

Prick each popover. This lets the steam escape so the popovers crisp in the oven.

Old-Fashioned Popovers

*1 tablespoon shortening or
nonstick spray coating
2 eggs
1 cup milk
1 tablespoon cooking oil
¾ cup all-purpose flour
½ teaspoon salt*

Using ½ *teaspoon* shortening for each cup, grease the bottom and sides of six cups of a popover pan or five 6-ounce custard cups. (*Or,* generously spray with nonstick coating.) Place the custard cups on a baking sheet. Set aside.

In a medium mixing bowl use a wire whisk or a rotary beater to beat eggs; beat in milk and cooking oil. Add flour and salt; beat till mixture is blended but still slightly lumpy. Fill the greased popover or muffin cups half full. Bake, uncovered, in a 400° oven about 40 minutes or till crusts are very firm.

Turn off oven. Using the tines of a fork, *immediately* prick each popover to let steam escape (see how-to photo, *above*). Return the popovers to the oven for 5 to 10 minutes more or till of desired crispness. (Be sure the oven is turned off.) Serve hot. Makes 5 or 6 popovers.

Nutrition information per popover: 164 cal., 8 g fat, 89 mg chol., 6 g pro., 16 g carbo., 0 g fiber, 263 mg sodium. RDA: 15% thiamine, 21% riboflavin.

Eggnog Popovers: Prepare popovers as directed, *except* add 1 tablespoon *dry instant eggnog,* 1 tablespoon *rum or ¼ teaspoon rum extract,* and ¼ teaspoon *ground nutmeg* to batter.

Caraway Rye Popovers: Prepare popovers as directed, *except* decrease all-purpose flour to *½ cup.* Add ¼ cup *rye or whole wheat flour* and ½ teaspoon *caraway seed* with the all-purpose flour.

Fruit and Honey-Bran Muffins

1½ cups all-purpose flour
1 cup whole bran cereal or ½ cup oat, rice, or toasted wheat bran
¼ cup packed brown sugar
1 tablespoon baking powder
1 teaspoon ground cinnamon
¼ teaspoon salt
1 egg
1¼ cups milk
¼ cup honey
¼ cup cooking oil
½ cup raisins or chopped dried fruit (apricots, dates, figs, cherries, blueberries, or cranberries)

In a mixing bowl stir together flour, whole bran cereal or bran, brown sugar, baking powder, cinnamon, and salt. Make a well in the center.

In a small mixing bowl beat egg slightly. Stir in milk, honey, and oil. Add egg mixture all at once to flour mixture. Stir just till moistened (the bat-

◆ Current-Orange Scones, Fruit and Honey-Bran Muffins

Fruit and Honey-Bran
Muffins
◆◆◆
Currant-Orange
Scones

Be your own guest with make-ahead muffin batter and scones that get a running start from piecrust mix.

ter will be lumpy). Fold in raisins or dried fruit. Store in a covered container in the refrigerator for up to 3 days. Makes 14 to 16 muffins.

Using a spoon and spatula, fill each muffin cup ⅔ full with batter. The muffins will rise above the cups during baking.

Baking directions: Gently stir batter. Grease desired number of muffin cups. Fill ⅔ full (see how-to photo, *above*). Bake, uncovered, in a 400° oven for 15 to 20 minutes or till golden. Remove from pans. Serve warm.

continued on page 162

Baker's Hints

These easy tips will pave your road to baking success.

1. Preheat your oven before you mix the ingredients or, for yeast breads, after rising. Check your oven temperature occasionally with an oven thermometer to make sure it's accurate.

2. Bake breads, cookies, and pies uncovered, unless the recipe directs otherwise.

3. Measure liquid ingredients in a glass measure on a flat surface, lining up the markings at eye level.

4. Measure dry ingredients in a dry measuring cup, leveling the top with a straight-edged blade.

5. Stir all-purpose flour before measuring. It is not necessary to sift it. Cake flour does need sifting.

6. Choose your bakeware according to its browning ability. Shiny bakeware reflects heat and slows the browning process, making it ideal for shortbread and soft crust breads. Cookware with a dull finish and glass baking dishes will absorb more heat and brown crusts much quicker, which is perfect for piecrusts, cookies, coffee cakes, and crusty breads.

7. When making cutouts, try to get as many biscuits or cookies as you can from the first rolling. Too many rerollings may cause them to become tough and dry.

8. For yeast breads, use fresh yeast and a thermometer to make sure the heat of the liquid won't kill the yeast.

9. Grease muffin cups and baking pans on the bottoms and only halfway up the sides to prevent unwanted rims around the edges of quick breads.

10. For even baking, bake on one rack of your oven and allow space between baking sheets or dishes for the warm air to circulate.

11. To avoid soggy sides and bottoms, cool baked foods in the pans only as long as the recipe directs, then transfer the baked goods to a wire rack to finish cooling.

12. For tips on baking at high altitudes, see opposite page.

continued from page 161

Microwave directions: Gently stir batter. Line one or two 6-ounce custard cups with paper bake cups. Spoon *2 slightly round tablespoons* of batter into *each* cup. For 1 muffin, micro-cook, uncovered, on 100% power (high) for 30 to 60 seconds or till done. For 2 muffins, cook on high for 1 to 1½ minutes or till done. (To check for doneness, scratch the slightly wet surface with a wooden toothpick. The muffin should look cooked underneath.) Remove from cups; let stand on a wire rack for 5 minutes. Carefully remove paper bake cups. Serve warm.

Nutrition information per muffin: 158 cal., 5 g fat, 17 mg chol., 3 g pro., 28 g carbo., 2 g fiber, 184 mg sodium. RDA: 13% iron, 12% vit. A, 18% thiamine, 16% riboflavin, 13% niacin.

Pumpkin-Nut Muffins: Prepare muffin batter as directed, *except* add ¼ teaspoon *ground nutmeg* and ¼ teaspoon *ground ginger* to the flour mixture. Decrease the milk to *1 cup*. Add ½ cup *canned pumpkin* to the egg mixture. Stir ¼ cup chopped *walnuts or pecans* into the batter.

Buttermilk Biscuits

1 package piecrust mix (for 2-crust pie)
1½ teaspoons baking powder
⅛ teaspoon baking soda
½ cup buttermilk or sour milk*
Milk (optional)
1 tablespoon sugar (optional)
¼ teaspoon ground cinnamon (optional)

In a medium mixing bowl stir together piecrust mix, baking powder, and baking soda. Make a well in the center;

For scones, cut dough into 8 or 10 wedges and arrange them on the baking sheet, leaving space between the wedges.

add buttermilk or sour milk all at once. Using a fork, stir just till dough clings together. (The dough will be sticky.)

On a well-floured surface, knead dough gently for 10 to 12 strokes. Roll or pat dough to ½-inch thickness. Cut with a 2½-inch biscuit cutter, dipping the cutter into flour between cuts. For shiny crusts, brush tops of biscuits with milk. If desired, stir together sugar and cinnamon; sprinkle atop biscuits.

Transfer biscuits to an ungreased baking sheet. Bake in a 450° oven for 8 to 10 minutes or till golden. Serve warm. Makes 10 to 12 biscuits.

Nutrition information per biscuit: 200 cal., 13 g fat, 0 mg chol., 2 g pro., 17 g carbo., 0 g fiber, 296 mg sodium.

Applesauce-Walnut Biscuits: Prepare biscuits as directed, *except* add ½ teaspoon *ground cinnamon* and substitute ½ cup *chunk-style applesauce* for the buttermilk. Stir ⅓ cup chopped *walnuts* into the dough.

Currant-Orange Scones: Prepare biscuit dough as directed, *except* add 1 tablespoon *sugar* and 1 teaspoon finely shredded *orange peel* to dry ingredients.

In a small mixing bowl combine the buttermilk and ½ cup *currants* or chopped pitted *dates or raisins;* let stand for 5 minutes. Stir buttermilk mixture into dry ingredients.

On a floured surface, knead dough for 10 to 12 strokes. Roll into an 8-inch circle; cut into 8 or 10 wedges. Transfer to a lightly greased baking sheet, allowing space between the wedges (see how-to photo, *left*). Bake, uncovered, in a 425° oven for 12 to 15 minutes or till golden. Serve warm. Makes 8 or 10 scones.

*Note: To make sour milk, add milk to 1½ teaspoons lemon juice to equal ½ cup. Let stand for 5 minutes.

Creamy Caramel-Pecan Rolls

SAVE TIME AND EFFORT BY STARTING with thawed frozen bread dough, then let the rolls rise in the refrigerator overnight—

1¼ cups sifted powdered sugar
½ cup whipping cream
1 cup coarsely chopped pecans
2 14- to 16-ounce loaves frozen sweet or white bread dough, thawed
3 tablespoons margarine or butter, melted
½ cup packed brown sugar
1 tablespoon ground cinnamon
¾ cup light or dark raisins (optional)

For topping, in a small mixing bowl stir together powdered sugar and whipping cream. Divide evenly between two 9x1½-inch round baking pans. Sprinkle pecans evenly over sugar mixture.

On a lightly floured surface, roll each loaf of dough into a 12x8-inch rectangle. Brush with melted margarine or butter.

continued on page 164

High Altitude Baking

Above 3,000 feet, baked products tend to rise higher and dry out faster. If you live at such high altitudes, you may need to adjust some of the recipes in this story.

Yeast breads: Yeast doughs may rise faster than the time given in the recipe. Let them rise till just nearly double. If you'd like more yeast flavor, punch the dough down once, then let rise a second time. Also, breads are drier at high altitudes, so knead in only enough flour to reach the desired stiffness.

Biscuits, muffins, and cookies: To prevent overrising and dryness, cut back a little on the sugar and leavening (baking powder or soda) and increase the liquid slightly. For cookies, increase the oven temperature about 25° and decrease the baking time slightly to prevent them from getting too dry.

For more information: Contact your local extension agent or write to: Colorado State University, Bulletin Room, Fort Collins, CO 80523.

continued from page 163

In a small mixing bowl stir together brown sugar and cinnamon; sprinkle over dough. If desired, top with raisins. Roll up rectangles, jelly-roll style, starting from a long side (see how-to photo, *below right*). Pinch to seal. Cut each into 10 to 12 slices.

Place rolls, cut side down, atop mixture. Cover with a towel. Let rise in a warm place till nearly double, about 30 minutes. (*Or,* cover with oiled waxed paper, then with plastic wrap. Refrigerate 2 to 24 hours. Before baking, let chilled rolls stand, covered, 20 minutes at room temperature. Puncture any surface bubbles with a greased toothpick.)

Bake rolls, uncovered, in a 375° oven till golden, allowing 20 to 25 minutes for unchilled rolls and 25 to 30 minutes for chilled rolls. If necessary, cover rolls with foil the last 10 minutes to prevent overbrowning. Cool in pans 5 minutes on a wire rack. Invert onto a serving platter. Serve warm. Makes 20 to 24 rolls.

Nutrition information per roll: 224 cal., 9 g fat, 8 mg chol., 4 g pro., 32 g carbo., 0 g fiber, 43 mg sodium. RDA: 22% thiamine, 11% riboflavin, 10% niacin, 11% iron.

Jumbo Creamy Caramel-Pecan Rolls: Prepare rolls as directed, *except* use a 12-inch deep-dish pizza pan or a 13x9x2-inch baking pan. Roll up rectangles from short sides; cut each into 4 slices. Let rise as directed. Bake, uncovered, in a 375° oven, allowing 25 to 30 minutes for unchilled and 30 to 35 minutes for chilled rolls. If necessary, cover with foil last 10 minutes. Cool. Makes 8 jumbo rolls.

Creamy Caramel-Pecan Rolls

Bake these nutty sweet rolls big and bodacious for hearty appetites, or scale them down for an ordinary, everyday size. Pop them into the oven first thing, after they rise overnight.

Roll up each rectangle with filling, jelly-roll style, running fingers from center to edges to keep the roll evenly shaped.

Creamy Caramel-Pecan Rolls ◆

Cranberry-Pear Pie

USE BOSC, BARTLETT, OR ANJOU PEARS
in this winning pie—

4 medium pears
1 cup sugar
¼ cup all-purpose flour
1 tablespoon finely shredded orange peel
1 teaspoon ground cinnamon
2 cups cranberries
Pastry for a double-crust pie
1 tablespoon margarine or butter, cut up
Glazed Nut Topping
Sweetened whipped cream (optional)

Peel, core, and slice pears (should have 5 cups). In a mixing bowl combine sugar, flour, orange peel, and cinnamon. Add pears and cranberries; toss to coat. Set aside.

For pie shell, prepare double-crust pastry. Roll out *half* of the pastry; line a 9-inch pie plate with pastry. Fill the pastry-lined pie plate with pear mixture. Dot filling with margarine or butter. Trim bottom pastry to ½ inch beyond edge of plate. Roll out remaining pastry; cut into ½-inch-wide strips. Weave strips on top of filling to make a lattice. Press ends of strips into rim of bottom crust. Fold bottom pastry over strips; seal and crimp edge. Cover edge of pie with foil.

Bake in a 375° oven for 25 minutes. Remove foil; bake for 25 to 30 minutes more or till crust is golden. Spoon Glazed Nut Topping evenly over warm

pie. Cool pie on wire rack before serving. Serve with sweetened whipped cream, if desired. Makes 8 servings.

Glazed Nut Topping: In a small saucepan combine ½ cup chopped *walnuts* and 2 tablespoons *margarine or butter*. Cook and stir over medium heat till walnuts are lightly browned. Stir in 3 tablespoons *brown sugar*. Heat and stir till sugar is dissolved. Stir in 1 tablespoon *milk*.

Nutrition information per serving: 529 cal., 27 g fat, 0 mg chol., 5 g pro., 72 g carbo., 3 g fiber, 188 mg sodium.

RDA: 15% iron, 14% vit. C, 28% thiamine, 17% riboflavin.
$200 WINNER
Mrs. Marilu Locche,
New Hartford, Conn.

◆ Cranberry-Pear Pie, *above*

Quick Veggie Chili con Queso, *facing page, right,* ◆
Chocolate and Pear Bread Pudding
facing page, left

Chocolate and Pear Bread Pudding

TOP THIS PEAR DESSERT WITH PUR-
chased chocolate sauce or sweetened
whipped cream—

1 8-ounce package cream cheese, softened
⅔ cup sugar
1 teaspoon finely shredded lemon peel
1 teaspoon vanilla
¼ teaspoon ground nutmeg
¼ teaspoon ground cinnamon
4 eggs
1½ cups milk, half-and-half,
or light cream
3 cups dry bread cubes
(about 4 slices bread)
4 medium pears, peeled, cored,
and thinly sliced (2 cups)
⅓ cup miniature semisweet
chocolate pieces
1 teaspoon sugar

⅛ teaspoon ground nutmeg
⅛ teaspoon ground cinnamon

In a large mixing bowl beat cream
cheese, the ⅔ cup sugar, lemon peel,
vanilla, and the ¼ teaspoon nutmeg and
cinnamon with an electric mixer on low
speed till smooth. Beat in eggs, one at a
time, beating just till combined after
each addition. With a large spoon, stir in
milk or cream, bread, pears, and chocolate. Pour mixture into an ungreased
8x8x2-inch baking dish, stirring gently to
distribute chocolate.

In a small bowl combine remaining
sugar, nutmeg, and cinnamon. Sprinkle
over pear mixture. Place dish in a
13x9x2-inch baking pan; set on oven
rack. Pour *hot water* into the 13x9x2-
inch baking pan to a depth of 1 inch.
Bake in a 350° oven about 45 minutes or
till knife inserted in custard near the cen-

ter of dish comes out clean. Serve warm
or cool. Makes 9 servings.

Nutrition information per serving:
316 cal., 16 g fat, 141 mg chol., 8 g pro.,
37 g carbo., 1 g fiber, 204 mg sodium.
RDA: 14% calcium, 25% vit. A, 10%
thiamine.
$100 WINNER
Sally Vog, Springfield, Oreg.

Quick Veggie Chili con Queso

1 28-ounce can crushed tomatoes
2 15-ounce cans pinto beans
1 15-ounce can red kidney beans
1 15-ounce can garbanzo beans
1 14½-ounce can hominy
1 6-ounce can tomato paste
1 4-ounce diced green chili peppers
2 medium onions, chopped (1 cup)
2 medium zucchini, halved
lengthwise and sliced (2½ cups)
1 to 2 tablespoons chili powder
1 teaspoon ground cumin
¾ teaspoon garlic powder
½ teaspoon sugar
1½ cups shredded Monterey Jack
cheese (6 ounces)

continued on page 168

continued from page 167
In a Dutch oven combine tomatoes, *undrained* pinto and kidney beans, *drained* garbanzo beans and hominy, tomato paste, *undrained* chili peppers, onions, zucchini, chili powder, cumin, garlic powder, sugar, and *salt* to taste, if desired. Heat to boiling; reduce heat. Simmer, covered, 30 minutes. Remove from heat. Add cheese; stir till melted. Serve with sour cream and garnish with cilantro, if desired. Makes 8 servings.

Nutrition information per serving: 360 cal., 9 g fat, 19 mg chol., 22 g pro., 56 g carbo., 12 g fiber, 760 mg sodium. RDA: 34% calcium, 33% iron, 40% vit. A, 67% vit. C.

$200 WINNER
Abigail Kurtz Mahoney,
San Marcos, Calif.

Fruit-and-Nut Chili

THIS MIX OF CURRY, APPLES, ALMONDS, cocoa, and cinnamon, plus all of the usual chili fixings, gives this recipe an updated taste—

◆ Fruit-and-Nut Chili,

1½ pounds lean ground beef
4 medium onions, chopped (2 cups)
3 cloves garlic, minced
2 16-ounce cans tomatoes, cut up
1 15-ounce can tomato sauce
1 14½-ounce can chicken broth
3 medium green, red, and/or yellow sweet peppers, chopped (2¼ cups)
2 4-ounce cans diced green chili peppers, drained
2 cooking apples (such as Granny Smith or Jonathan), cored and chopped
3 tablespoons chili powder
2 tablespoons unsweetened cocoa powder
1 tablespoon curry powder
1 teaspoon ground cinnamon

1 15-ounce can red kidney beans, drained
⅔ cup slivered almonds
Raisins, cheddar cheese, and plain yogurt or sour cream (optional)

In a large Dutch oven cook beef, onions, and garlic till meat is brown. Drain off fat. Stir in *undrained* tomatoes, tomato sauce, broth, peppers, green chili peppers, apples, chili powder, cocoa, curry, and cinnamon. Bring to boiling; reduce heat. Cover; simmer for 1 hour. Add kidney beans and almonds. Heat through. Serve with raisins, cheddar cheese, and yogurt or sour cream, if desired. Makes 8 main-dish servings.

Nutrition information per serving: 330 cal., 15 g fat, 54 mg chol., 25 g pro., 31 g carbo., 8 g fiber, 1,097 mg sodium. RDA: 13% calcium, 33% iron, 69% vit. A, 108% vit. C.

$100 WINNER
Scott Weaner,
Wichita Falls, Tex.

November

Better Homes and Gardens cover — November 1992

Light Appetizers & Desserts

Holiday Recipes from Top Chefs

Prize Tested Recipes®

Pumpkin-Pear Cake, Pumpkin Flan, Creamy Pesto Pasta,

Pasta with Red Clam Sauce

Light Appetizers & Desserts

Holiday Recipes from Top Chefs

Deck your holiday table with an all-new style of festive party fare. It's lighter, leaner, and still as luscious as ever. To help you create a guilt-free spread, nationally renowned chefs and food writers share their best-ever finger foods and desserts. Your friends will relax and enjoy the party, knowing that these richly flavored recipes are low in fat and calories.

Salmon-Dill Canapés

BLEND THIS CREAMY SPREAD THE DAY before and chill, or make and freeze it for up to a month—

1 fresh salmon steak, ¾ to 1
inch thick (8 ounces)
1 8-ounce package light cream cheese
(Neufchâtel)
3 tablespoons fresh dill or
1 tablespoon dried dillweed
2 tablespoons lemon juice
¼ teaspoon salt
¼ teaspoon white or black pepper
Bibb lettuce or leaf lettuce (optional)
1 3½-ounce jar capers, drained
1 small red or white onion,
finely chopped (¼ cup)

continued on page 172

Salmon-Dill Canapés

Invite guests to build their own appetizers. They won't be able to resist piling crusty bread and cucumbers with fresh salmon spread, capers, and onions.

Carolyn O'Neil, R.D., "On The Menu," CNN, Atlanta, Ga.

Salmon-Dill Canapés, Shrimp Kabobs with Sesame◆ Dipping Sauce, Garlic-Ginger Chicken Strips, Herbed Cheese and Greens

continued from page 170
1 large cucumber,
cut into ¼-inch-thick slices
1 loaf baguette-style French bread,
thinly sliced
Lemon slices (optional)
Fresh dill sprigs (optional)

Place the salmon steak on the unheated rack of a broiler pan. Broil 4 inches from heat for 5 to 7 minutes on each side or till salmon flakes easily when tested with a fork; cover and chill till cool or till needed.

Remove skin and bones from the cooled salmon. Place salmon in a food processor bowl or blender container. Add cream cheese, dill, lemon juice, salt, and pepper. Cover and process or blend mixture till smooth and combined. Cover and chill the spread up to 24 hours before serving.

To serve, if desired, line the center of a large platter with lettuce. Mound salmon spread in the center of the lettuce. Arrange capers and onions next to salmon spread. Fill the rest of the platter with cucumber and bread slices. To assemble canapés, spread cucumber or bread slices with salmon spread and top with capers and onions. If desired, top platter or canapés with lemon slices and fresh dill. Makes about 40 appetizers.

Nutrition information per serving: 41 cal., 2 g fat, 7 mg chol., 2 g pro., 4 g carbo., 0 g fiber, 92 mg sodium.

Garlic-Ginger Chicken Strips

4 skinless, boneless chicken breast halves (1 pound total)
¼ cup lower-sodium soy sauce
¼ cup dry sherry

Garlic-Ginger Chicken Strips

"At our cooking school, we boost flavor with spices instead of fat. These chicken strips marinate in a blend of oriental flavors, including ginger and garlic."
Martin Yan, "Yan Can Cook" TV show, Foster City, Calif.

1 tablespoon snipped fresh basil or 1 teaspoon dried basil, crushed
6 to 8 cloves garlic, minced
1 tablespoon honey
2 teaspoons grated gingerroot
½ teaspoon pepper
½ teaspoon crushed red pepper
¼ teaspoon five-spice powder
Green and purple kale leaves (optional)
Red sweet pepper knots
(see directions, right)

Cut each chicken breast half lengthwise into 4 long strips (16 total). In a large nonmetal bowl combine soy sauce, sherry, basil, garlic, honey, gingerroot, pepper, crushed red pepper, and five-spice powder. Add chicken strips; stir to coat. Cover and marinate for 30 minutes at room temperature or for 4 to 24 hours in the refrigerator.

Drain chicken, reserving marinade. Place chicken strips on the unheated rack of a broiler pan. Broil 4 to 5 inches from the heat about 5 minutes or till light brown, brushing once with reserved marinade. Turn and brush again with marinade. Broil 3 to 5 minutes more or till chicken is golden brown and no longer pink inside.

To serve, line a serving platter with kale, if desired. Transfer chicken strips to platter; top with red sweet pepper knots, if desired. Serve warm. Makes 8 appetizer servings.

Red sweet pepper knots: Cut red sweet pepper into short, very thin strips, about 1¼x⅛ inches. Place in a bowl of boiling water for 1 minute or just till limp. Drain; cool. Tie into knots.

Nutrition information per serving: 88 cal., 2 g fat, 30 mg chol., 12 g pro., 4 g carbo., 0 g fiber, 307 mg sodium. RDA: 29% niacin.

Shrimp Kabobs with Sesame Dipping Sauce

THESE EASY KABOBS COMBINE THREE low-fat sauces—hoisin, tomato, and plum sauce—in the tangy marinade—

1 pound fresh or frozen medium-size raw shrimp, peeled and deveined
¼ cup hoisin sauce
¼ cup tomato sauce
¼ cup plum sauce or snipped chutney
1 tablespoon lemon juice
2 teaspoons grated gingerroot
2 teaspoons minced garlic
⅛ teaspoon white or black pepper
16 6-inch bamboo skewers or eight 12-inch bamboo skewers, cut in half
1 fresh pineapple or one 8-ounce can pineapple chunks (juice pack), drained
1 medium red and/or green sweet pepper, cut into 1-inch squares (1 cup)
Sesame Dipping Sauce

Thaw shrimp, if frozen. For marinade, in a medium mixing bowl combine hoisin sauce, tomato sauce, plum sauce or chutney, lemon juice, gingerroot, garlic, and white or black pepper. Add shrimp and stir to coat. Cover and chill for 1 hour. (Do not marinate longer.) Soak bamboo skewers in water for 30 minutes.

If using a fresh pineapple, cut in half lengthwise through crown. Set one half aside. With a knife (preferably a pineapple knife or sturdy grapefruit knife), cut around the shell of the other half to loosen fruit. Remove fruit; cut into quarters. Trim core; cut fruit into chunks. Reserve 16 chunks; save any extra for another use.

Drain shrimp, reserving marinade. On each skewer, thread 1 shrimp, 1 pineapple chunk, 1 sweet pepper square, and 1 more shrimp, leaving ¼-inch space between items. Repeat with remaining skewers and ingredients. Brush skewers with some of the reserved marinade.

To broil, place skewers on the unheated rack of a broiler pan. Broil 4 inches from the heat about 4 minutes or till shrimp turn pink, turning skewers once and brushing with marinade.

Or, to grill, brush grill rack with *cooking oil;* place skewers on rack directly over *hot* coals. Grill, uncovered, for 4 minutes. Turn and brush with reserved marinade. Grill 4 to 6 minutes more or till shrimp turn pink.

To serve kabobs, if desired, stick the sharp ends of the skewers into the outer shell of the reserved pineapple half, so that the kabobs can easily be removed by guests. Serve kabobs with Sesame Dipping Sauce. Makes 16 servings.

Shrimp Kabobs with Sesame Dipping Sauce

Shrimp makes a tempting low fat appetizer but can get pricey. To keep costs low and to add color, Martin Yan skewers marinated shrimp with pineapple and sweet pepper. Dip them into tangy sesame sauce before nibbling.

Herbed Cheese and Greens

"When elegant also needs to be easy, I stir together two low-fat cheeses and serve this creamy blend on crisp greens instead of on high fat crackers."
Anne Lindsay, cookbook author, Toronto, Canada

Sesame Dipping Sauce: In a small serving bowl stir together ⅓ cup *rice vinegar or white vinegar,* ¼ cup *honey,* ¼ cup *lower-sodium soy sauce,* 2 tablespoons toasted *sesame seed,* and 2 teaspoons *toasted sesame oil.* Cover and set aside or chill for 30 minutes to allow flavors to blend.

Nutrition information per serving: 65 cal., 2 g fat, 33 mg chol., 5 g pro., 9 g carbo., 1 g fiber, 239 mg sodium. RDA: 10% vit. C.

Herbed Cheese and Greens
THESE DAINTY APPETIZERS ARE EASY FOR guests to handle at stand-up parties—

2 large heads Belgian endive
4 ounces soft goat's cheese (chévre)
⅓ cup skim-milk ricotta cheese
¼ cup finely snipped parsley
1 teaspoon milk
¼ teaspoon salt
⅛ teaspoon pepper
30 small fresh basil leaves
1 small red onion, cut into thin,
½-inch-long strips

Divide endive into individual leaves; wash and drain well.

In a small mixing bowl combine goat's cheese, ricotta, parsley, milk, salt, and pepper; mix well.

Line wide end of *each* endive leaf with a basil leaf. Place cheese mixture into a pastry bag fitted with a large star tip. Pipe about *1 teaspoon* cheese mixture over the wide end of each basil leaf. (*Or,* spoon the same amount of cheese mixture atop basil leaves.) Top each appetizer with red onion strips. Makes about 30.

Nutrition information per appetizer: 16 cal., 1 g fat, 3 mg chol., 1 g pro., 1 g carbo., 0 g fiber, 36 mg sodium.

Black Bean Chili in Phyllo Cups

Jill's spicy appetizer tarts take a playful twist on all American chili. For easy serving and extra appeal, spoon chicken chili into low fat pastry cups made from phyllo dough.

Jill D. O'Connor, pastry chef/author, Bainbridge Island, Wash.

Dried Tomato Crostini

Blend true Italian flavors, including tomatoes, olives, and capers, for this naturally low fat antipasto. Just before serving, spread the tomato topper on the pretoasted croutons.

Tracy Pikhart Ritter, consulting chef/writer, San Diego, Calif.

◆ Black Bean Chili in Phyllo Cups, Dried Tomato Crostini

Dried Tomato Crostini

12 dried tomato halves (dry pack)
¼ cup boiling water
2 tablespoon balsamic or red wine vinegar
1 ripe medium tomato, peeled,
  seeded, and chopped (½ cup)
¼ cup finely chopped red onion
4 pitted ripe olives, minced (optional)
1 tablespoon olive oil or cooking oil
1½ teaspoons snipped parsley
1 clove garlic, minced
½ teaspoon capers, drained and chopped
Cracked black pepper
1 8-ounce loaf baguette-style French bread
Shredded Parmesan cheese or
  mozzarella cheese (optional)
Fresh thyme sprigs (optional)

In a bowl combine dried tomatoes, water, and vinegar. Let stand for 15 to 20 minutes to soften tomatoes. Drain; discard liquid. Cut dried tomatoes into thin strips; return to bowl. Stir in ripe tomato, onion, olives, oil, parsley, garlic, and capers. Season with pepper.

Bias-slice bread into 24 pieces, about ½ inch thick. Place bread slices on a baking sheet. Bake in a 350° oven for 3 to 5 minutes or till light brown. Turn bread over; bake for 3 to 5 minutes more or till light brown.

Spoon tomato mixture onto toasted bread and serve immediately. *Or,* if desired, sprinkle shredded Parmesan or mozzarella cheese over tomato mixture; return to oven for 3 to 5 minutes more or till cheese is melted. To serve, garnish with thyme, if desired. Serve immediately. Makes 24 appetizer servings.

Nutrition information per serving: 35 cal., 1 g fat, 0 mg chol., 1 g pro., 6 g carbo., 0 g fiber, 61 mg sodium.

Black Bean Chili in Phyllo Cups

FOR BUFFET PARTIES, SET OUT A TRAY OF Phyllo Cups and a pot of chili, so guests can fill their own—

6 to 8 ounces skinless, boneless
chicken breast
¾ cup water
1 small onion, finely chopped
1 or 2 cloves garlic, minced
1 tablespoon olive oil or cooking oil
1 teaspoon chili powder
1 teaspoon dried oregano, crushed
1 14½-ounce can stewed tomatoes
½ cup beer
2 tablespoons lime juice
1 15-ounce can black beans,
rinsed and drained
1 or 2 fresh jalapeño peppers, seeded and
diced, or 2 tablespoons diced
canned jalapeño peppers
1 teaspoon crushed red pepper (optional)
Phyllo Cups
Plain nonfat yogurt (optional)
Fresh cilantro or parsley sprigs (optional)

Place chicken in a medium skillet with water. Bring to boiling; reduce heat. Cover and simmer for 12 to 14 minutes or till no longer pink. Drain and cool. Use a fork to pull chicken apart into long, thin shreds; set aside.

In a 2-quart saucepan cook onion and garlic in hot oil over medium-high heat till tender but not brown. Stir in chili powder and oregano; cook for 1 minute more. Drain stewed tomatoes, reserving juices; set aside. Add reserved tomato juice, beer, and lime juice to onion mixture; bring to boiling. Reduce heat; simmer, uncovered, for 5 minutes.

Meanwhile, coarsely chop the stewed tomatoes. Add tomatoes, shredded

Curried Crab Dip with Herb Crisps

"Chips with dip are a 'must-have' at most parties. That's why I created these zero-fat chips from egg roll wrappers. Pair them with a bowlful of yogurt crab dip."

Susie Heller, recipe consultant,

Shaker Heights, Ohio

chicken, black beans, jalapeños, and red pepper to onion mixture. Simmer mixture, uncovered, for 15 to 20 minutes more or till most of the liquid is absorbed (mixture should be thick).

◆ Curried Crab Dip with Herb Crisps

Season with salt and pepper.

Just before serving, spoon about *1 tablespoon* chili into each Phyllo Cup. Top with yogurt and cilantro sprigs, if desired. Serve immediately to keep the Phyllo Cups from getting soft. Makes 36 to 40 appetizers.

Phyllo Cups: Thaw eight 17x12-inch sheets of frozen *phyllo dough*. Spray *one* sheet lightly with *nonstick spray coating*. (Keep remaining phyllo dough covered with a damp cloth until you're ready to use it.) Top with a second sheet of phyllo dough and spray with nonstick coating. Repeat with 2 more sheets of phyllo and additional spray coating. You should have 4 layers of phyllo.

With a sharp knife, cut layered phyllo lengthwise into 4 strips. Cut each strip into 5 squares, keeping layers intact. Press each square gently into a 1¾-inch muffin pan, creasing as needed to fit.

Repeat with remaining four sheets of phyllo dough and nonstick coating to make 40 cups total. Bake Phyllo Cups in a 350° oven for 8 to 10 minutes or till crisp and golden. Cool Phyllo Cups for 5 minutes in the pan, then transfer to a wire rack and cool them completely.

To store, transfer cups to a tightly covered container; chill for up to 2 days or freeze for up to 1 month.

Nutrition information per serving: 39 cal., 1 g fat, 4 mg chol., 3 g pro., 6 g carbo., 1 g fiber, 86 mg sodium.

Curried Crab Dip

IT'S IMPORTANT TO DRAIN THE PLAIN yogurt to give this dip a creamier, thicker texture. Make sure the yogurt does not contain gelatin—

2 8-ounce cartons plain nonfat yogurt
(without gelatin)
1 cup cooked crabmeat (6 ounces)
2 tablespoons chopped green onions
1 to 2 tablespoons snipped chutney
1 teaspoon curry powder
¼ teaspoon salt
Dash ground red pepper
2 tablespoons toasted sliced almonds
Herb Crisps (see recipe, right) or
low-fat crackers

Line a large strainer with a double thickness of 100% cotton cheesecloth and place it over a medium mixing bowl. Spoon the yogurt into the strainer. Cover and refrigerate overnight. Discard any liquid in the bowl; clean the bowl.

In the mixing bowl combine the drained yogurt, crabmeat, green onion, chutney, curry powder, salt, and red pepper. Cover and chill till serving time, up to 4 hours. Place in a serving bowl.

Lean Entertaining Tips

Lighten your holiday fare without losing the flavors you love—

◆ Strive for balance in your menu. It's OK to serve one or two favorite splurge foods. Just fill in with lighter, more healthful dishes.

◆ Place nutritious nibbles within arm's reach. Set trays of cut-up fresh vegetables or fruits around the room. For a simple dip, stir herbs into lower-fat mayonnaise or fruit preserves into nonfat yogurt.

◆ Use the leanest meat cuts available and use less. Stretch the reduced amount of meat by cutting it into smaller pieces or by adding vegetables, rice, or grains.

◆ Start with less. When recipes call for a high amount of fat, try using less, especially in salad dressings, marinades, and sauces.

◆ Use nonstick spray coating for greasing baking pans and frying.

◆ Lighten up dairy-rich dishes with low-fat options. Look for part-skim cheeses and lower-fat versions of cheddar, Swiss, and other cheeses. Replace cream cheese with light cream cheese and cream with low-fat milk or evaporated skim milk.

◆ Turn light desserts into showstoppers with creative garnishing. To paint plates with delicious designs, place pureed fruit in plastic squirt bottles and paint away. Or, add a glistening glaze to fresh or poached fruit with melted jelly.

Garnish with toasted sliced almonds. Serve with Herb Crisps or crackers. Makes about 2 cups.

Nutrition information per tablespoon dip: 17 cal., 0 g fat, 5 mg chol., 2 g pro., 2 g carbo., 0 g fiber, 45 mg sodium.

Herb Crisps

YOU CAN ALSO PREPARE THESE CRUNCHY, golden chips by substituting wonton wrappers for the egg roll wrappers. Since wonton wrappers come in smaller squares, you do not have to cut them—

6 egg roll wrappers (7x7 inches)
Nonstick spray coating
1½ teaspoons dried Italian seasoning,
crushed, or dried oregano, crushed
½ teaspoon garlic salt

Cut each egg roll wrapper into 4 squares (you should end up with 24 small squares total). Fill a Dutch oven or large pot about half-full with water; bring to boiling. Drop in egg roll wrappers, 1 or 2 at a time. Cook for 15 to 20 seconds or till the wrappers look like cooked noodles. (The cooking time will vary depending on the thickness of the wrapper.) Using a slotted spoon, gently remove one wrapper at a time. Place wrappers in a single layer on paper towels to drain. If wrappers stick together, hold under cold water a few seconds.

Spray a baking sheet with nonstick coating. Arrange the coated wrappers in a single layer on a baking sheet; sprinkle with Italian seasoning or oregano and garlic salt.

Bake in a 375° oven for 5 minutes. Turn wrappers; bake for an additional 3 to 4 minutes or till golden and crisp.

continued on page 178

continued from page 177
Remove from the oven. Cool on a wire rack. Makes 24 chips.

Nutrition information per chip: 25 cal., 0 g fat, 6 mg chol., 1 g pro., 5 g carbo., 0 g fiber, 19 mg sodium.

Fresh Raspberry Kuchen

KUCHEN (koo ken) IS A GERMAN WORD for cake or pastry. In this version, a layer of cake is topped with colorful berries baked in a lemon cream—

> 2 cups fresh or frozen raspberries*
> 1 cup all-purpose flour
> ½ cup sugar
> 1 teaspoon baking powder
> ¼ cup margarine, melted
> 2 egg whites
> 1 teaspoon vanilla
> 1½ cups plain lower-fat or nonfat yogurt
> 2 tablespoons all-purpose flour
> ½ cup sugar
> 2 slightly beaten egg yolks
> 1 slightly beaten egg
> 1½ teaspoons finely shredded lemon peel
> 1 teaspoon vanilla
> Lemon leaves (optional)

If using frozen raspberries, thaw at room temperature 15 minutes; drain.

In food processor bowl or medium mixing bowl, stir together the 1 cup flour, the first ½ cup sugar, and baking powder. Add margarine, the 2 egg whites, and the first teaspoon vanilla. Cover; process or stir by hand till well mixed. Spread onto bottom of a 9-inch springform pan; sprinkle with berries.

For filling, drain excess liquid from yogurt; measure yogurt. Place in a large mixing bowl; sprinkle with 2 table-spoons flour. Add remaining sugar, yolks, whole egg, peel, and remaining vanilla. Mix till smooth; pour over berries in springform pan.

Bake in 350° oven about 55 minutes or till center appears set when shaken gently. Cool for 15 minutes; remove sides of pan. Cover; chill till serving time, up to 24 hours. To serve, transfer to a serving platter, removing bottom of pan, if desired. Garnish with lemon leaves, if desired. Serves 12.

Note: Frozen raspberries may make the creamy filling softer because they tend to water out.

Nutrition information per serving: 183 cal., 6 g fat, 55 mg chol., 4 g pro., 29 g carbo., 1 g fiber, 105 mg sodium. RDA: 10% calcium, 10% vit. A, 10% thiamine, 15% riboflavin.

Fresh Raspberry Kuchen ◆

Fresh Raspberry Kuchen

"Party goers appreciate a dessert they can feel good about. To lighten up this cake, I cut back on margarine and use egg whites. The topping gets its creaminess from yogurt."
Anne Lindsay, cookbook author, Toronto, Canada

Old-Fashioned Pumpkin Gingerbread

YOU CAN MAKE THIS MOIST GINGER-bread the day before or freeze it for up to 3 months wrapped tightly in heavy foil or freezer wrap. To serve, thaw the frozen cake at room temperature, then wrap in foil and reheat in a 300° oven for 10 to 12 minutes. Reheat individual servings in the microwave oven on 50% power (medium) for 40 seconds—

½ cup packed brown sugar
¼ cup margarine, softened
2 tablespoons sugar
1½ teaspoons finely shredded orange peel
3 egg whites
1 cup canned pumpkin
¼ cup light corn syrup
2 tablespoons molasses
1¼ cups sifted cake flour*
1 teaspoon baking soda
½ teaspoon baking powder
½ teaspoon ground cinnamon
½ teaspoon ground ginger
¼ teaspoon salt
1 tablespoon powdered sugar
Orange peel curls (optional)

In a large mixing bowl combine brown sugar, margarine, sugar, and orange peel. Beat with an electric mixer on high speed till smooth. Add egg whites, *one* at a time, beating about 1 minute after each addition. Mix in pumpkin, corn syrup, and molasses on medium speed till mixture is smooth.

In a small mixing bowl stir together sifted cake flour, baking soda, baking powder, cinnamon, ginger, and salt. Gradually beat flour mixture into sugar mixture; beat till smooth. Pour batter into a greased 8x8x2-inch baking pan.

◆ Old-Fashioned Pumpkin Gingerbread

Bake in a 350° oven about 30 minutes or till cake pulls slightly away from sides of pan and toothpick inserted in center comes out clean. *Do not over bake.* Transfer pan to a wire rack and cool in pan about 15 minutes or till warm. Dust with powdered sugar. Serve warm or cool, cut in squares. Garnish with curled strips of orange peel, if desired. Makes 9 servings.

*Note: To substitute all-purpose flour for the cake flour, use 1 cup plus 2 tablespoons *sifted all-purpose flour* in place of all the sifted cake flour.

Nutrition information per serving: 212 cal., 5 g fat, 14 mg chol., 3 g pro., 39 g carbo., 1 g fiber, 200 mg sodium. RDA: 17% iron, 81% vit. A, 13% thiamine, 11% riboflavin.

Old-Fashioned Pumpkin Gingerbread

Abby's love for moist, hearty gingerbread goes back to childhood. For a lightened-up version, she replaces most of the fat with pumpkin, which adds a wonderful flavor of its own.

Abby Mandel, cookbook author and columnist, Winnetka, Ill.

◆ Chocolate Pumpkin Brownies

baking powder, cocoa powder, cinnamon, allspice, salt, and nutmeg. Beat on low speed till smooth. Stir in semisweet chocolate pieces.

Spray an 11x7x1½-inch baking pan with nonstick coating. Pour batter into pan; spread evenly. Bake in a 350° oven for 15 to 20 minutes or till a toothpick inserted near the center comes out clean. Cool in pan on a wire rack. Cut into 2-inch squares. Makes 15 squares.

Nutrition information per square: 82 cal., 3 g fat, 11 mg chol., 1 g pro., 14 g carbo., 0 g fiber, 53 mg sodium. RDA: 18% vit. A.

Lemon Yogurt Creme

TO DECORATE THIS COLORFUL DESSERT, look for small flowers that are safe to eat and were grown without pesticides. Your safest sources are the supermarket and growing your own—

1 32-ounce carton plain nonfat yogurt
(without gelatin)
¼ cup cold water
1 envelope unflavored gelatin
1 cup sifted powdered sugar
Seeds from ½ of a vanilla bean*
or 2 tablespoons vanilla
1 teaspoon finely shredded lemon peel
Edible flowers such as nasturtiums,
marigolds, bachelor's buttons,
and/or pansies (optional)
Assorted fresh fruits such as grapes, sliced
pear halves, apple wedges,
and/or kumquats (optional)
Lemon leaves (optional)

continued on page 183

Chocolate Pumpkin Brownies

When simple ranks as high as healthful and delicious on your holiday wish list, Vincent's blond brownies satisfy.

Vincent Guerithault,

chef/owner,Vincent

on Camelback Restaurant,

Phoenix, Ariz.

Chocolate Pumpkin Brownies

THESE COOKIE SQUARES ARE DOTTED with chocolate pieces—

⅔ cup packed brown sugar
½ cup canned pumpkin
1 whole egg
2 egg whites
2 tablespoons cooking oil
1 cup all-purpose flour
1 teaspoon baking powder
1 teaspoon unsweetened cocoa powder
½ teaspoon ground cinnamon
½ teaspoon ground allspice
¼ teaspoon salt
¼ teaspoon ground nutmeg
⅓ cup miniature semisweet chocolate pieces
Nonstick spray coating

In a large mixing bowl combine brown sugar, pumpkin, egg, egg whites, and oil. Beat with an electric mixer on medium speed till blended. Add flour,

Lemon Yogurt Creme

"I love creating fabulous desserts, especially healthful ones. While experimenting with nonfat yogurt cheese, which is simply drained yogurt. I came up with this flower-studded dessert creme. Showcase it as a colorful center piece for your table, then serve it as a delicious finale."

Lori McKean, chef and food writer,

Cannon Beach, Oreg.

Chocolate Hazelnut Meringue Torte

Treat your guests to layers of rich, chocolaty mousse, toasted hazelnut meringue, and vivid red raspberry sauce. Lori's exquisite torte offers all the flavor of a decadent dessert, yet it's low in fat and cholesterol.

◆ Lemon Yogurt Creme, Chocolate Hazelnut Meringue Torte

continued from page 181

Line a large strainer with a double thickness of 100% cotton cheesecloth and place over a medium mixing bowl. Spoon the yogurt into the strainer; cover and chill at least 4 hours or overnight. Discard any liquid left in the bowl.

In a small saucepan combine cold water and gelatin; let stand for 5 minutes to soften. Cook and stir over low heat till gelatin is dissolved. Remove from heat.

In a large mixing bowl combine drained yogurt, gelatin mixture, powdered sugar, vanilla bean seeds or vanilla, and lemon peel. Line *one* 4-cup heart-shaped mold or baking pan, *one* 8x1½-inch round baking pan, or *eight* ½-cup heart-shaped molds with plastic wrap, using enough so the wrap hangs over sides of mold(s) or pan.

Place edible flowers face down in bottom of the mold(s) in a decorative pattern. Carefully spoon yogurt mixture over flowers. Smooth top(s). Cover with plastic wrap; chill for at least 4 hours or overnight in the refrigerator till set.

To serve, place platter (or plates for the smaller molds) on top of mold(s) or pan and invert. Carefully remove mold(s) or pan. The flowers should be on top. Carefully remove plastic wrap. Serve with assorted fresh fruit. Garnish with lemon leaves, if desired. Makes 8 servings.

*Note: To use vanilla bean, cut one bean in half; store the unused half, tightly wrapped, in the refrigerator for up to six months. Split the other half of the bean with a sharp knife and scrape out the powder-fine seeds.

Nutrition information per serving: 125 cal., 0 g fat, 2 mg chol., 7 g pro., 22 g carbo., 0 g fiber, 88 mg sodium. RDA: 28% calcium, 20% riboflavin.

Chocolate Hazelnut Meringue Torte

THIS CHOCOLATE-FILLED TORTE IS PROOF that low-fat ingredients, such as egg whites, yogurt, and cocoa, can create a luscious dessert that's perfect for entertaining—

> *1 16-ounce carton plain nonfat yogurt (without gelatin)*
> *6 egg whites*
> *1 teaspoon white wine vinegar*
> *Dash salt*
> *Dash cream of tartar*
> *1½ cups sugar*
> *½ cup hazelnuts or almonds, toasted and finely chopped*
> *Cornstarch*
> *½ cup unsweetened European cocoa powder* or regular unsweetened cocoa powder, sifted*
> *¼ cup sugar*
> *6 egg whites*
> *1 cup sugar*
> *3 tablespoons crème de cacao or orange liqueur*
> *1 tablespoon cold water*
> *1 envelope unflavored gelatin*
> *Raspberry Sauce*

Line a strainer with a double thickness of 100% cotton cheesecloth and place it over a bowl. Place the yogurt into the strainer; cover and chill overnight. Discard any liquid.

For meringue, in a mixing bowl beat the first 6 egg whites, vinegar, salt, and cream of tartar with an electric mixer on medium speed till soft peaks form (tips curl). Add the 1½ cups sugar, ¼ *cup* at a time, beating on high speed. Continue beating on high speed till very stiff peaks

continued on page 184

continued from page 183

form (tips stand straight). Gently fold nuts into meringue.

Line 3 baking sheets with parchment paper or plain brown paper. Grease paper and dust it with cornstarch. On each of the 3 baking sheets, trace a 9-inch circle using your finger or a pen. With a spatula, spread the meringue mixture evenly over the 3 circles.

Bake in a 300° oven about 40 minutes or till crisp and barely golden. (If necessary, chill *one-third* of the meringue mixture while the other two meringues bake. Spread chilled meringue on a baking sheet and bake as directed.) Cool baked meringues on the baking sheet.

To make meringues ahead, wrap cooled meringues tightly in plastic wrap; chill for up to 24 hours. To freeze, place meringues on a baking sheet; freeze for 1 hour or till frozen. Wrap individually in freezer wrap and freeze for up to 1 month.

For filling, in an extra-large mixing bowl combine drained yogurt, cocoa powder, and the ¼ cup sugar. Set mixture aside.

In the top of a double boiler combine remaining egg whites and the 1 cup sugar. Place over, but not touching, boiling water. Insert candy thermometer. Heat, whisking constantly, till mixture reaches 165° (about 7 minutes). Transfer egg white mixture immediately to a large mixing bowl. Beat with an electric mixer on high speed till stiff peaks form and mixture is glossy (5 to 7 minutes). Set aside.

Clean the top of the double boiler and add liqueur and cold water. Sprinkle gelatin atop. Let stand 5 minutes to soften. Place over, but not touching, boiling water; heat and stir till gelatin is dissolved. Stir into yogurt mixture.

Sweet-Potato-Banana Custards

At her restaurant, Leah takes pride in low fat menu items, including dessert. This Southern-style custard uses sweet potato and banana for flavor and as substitutes for some of the eggs.

Leah Chase, owner,

Dooky Chase's Restaurant,

New Orleans, La.

Working quickly, whisk the egg white mixture, one-third at a time, into yogurt mixture. Chill, uncovered, till the mixture mounds when dropped from a spoon, about 20 minutes. Do not chill any longer or the mixture will get too stiff.

To assemble the torte, place *one* layer of meringue on a cake plate and spoon *half* of the filling evenly over the meringue. Top with another meringue layer; spoon the remaining filling over the second layer. Top with the third meringue layer. Loosely cover the torte with plastic wrap; chill for at least 1½ hours but no more than 4 hours (chilling longer may cause the meringue layers to start to dissolve).

To serve, lightly dust the top of the torte with cocoa. Serve with Raspberry Sauce. Makes 12 servings.

◆ Sweet-Potato-Banana Custards

*Note: If using European unsweetened cocoa, the filling will have a more intense chocolate flavor and a deeper brown color, as pictured on page 182. Look for this type of cocoa in specialty food markets.

Raspberry Sauce: In a food processor bowl or blender container combine 2 cups fresh or frozen *raspberries,* ¼ cup *water,* 1 tablespoon *sugar,* and 1 teaspoon *vanilla.* Cover and process or blend till smooth. Strain through a sieve.

Nutrition information per serving: 276 cal., 4 g fat, 1 mg chol., 8 g pro., 55 g carbo., 1 g fiber, 98 mg sodium. RDA: 18% calcium, 10% vit. C, 21% riboflavin.

Sweet-Potato-Banana Custards

2 cups mashed cooked sweet potato (3 to 4 medium sweet potatoes)
⅔ cup mashed ripe banana
1 12-ounce can (1½ cups) evaporated skim milk

◆ Orange and Rice Custard

¼ cup packed brown sugar
2 beaten eggs
½ teaspoon salt
Nonstick spray coating
½ cup raisins
1 tablespoon sugar
½ teaspoon ground cinnamon

In a mixing bowl combine sweet potato and banana. Add milk; mix well. Add brown sugar, eggs, and salt; mix well.

Spray eight 1/2 cup ramekins, soufflé dishes, or 6-ounce custard cups with nonstick coating. Divide mixture among the ramekins or cups. Sprinkle raisins in each cup. Arrange ramekins or cups on a baking sheet.

Combine sugar and cinnamon; sprinkle atop mixture in each ramekin or cup. Bake in a 325° oven about 35 minutes or till a knife inserted near the centers comes out clean. Serve warm. Makes 8 servings.

Nutrition information per serving: 228 cal., 2 g fat, 55 mg chol., 7 g pro., 48 g carbo., 3 g fiber, 218 mg sodium. RDA: 22% calcium, 185% vit. A, 29% vit. C, 28% riboflavin.

Orange and Rice Custard

Dotty stirred two favorites, custard and rice pudding, into one terrific new dessert. Because this recipe uses buttermilk, egg product, and rice, it contains half the fat of regular custard. Yet dessert lovers won't miss a thing.

Dotty Griffith, food editor for *THE DALLAS MORNING NEWS,* Dallas, Texas

Orange and Rice Custard
SERVE THIS CITRUS-FLAVORED CUSTARD in squares for casual gatherings, or spoon it into goblets for fancy affairs—

½ teaspoon finely shredded orange peel
¾ cup orange juice
¾ cup water
⅔ cup medium- or short-grain white rice*
1 tablespoon sugar
Nonstick spray coating
¾ cup frozen egg product, thawed, or 3 slightly beaten eggs
1 cup sugar
1 tablespoon margarine, melted
2 cups buttermilk

2 tablespoons orange juice
Thin strips of orange peel (optional)
Fresh mint sprigs (optional)

In a small saucepan combine ¾ cup orange juice and the water; heat to boiling. Stir in ¼ *teaspoon* of the shredded peel, *uncooked* rice, and the 1 tablespoon sugar. Reduce heat; simmer, covered, for 15 to 20 minutes or till liquid is absorbed and rice is tender.

Spray a 2-quart square baking dish with nonstick coating. Spoon rice mixture into dish; spread evenly. Set aside.

In a large mixing bowl combine egg product or eggs, the 1 cup sugar, margarine, buttermilk, the 2 tablespoons orange juice, and remaining ¼ teaspoon shredded peel. Mix till sugar is dissolved.

Carefully pour egg mixture over rice. Place dish in a large baking pan; pour hot water into baking pan to a depth of 1 inch. Bake in a 350° oven for 40 to 45 minutes or till firm around edges and almost set in center. Remove large pan from oven. Carefully lift custard dish from water; transfer to a wire rack. Cool about 30 minutes or till room temperature. Cover; chill the custard for 4 hours before serving.

To serve, spoon custard into dessert dishes or cut into squares. Garnish with orange peel strips and mint, if desired. Makes 10 to 12 servings.

*Note: Short-grain or medium-grain rice works best for this dessert because each gives it a softer, fluffier texture.

Nutrition information per serving: 178 cal., 2 g fat, 5 mg chol., 5 g pro., 35g carbo., 0 g fiber, 98 mg sodium. RDA: 14% vit. C, 11% thiamine, 11% riboflavin.

Pumpkin-Pear Cake

WHEN YOU TURN THIS CAKE UPSIDE down, a caramel-pear topping appears—

⅔ cup packed brown sugar
¼ cup margarine or butter, melted
1 teaspoon cornstarch
1 16-ounce can pear halves in light syrup
1½ cups all-purpose flour
1½ teaspoons pumpkin pie spice
1 teaspoon baking soda
¾ teaspoon baking powder
4 egg whites
1 cup granulated sugar
1 cup canned pumpkin
½ cup cooking oil

In a small bowl combine brown sugar, melted margarine or butter, and cornstarch. Drain pears, reserving 3 *tablespoons* of the syrup. Stir reserved syrup into brown sugar mixture. Pour mixture into a 10-inch round baking pan or a 9x9x2-inch baking pan. (If desired, cut pears into fans by cutting 3 or 4 lengthwise cuts ½ inch from the top of pear to the bottom of the pear.) Arrange pear halves, small ends to the center and rounded side down, atop syrup in pan.

In a small bowl combine flour, pumpkin pie spice, baking soda, and baking powder; set aside. In another mixing bowl beat egg whites with electric mixer on medium speed till soft peaks form. Gradually add granulated sugar, beating till stiff peaks form. Using low speed, blend in pumpkin and oil. Fold flour mixture into pumpkin mixture just till

◆ Pumpkin-Pear Cake

moistened; carefully spoon over pears. Spread mixture evenly with back of spoon. Bake in 350° oven for 50 to 60 minutes or till a toothpick inserted near center comes out clean. Cool about 5 minutes. Loosen from sides of pan; invert onto serving plate. Serve warm. Makes 10 to 12 servings.

Nutrition information per serving: 370 cal., 16 g fat, 0 mg chol., 4 g pro., 56 g carbo., 1 g fiber, 191 mg sodium. RDA: 12% iron, 75% vit. A, 14% thiamine, 13% riboflavin.

$200 WINNER
Mrs. Kim Landhuis,
Fort Dodge, Iowa

Pumpkin Flan

THIS LUSCIOUS CUSTARD TASTES LIKE A crustless pumpkin pie with caramel sauce—

1 cup sugar
4 beaten eggs
1 16-ounce can pumpkin
1 12-ounce can evaporated milk
½ cup sugar
1 teaspoon ground cinnamon
1 teaspoon vanilla
½ teaspoon ground ginger
½ teaspoon ground nutmeg
¼ teaspoon salt
Sweetened whipped cream (optional)
Ground nutmeg (optional)

In a large heavy skillet cook the 1 cup sugar over medium-high heat till sugar begins to melt; *do not stir,* just shake skillet occasionally. When sugar starts to melt, reduce heat to low; cook, stirring frequently, till sugar is golden brown. Quickly pour sugar into a 10-inch deep pie plate or a 10-inch quiche dish. Tilt to evenly coat bottom. Place pie plate or quiche dish into a large roasting pan. Place on rack in oven.

In a large mixing bowl stir together eggs, pumpkin, milk, the ½ cup sugar, cinnamon, vanilla, ginger, nutmeg, and salt. Pour pumpkin mixture atop sugar in pie plate or quiche dish. Pour *boiling* water into roasting pan around pie plate or quiche dish to a depth of ½ inch. Bake in a 350° oven for 50 to 55 minutes for pie plate or 45 to 50 minutes for quiche dish, or till a knife inserted near center comes out clean. Cool. Chill, covered, for 4 to 24 hours. To serve, loosen edges of flan with a knife, slipping point of knife down sides of flan to let air in. Invert flan onto a serving platter. Top with sweetened whipped cream and nutmeg, if desired. Makes 10 servings.

Nutrition information per serving: 186 cal., 2 g fat, 87 mg chol., 6 g pro., 37 g carbo., 1 g fiber, 125 mg sodium. RDA: 17% calcium, 135% vit. A, 19% riboflavin.

$100 WINNER
Mrs. Allen Silvi,
Fairport Harbor, Ohio

Creamy Pesto Pasta

COMBINE BASIL WITH LOWER-FAT CREAM cheese and cottage cheese for a lightened-up sauce—

12 ounces pasta, such as rigatoni,
rotini, or mostaccioli
4 teaspoons dried basil, crushed or ¼ cup
chopped fresh basil
2 cloves garlic, minced
2 tablespoons olive oil or cooking oil
½ of an 8-ounce package light cream cheese
(Neufchâtel)
½ cup low-fat cottage cheese
⅓ cup grated Parmesan cheese
⅓ cup dry white wine
¼ cup snipped parsley
⅓ cup water

◆ Pumpkin Flan, *top*
◆ Creamy Pesto Pasta, *above*

continued on page 188

Pasta with Red Clam Sauce

◆ Pasta with Red Clam Sauce
continued from page 187

Cook pasta according to package directions. Drain well. Keep warm.

Meanwhile, in a medium skillet cook basil and garlic in hot oil about 1 minute. Reduce heat. Add cream cheese, cottage cheese, and Parmesan cheese. Heat and stir till fairly smooth. Stir in wine, parsley, and water. Cook, uncovered, for 3 minutes or till slightly thickened. Serve sauce over hot cooked pasta. Garnish with fresh *basil*, if desired. Makes 4 main-dish servings.

Nutrition information per serving: 285 cal., 11 g fat, 20 mg chol., 12 g pro., 31 g carbo., 0 g fiber, 258 mg sodium. RDA: 16% calcium, 13% iron, 12% vit. A, 20% thiamine.

$200 WINNER
Claudia N. Ebeling,
Lewisburg, Pa.

Pasta with Red Clam Sauce

SUE ANN MODIFIED HER FATHER'S RED clam sauce recipe into this, simpler version—

3 cloves garlic, minced
1 tablespoon olive oil or cooking oil
½ teaspoon coarsely ground black pepper
¼ teaspoon crushed red pepper
1 10-ounce can whole baby clams
*2 14½- or 16-ounce cans whole Italian-
style tomatoes, cut up*
2 teaspoons dried parsley flakes
½ teaspoon dried basil, crushed
½ teaspoon anchovy paste (optional)
*8 ounces pasta, such as medium shell,
mostaccioli, or cavatelli*

In a large skillet cook garlic in hot oil over medium heat about 30 seconds. Add black and red pepper. Cook and stir for 30 seconds more.

Drain clams, reserving juice. Set clams aside. Add reserved clam juice and *undrained* tomatoes to skillet. Stir in parsley, basil, and anchovy paste, if desired. Bring to boiling; reduce heat. Simmer, uncovered, for 30 to 35 minutes or to desired consistency. Stir in clams; heat through.

Meanwhile, cook pasta according to package directions. Drain well. Serve sauce over hot cooked pasta. Makes 4 main-dish servings.

Nutrition information per serving: 334 cal., 6 g fat, 44 mg chol., 16 g pro., 57 g carbo., 2 g fiber, 395 mg sodium. RDA: 15% calcium, 45% iron, 18% vit. A, 56% vit. C, 40% thiamine, 23% riboflavin, 34% niacin.

$100 WINNER
Sue Ann Scarcia-Barry,
Lititz, Pa.

December

Delicious Memories
Prize Tested Recipes®

Chocolate Mousse Torte, Scarlet Pears,

Peppy Chick-Pea Dip, French-Style Cream Cheese Spread

Delicious Memories

We all have foods that we cherish—dishes we expect to see every time we gather for a holiday meal. As the years go by, they become more than just foods, they become family traditions. To pay tribute to these special dishes, *Better Homes and Gardens®* staff members gathered their own recipes for this story. We indulged in one another's desserts and ethnic specialties, and laughed about the family stories they called to mind. On the following pages, we share these treasured recipes, hoping they will add warmth to your holiday season.

Double Mushroom-Pumpkin Soup

IF DESIRED, YOU CAN MAKE THIS SOUP the day before, then stash it in the refrigerator until ready to heat and eat—

¼ cup dried mushrooms
(such as porcini or shiitake)
3 cups water
1 large onion, finely chopped
1 cup chopped or sliced fresh mushrooms
1 tablespoon margarine or butter
1 16-ounce can pumpkin
2 teaspoons instant chicken
bouillon granules
¼ teaspoon ground nutmeg
¼ teaspoon salt

¼ teaspoon pepper
Fresh chives (optional)
Half-and-half or light cream,
warmed (optional)

In a 2-cup glass measure combine dried mushrooms and *1 cup* of the water. Micro-cook, uncovered, on 100% power (high) for 3 minutes or till boiling. (*Or,* pour *1 cup* boiling water over dried mushrooms.) Let stand for 10 minutes. Drain mushrooms, reserving liquid; finely chop.

continued on page 192

Fresh Cranberry Relish, Marinated Prime Rib,◆
Sweet-and-Sour Red Cabbage, Cloverleaf Rye Rolls,
Cheesy Mashed Potatoes, Double
Mushroom- Pumpkin Soup

continued from page 190

In a medium saucepan cook onion and fresh mushrooms in margarine or butter till tender but not brown. Stir in finely chopped, drained mushrooms; reserved liquid; remaining 2 cups water; pumpkin; bouillon granules; nutmeg; salt; and pepper.

Cook and stir over medium heat till heated through. If desired, garnish with chives and additional mushrooms; top with a little warm half-and-half or light cream. Makes 6 to 8 servings.

To make ahead: Prepare soup; cover and chill overnight. To serve, heat through and serve as directed.

Nutrition information per serving: 93 cal., 4 g fat, 6 mg chol., 3 g pro., 13 g carbo., 2 g fiber, 414 mg sodium. RDA: 12% iron, 214% vit. A, 10% vit. C, 15% riboflavin, 14% niacin.

Marinated Prime Rib

¾ cup dry red wine
½ cup chopped onion
¼ cup lemon juice
¼ cup water
1 tablespoon Worcestershire sauce
½ teaspoon dried rosemary, crushed
½ teaspoon dried marjoram, crushed
¼ teaspoon garlic salt
1 4- to 6-pound beef rib roast
Fresh rosemary (optional)

For marinade, in a mixing bowl stir together wine, onion, lemon juice, water, Worcestershire sauce, rosemary, marjoram, and garlic salt.

Place meat in a plastic bag in a shallow dish. Add marinade, close bag. Marinate in the refrigerator for 6 to 24 hours, turning bag occasionally.

Double Mushroom-Pumpkin Soup

The official family soup on Christmas Eve at Joy Taylor's house.

Marinated Prime Rib

A favorite entrée from Nancy Byal's Missouri upbringing.

Cheesy Mashed Potatoes

Lisa Holderness' Aunt Joani always brings a big batch of her "secret" recipe.

Sweet-and-Sour Red Cabbage

Proof of Nancy's German heritage.

Fresh Cranberry Relish

Joy's daughter, Anna, now helps fix this hand-me-down recipe.

Cloverleaf Rye Rolls

With sleeves rolled past her elbows, Kristi Fuller always helped her mom shape these.

Drain meat, discarding marinade. Place meat, fat side up, in a large roasting pan. Insert a meat thermometer into center, not touching bones.

Roast in a 325° oven to desired doneness, allowing 1¾ to 3 hours for rare (140°), 2¼ to 3¾ hours for medium (160°), or 2¾ to 4¼ hours for well-done (170°). Transfer meat to a cutting board. Cover with foil and let stand for 15 minutes before carving. If desired, garnish with fresh rosemary. Serves 12 to 16.

To make ahead: Marinate the beef roast overnight. Roast and serve as directed above.

Nutrition information per serving: 266 cal., 15 g fat, 89 mg chol., 30 g pro., 0 g carbo., 96 mg sodium, 0 g fiber. RDA: 19% iron, 18% riboflavin, 30% niacin.

Cheesy Mashed Potatoes

INSTEAD OF MASHING THESE POTATOES with a potato masher, they are shredded after cooking—

9 medium baking potatoes (3 pounds)
2 cups shredded regular or lower-fat cheddar cheese (8 ounces)
¼ cup margarine or butter
1 8-ounce carton regular or lower-fat dairy sour cream
1 tablespoon chopped green onion
½ teaspoon salt
¼ teaspoon pepper
Paprika

In a Dutch oven add water to unpeeled potatoes just to cover; sprinkle with *salt*. Bring to boiling; reduce heat. Cover and simmer for 30 to 35 minutes or till almost tender. Drain; cool slightly. Peel and shred potatoes with a grater.

In a large mixing bowl combine potatoes, cheese, and margarine or butter; stir till margarine is melted. Stir in sour cream, green onion, the ½ teaspoon salt, and the pepper. Transfer to a greased 2-quart casserole.

Bake, uncovered, in a 325° oven for 45 to 50 minutes or till heated through. Sprinkle with paprika. Makes 8 servings.

To make ahead: Before baking, cover and chill the potato mixture overnight. To heat, bake in a 325° oven, covered, for 1¼ to 1½ hours, stirring twice. (Or, heat in the microwave oven on 100% [high] power for 15 to 20 minutes, stirring once.) Sprinkle with paprika before serving.

Nutrition information per serving: 371 cal., 21 g fat, 42 mg chol., 11 g pro., 35 g carbo., 0 g fiber, 400 mg sodium. RDA: 32% calcium, 29% vit. A, 21% vit. C, 17% thiamine, 14% riboflavin, 15% niacin.

Sweet-and-Sour Red Cabbage

A COLORFUL VEGETABLE DISH FOR THE holidays or any day—

*1 medium head red cabbage,
shredded (6 cups)
1 medium apple, peeled and
finely chopped
¼ cup raisins
¼ cup sugar
¼ cup vinegar
½ teaspoon salt
⅛ teaspoon pepper
1 tablespoon margarine or butter*

In a large skillet cook cabbage, apple, and raisins, covered, in a small amount of boiling water for 5 to 7minutes or till crisp-tender; drain.

In a small mixing bowl combine sugar, vinegar, salt, and pepper; stir till sugar is dissolved. Add to cabbage mixture in skillet. Add margarine or butter. Cook, covered, for 3 to 4 minutes or till heated through, stirring twice. Makes 6 to 8 servings.

Nutrition information per serving: 93 cal., 2 g fat, 0 mg chol., 1 g pro., 20 g carbo., 3 g fiber, 219 mg sodium. RDA: 39% vit. C.

Fresh Cranberry Relish

*¾ cup apple juice or orange juice
½ to ⅔ cup sugar
¼ teaspoon ground cinnamon
¼ teaspoon ground nutmeg
Dash ground cloves
1 12-ounce package (3 cups) cranberries
½ cup light raisins
½ cup chopped pecans
Flowering kale or leaf lettuce (optional)*

In a medium saucepan combine juice, sugar, cinnamon, nutmeg, and cloves. Cook and stir over medium heat till sugar is dissolved. Add cranberries and raisins. Bring to boiling; reduce heat. Cook and stir for 3 to 4 minutes or till cranberries pop. Remove from heat. Stir in pecans. Transfer to a serving bowl. Cover and chill thoroughly. If desired, garnish with kale or lettuce. Makes 8 (⅓-cup) servings.

Nutrition information per ⅓-cup serving: 149 cal., 5 g fat, 0 mg chol., 1 g pro., 28 g carbo., 1 g fiber, 2 mg sodium. RDA: 10% vit. C.

Cloverleaf Rye Rolls

THE ROLLS CAN BE BAKED AHEAD AND stored in the freezer—

*3½ to 4 cups all-purpose flour
2 packages active dry yeast
¼ cup sugar
1 teaspoon salt
2 cups water
2 tablespoons shortening
2 cups rye flour
Melted margarine or butter (optional)*

In a large mixing bowl stir together 2¾ cups of the all-purpose flour, the yeast, sugar, and salt. Set aside.

In a small saucepan heat and stir water and shortening till warm (120° to 130°) and shortening is almost melted. Add shortening mixture to flour mixture. Beat with an electric mixer on low speed for 30 seconds, scraping bowl. Beat on high speed for 3 minutes. Using a spoon, stir in rye flour and as much remaining all-purpose flour as you can.

Turn dough out onto a lightly floured surface. Knead in enough remaining all-purpose flour to make a moderately stiff dough that is smooth and elastic (6 to 8 minutes). Shape into a ball. Place in a greased bowl; turn once. Cover; let rise in warm place till double (about 1 hour).

Punch dough down. Turn out onto a lightly floured surface. Divide in half. Cover; let rest for 10 minutes.

Lightly grease 24 muffin cups. Divide each *half* of dough into 36 pieces. Shape each piece into a ball, pulling edges under to make a smooth top. Place *3* balls in *each* cup, smooth side up. Cover; let rise in a warm place till double (about 30 minutes).

continued on page 194

Royal Christmas Cake

THE CAKE IS FILLED WITH FRUITS AND nuts, spread with almond paste, then topped with Royal Icing—

2 cups all-purpose flour
1 teaspoon ground cinnamon
½ teaspoon baking powder
¼ teaspoon baking soda
¼ teaspoon ground nutmeg
¼ teaspoon ground cloves
1½ cups currants
1½ cups dark or light raisins
1½ cups diced mixed candied
fruits and peels
1 cup candied red and/or green cherries
½ cup ground almonds (2 ounces)
4 eggs
1 cup sugar
¾ cup margarine or butter, melted
½ cup rum, brandy, or orange juice
3 tablespoons lemon juice
Rum, brandy, or orange juice
1 8-ounce can almond paste
Royal Icing
Fresh bay leaves (optional)

Grease two 9x1½-inch round baking pans. Line bottom and sides with parchment or waxed paper to prevent over-browning; grease paper.

In a large mixing bowl stir together flour, cinnamon, baking powder, baking soda, nutmeg, and cloves. Stir in currants, raisins, fruits and peels, cherries, and almonds. Set aside.

In a mixing bowl beat eggs slightly with a fork. Add sugar, margarine or butter, ½ cup rum, and lemon juice; stir till combined. Stir egg mixture into fruit mixture; pour into pans.

Bake in a 300° oven for 1¼ to 1½ hours or till a toothpick inserted near the center comes out clean. (Cover pans

continued from page 193

Bake in a 375° oven for 15 to 18 minutes or till golden. If desired, brush with melted margarine or butter. Remove from pans; cool on a wire rack or serve warm. Makes 24 rolls.

To make ahead: Wrap the cooled, baked rolls in a single layer in heavy foil; seal, label, and freeze up to 2 months. To reheat, bake wrapped rolls in a 350° oven for 30 to 35 minutes.

Nutrition information per unbuttered roll: 111 cal., 1 g fat, 0 mg chol., 3 g pro., 22 g carbo., 1 g fiber, 90 mg sodium. RDA: 16% thiamine.

◆ Royal Christmas Cake

Royal Christmas Cake
Julia Malloy, Food Editor

"I remember licking the sweet marzipan filling from the Father Christmas figurine that always adorned our Christmas cake. Because it just wasn't Christmas without them, my mother wrote home for the family Christmas cake recipe and her figurine soon after she emigrated from England."

loosely with foil after 1 hour of baking to prevent overbrowning.) Cool in pans on a wire rack.

Remove cooled cake from pans. Wrap layers separately in rum, brandy, or juice-moistened 100% cotton cheesecloth. Overwrap with foil. Store in the refrigerator for 1 to 2 weeks. Remoisten cheesecloth with rum every 3 or 4 days or when dry.

To assemble, place one cake layer, top side down, on a serving plate. Spread with *half* of the almond paste. (*Or,* if paste is too thick to spread, divide into 2 balls. Place *each* ball between two sheets of waxed paper; flatten slightly. With a rolling pin, roll *each* portion from center to edges till 10 inches in diameter; trim to form a 9-inch circle. Remove one sheet of paper from one circle; invert onto cake. Peel off remaining paper.)

Spread *some* of the Royal Icing over almond paste on first cake layer. Add second cake layer, top side up; top with remaining paste. Frost top and sides of cake with remaining Royal Icing. If desired, garnish with bay leaves. Makes 16 servings.

Royal Icing: In a large mixing bowl combine 4 cups sifted *powdered surgar,* ½ cup *water,* ¼ cup *meringue powder,* and 1 teaspoon *vanilla.* Beat with an electric mixer on high speed for 7 to 10 minutes or till very stiff. Use immediately, covering icing in bowl with a damp paper towel. Makes 3½ cups.

To make ahead: Bake cake at least 1 week ahead to allow flavors to mellow. You can store the frosted cake for up to 1 week in the refrigerator or up to 6 weeks in the freezer.

Nutrition information per serving: 525 cal., 16 g fat, 53 mg chol., 8 g pro., 89 g carbo., 158 mg sodium, 1 g fiber. RDA: 10% calcium, 15% iron, 16% vit. A, 17% thiamine, 28% riboflavin, 12% niacin.

Candy Bar Pie

FOR EASIER SERVING, SET THE PIE ON A warm, damp towel for a couple of minutes before cutting the first wedge—

6 1- to 1.5-ounce bars milk chocolate with almonds, chopped
15 large marshmallows or 1½ cups tiny marshmallows
½ cup milk
1 cup whipping cream
½ teaspoon vanilla
Walnut Crust
Whipped cream (optional)
Coarsely chopped milk chocolate bars with almonds (optional)

For filling, in a medium saucepan combine the 6 candy bars, marshmallows, and milk; heat and stir over medium-low heat till chocolate is melted. Remove from heat; cool the chocolate mixture to room temperature. Chill a large mixing bowl and beaters.

In the chilled mixing bowl beat whipping cream and vanilla with an electric mixer on medium speed till soft peaks form (tips curl).

Fold whipped cream into cooled chocolate mixture. Spoon chocolate mixture into Walnut Crust. Freeze about 5 hours or till firm. Remove from the freezer about 10 minutes before serving. If desired, garnish with additional whipped cream and chopped chocolate. Makes 8 servings.

Walnut Crust: In a mixing bowl combine 1½ cups coarsely ground *walnuts* (6 ounces), 3 tablespoons melted *margarine or butter,* and 2 tablespoons *sugar.* Press mixture firmly onto bottom and up sides of a 9-inch pie plate. Bake in a 325° oven about 10 minutes or till edge is golden. Cool on a wire rack.

To make ahead: Make and freeze the pie up to 2 months before serving.

Nutrition information per serving: 445 cal., 35 g fat, 42 mg chol., 8 g pro., 30 g carbo., 1 g fiber, 98 mg sodium. RDA: 15% calcium, 28% vit. A, 16% riboflavin.

Martha Washingtons

ONCE YOU TEMPER (SLOWLY MELT) THE chocolate, you can store the candy at room temperature without it softening or discoloring. Use a thermometer to gauge the water temperature—

1 cup butter, softened
1½ teaspoons vanilla
6 cups sifted powdered sugar
1¼ pounds bittersweet chocolate or semisweet chocolate
3 tablespoons shortening
Walnut pieces

Line a 2-quart rectangular baking dish with foil, extending foil over edges of pan. Butter foil; set pan aside.

In a large mixing bowl beat softened butter and vanilla with an electric mixer on medium speed till fluffy. Gradually add powdered sugar, stirring till mixture is smooth and stiff. (If necessary, knead in some powdered sugar with your hands.) Pat mixture into prepared pan. Cover and chill about 1 hour or till firm.

continued on page 196

◆ Martha Washingtons, Candy Bar Pie
continued from page 195

Candy Bar Pie
◆ ◆ ◆
Martha Washingtons

Kristi Fuller, Food Editor

"Who can resist chocolate? At our house on Christmas, there were lots of chocolate goodies to be found. I always had room for my grandmother's frozen Candy Bar Pie and a few Martha Washingtons, too. We don't know how these hand-dipped candies came to be called Martha Washingtons, but my grandmother tells me my great-aunt gave her the recipe more than 60 years ago."

When candy mixture is firm, grasp foil to lift candy out of pan; cut candy into 1-inch squares. Cover and chill till ready to dip.

To temper the chocolate, in a medium glass mixing bowl combine chocolate and shortening. Pour *warm tap water* (100° to 110°) into a large mixing bowl to a depth of 1 inch. Place bowl of chocolate inside bowl of warm water. (The water should cover the bottom half of the smaller bowl.)

Stir the chocolate mixture *constantly* with a rubber spatula till the chocolate is completely melted and smooth. This takes about 15 to 20 minutes. Do not rush the process or the chocolate will not be properly tempered. If the water begins to cool, replace with more *warm water*. (Do not get water in the chocolate, as this can cause graininess. If water does get into the chocolate, stir in additional *shortening*, 1 teaspoon at a time, till mixture becomes shiny and smooth again.)

Use a 2-tined fork to carefully dip squares, one at a time, into melted chocolate. Draw fork across rim of bowl to remove excess chocolate. Invert candy onto a waxed-paper-lined baking sheet, twisting fork slightly as candy falls to swirl the top. (If excess chocolate pools at the base, next time let more chocolate drip off fork.)

If the chocolate becomes too thick while dipping, replace water in large bowl with *warm water*. Stir the chocolate till it reaches the right dipping consistency again.

Place 1 walnut piece on each candy. Allow candy to dry. Store candy, tightly covered, at room temperature for up to 2 weeks. Makes about 2½ pounds (77 pieces).

Nutrition information per piece: 107 cal., 7 g fat, 6 mg chol., 1 g pro., 13 g carbo, 0 g fiber, 25 mg sodium.

Soofganyah
•••
Potato Latkes

Sandy Soria, Design Editor

"We knew Babi (Yiddish for grandmother) delighted at being teased about her 'cooking muscles.' At 86, her arms were amazingly strong, not only from the vigorous hugs she gave so freely, but from years of turning potatoes to pulp and beating eggs. We lost our precious Babi last year, but preparing her folksy Jewish food still comforts us."

◆ Soofganyah, Potato Latkes

Potato Latkes

*3 large baking potatoes
(about 1¼ pounds)
2 slightly beaten eggs
½ teaspoon salt
⅛ teaspoon pepper
¾ cup cooking oil
Dairy sour cream (optional)*

Wash, peel, and shred potatoes. Place in a colander and rinse; squeeze by hand to drain liquid. In a large mixing bowl stir together potatoes, eggs, salt, and pepper. (The potatoes may turn slightly pink on standing.)

In a 12-inch skillet heat ½ *cup* of the oil over medium-high heat. Drop large spoonfuls (about ¼ *cup*) of the potato mixture into hot oil; flatten with a spoon to a thin cake (about 4 inches in diameter). Cook cakes, 3 or 4 at a time, for 2 to 3 minutes on each side or till golden brown. Adjust heat and add oil as necessary during cooking. Drain on paper towels. Serve warm with sour cream, if desired. Makes 12 latkes.

Nutrition information per latke: 133 cal., 10 g fat, 36 mg chol., 2 g pro., 9 g carbo., 1 g fiber, 101 mg sodium.

Soofganyah (Jelly Doughnuts)
FILL THESE DAINTY DOUGHNUTS WITH your favorite jelly or preserves—

*2¼ cups all-purpose flour
¾ cup sugar
1½ teaspoons baking powder
½ teaspoon salt
⅛ teaspoon ground cinnamon
⅛ teaspoon ground nutmeg*

*1 slightly beaten egg
½ cup desired fruit juice, such as orange,
apple, or white grape
2 tablespoons cooking oil
3 to 4 tablespoons desired fruit jelly or
preserves, such as strawberry, raspberry,
cherry, or grape
Cooking oil for deep frying
Sugar*

In a large mixing bowl stir together flour, ¾ cup sugar, baking powder, salt, cinnamon, and nutmeg. Add egg, juice, and cooking oil; stir till smooth.

On a floured surface, knead mixture into a soft dough. Roll to ¼-inch thickness; cut with a floured 2½-inch biscuit cutter. Reroll trimmings as necessary.

For each doughnut, spoon ½ teaspoon jelly in the center of *each* dough round. Moisten edges slightly with water. Bring
continued on page 198

♦ Cherry Tea Ring, Fairy Drops

Cherry Tea Ring

Fairy Drops

Lisa Holderness, Food Editor

"Baking reminds me of special people. As a child, I helped Mom shape hundreds of sugar-coated Fairy Drops. As a teen, I baked batch after batch with my best friend, Peggy. My grandmother inspired me to bake, too. She always has homemade sweet breads for us on Christmas morning."

½ cup butter
2 cups water
2 cups snipped dried cherries
Vanilla Glaze

In a small saucepan heat milk and ½ cup butter till butter is almost melted and milk is warm (105° to 115°).

In a large mixing bowl combine the ½ cup warm water and yeast; stir till yeast is dissolved. Add milk mixture, *3½ cups* of the flour, the ½ cup sugar, eggs, and salt; stir till smooth. Using a spoon, stir in as much of the remaining 3½ to 4 cups flour as you can.

Turn dough out onto a lightly floured surface. Knead in enough of the remaining flour to make a moderately stiff dough that is smooth and elastic (6 to 8 minutes). Shape into a ball. Place in a greased bowl; turn once to grease surface. Cover; let rise in a warm place till double (about 1½ hours).

continued from page 197

up edges around jelly to cover. Press to seal and form a ball.

In a 3-quart heavy saucepan or deep-fat fryer heat *3 inches* cooking oil to 365°. Fry doughnut balls, 2 or 3 at a time, in hot oil for 4 to 5 minutes or till golden brown, turning once. With a slotted spoon, remove doughnuts. Drain on paper towels. Roll in sugar. Serve warm. Makes 18 to 20.

Nutrition information per doughnut: 147 cal., 6 g fat, 12 mg chol., 2 g pro., 22 g carbo., 0 g fiber, 80 mg sodium. RDA: 11% thiamine.

Cherry Tea Ring

THIS ATTRACTIVE SWEET BREAD IS FILLED with dried cherries and a cinnamon-sugar mixture—

1½ cups milk
½ cup butter
½ cup warm water (105° to 115°)
2 packages active dry yeast
7 to 7½ cups all-purpose flour
½ cup sugar
2 slightly beaten eggs
1½ teaspoons salt
⅔ cup sugar
⅔ cup packed brown sugar
⅓ cup all-purpose flour
1 tablespoon ground cinnamon

Meanwhile, for filling, in a medium mixing bowl combine remaining ⅔ cup sugar and brown sugar, the ⅓ cup flour, and cinnamon. With a pastry blender or fork, cut in the remaining ½ cup butter till crumbly; set aside.

Punch dough down; turn out onto a lightly floured surface. Divide in half. Cover; let rest for 10 minutes.

In a small saucepan bring 2 cups water to boiling; remove from heat. Add cherries; let stand 5 minutes. Drain cherries; squeeze to remove excess water.

Roll *half* of the dough on the floured surface into a 15x9-inch rectangle. Sprinkle *half* of the cinnamon filling evenly over dough. Sprinkle with *half* of the cherries. Roll up from one of the long sides. Seal seams.

Place rolled dough on a greased baking sheet. Attach ends together to form a circle; pinch seam to seal. Using kitchen scissors or a sharp knife, cut a vertical slit from the outside of dough to center, leaving about 1 inch still attached at the center. Repeat at 1-inch intervals around the ring. Gently turn each slice so one of the cut sides is down. Cover; let rise till nearly double (about 30 minutes). Repeat with remaining dough, filling, and cherries to make another tea ring.

Bake in a 350° oven about 25 minutes or till tops sound hollow when tapped (the centers may be lighter in color). If necessary, to prevent over-browning, cover tea rings loosely with foil the last 5 to 10 minutes of baking. Transfer to a wire rack; cool. Before serving, drizzle with Vanilla Glaze. Makes 2 tea rings (24 servings).

To make-ahead: Bake the rings, but do not glaze before freezing. Seal, label, and freeze for up to 4 months. Thaw overnight in the refrigerator. Drizzle with glaze.

Vanilla Glaze: In a small mixing bowl stir together 2½ cups sifted *powdered sugar*, 2 teaspoons *light corn syrup*, ½ teaspoon *vanilla*, ½ teaspoon *almond extract*, and enough *evaporated milk, half-and-half, or light cream* (3 to 4 tablespoons) to make a glaze of drizzling consistency. If desired, stir in a few drops *red food coloring*.

Nutrition information per serving: 348 cal., 9 g fat, 19 mg chol., 5 g pro., 62 g carbo., 2 g fiber, 240 mg sodium. RDA: 14% iron, 22% vit. A, 27% thiamine, 20% riboflavin, 16% niacin.

Fairy Drops

DECORATE THESE COOKIES WITH A sprinkling of sugar or frost and trim with crushed red and green candy canes or colored sugar—

4½ cups all-purpose flour
1 teaspoon baking soda
1 teaspoon cream of tartar
1 teaspoon salt
1 cup butter
1 cup sifted powdered sugar
1 cup sugar
1 cup cooking oil
2 eggs
2 teaspoons almond extract
Colored or plain sugar (optional)
Almond Frosting (optional)
Crushed candy canes (optional)

In a medium mixing bowl stir together flour, baking soda, cream of tartar, and salt; set aside.

In a large mixing bowl beat butter with an electric mixer on medium-low speed till smooth. Add powdered sugar and the 1 cup sugar; beat on medium-high speed till fluffy. Add oil, eggs, and almond extract; beat just till combined. Gradually add dry ingredients, beating on medium speed just till combined. Cover; chill dough about 30 minutes or till needed.

To shape cookies, roll rounded teaspoonfuls of dough into balls. (The dough will be soft.) Arrange balls on ungreased cookie sheets. With the palm of your hand, the bottom of a glass, or a swirled or patterned cookie stamp, gently flatten the balls to about ¼-inch thickness. Sprinkle with sugar or leave plain, if planning to frost.

Bake in a 350° oven for 10 to 12 minutes or till edges are light brown. Transfer to a wire rack; cool completely. If desired, frost with Almond Frosting. Makes 55 to 60 cookies.

Almond Frosting: In a small mixing bowl beat ½ cup *butter* with an electric mixer on medium speed till fluffy. Beat in ½ teaspoon *almond extract* and ½ teaspoon *vanilla*. Alternately add 2½ to 3½ cups sifted *powdered sugar* and 3 tablespoons *light cream or milk,* beating till smooth and of spreading consistency. To tint, stir in a few drops *food coloring,* if desired. Makes about 2 cups.

To make ahead: Place unfrosted cookies in a freezer container; seal, label, and freeze for up to 12 months. Frost after thawing.

Nutrition information per cookie: 122 cal., 8 g fat, 17 mg chol., 1 g pro., 13 g carbo, 0 g fiber, 90 mg sodium.

Julekake

◆◆◆

Jule Glögg

Julia Malloy, Food Editor

"To my young mind, our Christmas lunch was almost better than opening presents. Grandma Martinusen would slice up fruity Julekake and top it with gjetost (Norwegian goat cheese) or rullepolse (spiced cured lamb). Years later, Grandma and I would fix batches of Glögg at Christmastime, then we'd sample a little to be sure it was just right."

Julekake (Norwegian Christmas Bread)

4¾ to 5¼ cups all-purpose flour
2 packages active dry yeast
1½ teaspoons ground cardamom
1¼ cups milk
½ cup sugar
⅓ cup margarine or butter
½ teaspoon salt
1 egg
1 cup currants or raisins
½ cup chopped candied red and/or green cherries
½ cup diced candied citron or mixed candied fruits and peels
1 egg
1 tablespoon water

In a large mixing bowl stir together *2 cups* of the flour, the yeast, and cardamom. In a saucepan combine milk, sugar, margarine or butter, and salt; heat and stir just till warm (120° to 130°) and margarine is almost melted.

Add milk mixture to flour mixture; add 1 egg. Beat with an electric mixer on low speed for 30 seconds, scraping sides of bowl constantly. Beat on high speed for 3 minutes. Using a wooden spoon, stir in currants or raisins, cherries, citron or mixed fruits, and as much remaining flour as you can.

Turn dough out onto a lightly floured surface. Knead in enough of the remaining flour to make a moderately stiff dough that is smooth and elastic (6 to 8 minutes total). Shape into a ball. Place in a lightly greased bowl; turn once to grease surface. Cover; let rise in a warm place till double (about 1½ hours).

Punch dough down. Turn out onto a lightly floured surface. Divide in half. Cover; let rest for 10 minutes.

Shape into 2 round loaves; place on greased baking sheet(s). Flatten each to an 8-inch diameter. Cover; let the dough rise in a warm place till almost double (45 to 60 minutes).

In a small mixing bowl beat egg and water; brush onto loaves. Bake in a 350° oven about 40 minutes or till loaves sound hollow when tapped, covering loosely with foil after 20 minutes to prevent overbrowning. Transfer to a wire rack; cool completely. Makes 2 loaves (24 servings).

To make ahead: Freeze baked breads in a storage container or freezer wrap for up to 6 months.

Nutrition information per serving: 171 cal., 3 g fat, 19 mg chol., 4 g pro., 32 g carbo., 1 g fiber, 87 mg sodium. RDA: 18% thiamine, 14% riboflavin, 10% niacin.

Jule Glögg

TIE THE SPICES TOGETHER IN A 100% cotton cheesecloth bag so they're easy to remove after cooking—

1 750-milliliter bottle (3¼ cups)
dry red wine
½ cup raisins
½ cup packed brown sugar
½ cup aquavit or vodka
6 inches stick cinnamon
12 whole cloves
¼ teaspoon cardamom seed
⅛ cup blanched whole almonds
Orange peel cutouts (optional)

In a large saucepan stir together wine, raisins, brown sugar, aquavit or vodka, cinnamon sticks, cloves, and cardamom seed. Bring to boiling; reduce heat. Simmer, uncovered, for 20 minutes, stirring occasionally.

Remove from heat. If desired, remove spices. Stir in almonds. Ladle into heatproof cups. If desired, garnish with orange peel cutouts. Makes 8 (4-ounce) servings.

Nutrition information per ½-cup serving: 205 cal., 3 g fat, 0 mg chol., 1 g pro., 23 g carbo., 1 g fiber, 11 mg sodium.

Phenomenal Fudge

YOU'LL NEED AN ACCURATE CANDY thermometer and two people to beat the fudge and drop it into creamy mounds. If you're on your own, you may want to pour the beaten fudge into a pan instead, because it sets up quickly—

3 tablespoons margarine or butter
3 tablespoons unsweetened cocoa powder
2½ cups sugar

¾ cup plus 2 tablespoons
evaporated milk
1 teaspoon light corn syrup

In a 2-quart heavy saucepan melt margarine. Add cocoa powder; stir till combined. Add sugar, milk, and corn syrup. Cook over medium-high heat till mixture is boiling, stirring constantly with a wooden spoon to dissolve sugar. (This should take about 5 minutes.) Avoid splashing the candy mixture onto sides of pan.

When mixture starts to boil, carefully clip a candy thermometer to the side. Reduce heat to medium-low. The mixture should continue to boil at a moderate steady rate over entire surface. Cook, stirring frequently, for 10 to 15 minutes or till the thermometer registers 230°.

Remove candy thermometer. Pour fudge mixture into a large mixing bowl, but *do not scrape* saucepan. Put thermometer in bowl. Cool till thermometer registers 100° and mixture is thick. (Depending on the room temperature, this can take between 1 and 2 hours, so check the thermometer frequently). *Do not scrape the bowl or stir during cooling.*

Meanwhile, line a baking sheet with waxed paper. (Beginning fudge makers may want to line a 9x5x3-inch loaf pan with foil, extending foil over edges of pan; butter foil.) Set aside.

Using a wooden spoon, beat cooled mixture about 7 minutes or till fudge becomes like a soft frosting. It should start to thicken and hold a swirl, yet still be glossy. *Immediately* drop by teaspoonfuls onto buttered foil (with the help of an assistant). If fudge starts to set before all candy is dropped, stir in ½ teaspoon *hot water* and continue dropping. (Beginning fudge makers may want to

◆ Phenomenal Fudge

Phenomenal Fudge
Bill Nolan, Building Editor

"None of the fudge I've ever eaten holds a candle to Grandma's. What makes hers so special? Its incredibly creamy, smooth richness—marvelously soft inside, and smooth as silk outside. I can still see Grandma spooning that heavenly stuff onto sheets of waxed paper to cool. She'd stack them on a plate to tempt us before our big holiday dinner."

pour the mixture into the loaf pan instead of dropping it. When firm, lift out of pan; cut into squares.) Cover; store in a cool, dry place up to 1 week. Makes 30 pieces.

Nutrition information per piece: 83 cal., 2 g fat, 2 mg chol., 1 g pro., 17 g carbo., 0 g fiber, 21 mg sodium.

◆ Pagache, Walnut Rolls

Pagache
◆ ◆ ◆
Walnut Rolls

Steve Greenhut, Building Editor

"Thanks to their grandmother's cooking, there's no chance that my wife and her sisters will ever lose the love for their Polish heritage (even though their last names are now Iranian, German, and Italian). After tasting Gram's holiday specialties—Pagache (which is a cheese-filled yeast bread) and Walnut Rolls—I've come to love their Polish foods, and Gram, even more."

Walnut Rolls

1¼ cups warm water (105° to 115°)
2 packages active dry yeast
1 teaspoon granulated sugar
6¼ to 6¾ cups all-purpose flour
⅔ cup granulated sugar
1 teaspoon salt
⅓ cup margarine or butter, melted
1 tablespoon shortening, melted
2 slightly beaten eggs
1 12-ounce can (1½ cups)
evaporated milk
4 cups ground walnuts (1 pound)
⅔ cup packed brown sugar
⅓ cup granulated sugar
½ teaspoon vanilla
3 tablespoons margarine
or butter, softened
1 slightly beaten egg
1 tablespoon milk

In a small mixing bowl combine water, yeast, and the 1 teaspoon sugar; stir to dissolve yeast. Set aside.

In a large mixing bowl stir together *2 cups* of the flour, the ⅔ cup sugar, and the salt; make a well in the center. Add the ⅓ cup margarine or butter and the shortening. Stir in eggs. Stir in yeast mixture and ¾ *cup* of the evaporated milk. Beat with an electric mixer on low speed for 30 seconds, scraping the sides of the bowl constantly. Beat on high speed for 3 minutes. Using a spoon, stir in as much remaining flour as you can.

Turn dough out onto a lightly floured surface. Knead in enough remaining flour to make a moderately soft dough that is smooth and elastic (3 to 5 minutes total). Shape into a ball. Place in a greased bowl; turn to grease surface. Cover; let rise in a warm place till double (about 1 hour).

Meanwhile, for filling, in a large mixing bowl stir together walnuts, brown sugar, ⅓ cup sugar, and vanilla. Stir in 3 tablespoons softened margarine or butter and enough of the remaining evaporated milk (about ¾ cup) to make a mixture that is easy to spread.

Punch dough down. Turn out onto a lightly floured surface. Divide into 4 portions. Cover; let rest 10 minutes.

Roll *one* portion of dough into a 16x10-inch rectangle. Dot rectangle with ⅔ *cup* of the filling; spread evenly to edges. Roll up *loosely*, jelly-roll style, from one of the long edges. (If rolled too tightly, the filling may cause the dough to crack during baking.) Moisten edges; pinch to seal. Repeat with remaining dough and nut filling to make 3 additional loaves.

Place loaves, seam side down, on a greased baking sheet. Prick tops with a fork. In a small bowl stir together 1 beaten egg and the 1 tablespoon milk; brush onto dough.

Bake in a 350° oven for 30 to 35 minutes or till done, covering with foil the last 20 minutes, if necessary, to prevent overbrowning. Cool on a wire rack. Makes 4 loaves (64 servings).

Nutrition information per slice: 134 cal., 7 g fat, 12 mg chol., 3 g pro., 16 g carbo., 1 g fiber, 62 mg sodium. RDA: 11% thiamine.

Pagache (Polish Pizza)

SERVE THIS CHEESY POTATO-FILLED bread on its own as an appetizer or with a hearty soup for dinner—

¼ cup warm water (105° to 115°)
1 package active dry yeast
1 teaspoon sugar

2½ to 3 cups all-purpose flour
2 tablespoons sugar
½ teaspoon salt
1 slightly beaten egg
½ cup milk
2 tablespoons margarine or butter, melted
2 tablespoons cooking oil
2 medium potatoes, peeled
and cut up (⅔ pound)
½ cup shredded sharp cheddar
cheese (2 ounces)
2 tablespoons margarine or butter
¼ teaspoon salt
1 tablespoon margarine or butter, melted

In a small mixing bowl combine warm water, yeast, and 1 teaspoon sugar; stir to dissolve yeast. Set aside.

In a large mixing bowl stir together 1½ cups of the flour, 2 tablespoons sugar, and the ½ teaspoon salt; make a well in the center. Stir in egg.

In a saucepan heat milk to 120° to 130°; stir into flour mixture. Stir in 2 tablespoons melted margarine or butter and the cooking oil. Stir in yeast mixture. Using a spoon, stir in as much remaining flour as you can.

Turn the dough out onto a lightly floured surface. Knead in enough of the remaining flour mixture to make a moderately stiff dough that is smooth and elastic (6 to 8 minutes total). Shape into a ball. Place in a greased bowl; turn once to grease surface. Cover; let rise in a warm place till double (about 1 hour).

Meanwhile, for filling, place potatoes in a medium saucepan; add water to cover. Sprinkle with *salt*. Bring to boiling; reduce heat. Cover and simmer for 20 to 25 minutes or till tender; drain. Add cheese, 2 tablespoons margarine or butter, and the ¼ teaspoon salt; mash till smooth. Set aside.

Punch dough down. Turn out onto a lightly floured surface. Divide in half. Cover; let rest for 10 minutes.

Roll *one* portion of dough into a 15x12-inch rectangle. Transfer rectangle to a lightly greased baking sheet. Spread filling over dough to within 1 inch of edges. Roll remaining dough to 15x12-inch rectangle; place over filling. Pinch edges to seal. Using a fork, prick dough every 2 inches in a grid pattern so steam can escape.

Bake in a 400° oven about 20 minutes or till golden brown, covering with foil the last 5 minutes, if necessary, to prevent overbrowning. Brush with 1 tablespoon melted margarine or butter. Cut into squares to serve. Serve warm or cool. Makes 24 to 30 appetizer servings.

Nutrition information per serving: 106 cal., 5 g fat, 12 mg chol., 3 g pro., 13 g carbo., 0 g fiber, 115 mg sodium. RDA: 11% thiamine.

Brown Sugar Spritz

1 cup butter
½ cup packed brown sugar
1 egg
½ teaspoon finely shredded lemon peel
½ teaspoon vanilla
¼ teaspoon almond extract
2⅔ cups all-purpose flour
1 teaspoon baking powder
Colored sugars (optional)
Assorted decorative sprinkles (optional)
Candied cherries, cut up (optional)

In a large mixing bowl combine butter and brown sugar; beat with an electric mixer for 30 seconds. Add egg, lemon peel, vanilla, and almond extract; beat till combined.

◆ Brown Sugar Spritz

Brown Sugar Spritz
Maryellyn Krantz,
Test Kitchen Home Economist

"My children, ages 12 and 10, are learning that giving is much more important than getting at Christmastime. That's why every December we bake dozens and dozens of festive cookies and homemade candies for some of our elderly neighbors. One of our favorite cookies is Brown Sugar Spritz."

In a small mixing bowl stir together flour and baking powder; gradually beat into sugar mixture. (If too stiff, use a spoon to stir in remaining flour.) *Do not chill.*

Force *unchilled* dough through a cookie press onto an ungreased cookie sheet. (*Or*, pipe dough through a large star tip into S shapes or circles for
continued on page 204

◆ Krumkake
continued from page 203

Krumkake

Susan McBroom,

Design Editorial Assistant

"My mother and I have revived the baking traditions of Norwegian holiday kaffee-klatsches held by my grandmother and her sisters years ago. Krumkake is our favorite, possibly because it's a necessity to have help—— and a good excuse for a get-together. When my granddaughter was only three days old, she attended her first krumkake session!"

wreaths.) If desired, decorate with colored sugars, sprinkles, or cherries.

Bake in a 375° oven for 9 to 10 minutes or till edges of cookies are firm but not brown. Transfer cookies to a wire rack; cool completely. Makes about 70 to 80 cookies.

Nutrition information per cookie: 47 cal., 3 g fat, 10 mg chol., 1 g pro., 5 g carbo., 0 g fiber, 32 mg sodium.

Krumkake (Cone Cookies)

EAT THESE DELICATE ROLLED COOKIES plain or fill them with whipped cream and other goodies—

3 eggs
½ cup sugar
½ cup butter
½ cup all-purpose flour
1 teaspoon vanilla
or ½ teaspoon almond extract
Dash ground nutmeg
Sweetened whipped cream (optional)
Chopped toasted almonds or chocolate-flavored sprinkles (optional)
Lingonberry, cherry, or strawberry preserves (optional)

In a medium mixing bowl beat eggs with an electric mixer on medium speed about 1 minute. Add sugar; beat about 3 minutes or till sugar is almost dissolved. Melt butter; cool slightly. Stir butter into egg mixture. Add flour, vanilla or almond extract, and nutmeg; stir just till mixture is smooth.

Heat a krumkake iron on the rangetop over medium-low heat. For a 6-inch iron, spoon about *1 tablespoon* of the batter onto the hot, ungreased iron. Close gently but firmly. Cook over medium-low heat about 30 seconds or till light golden brown. Turn iron and cook about 30 seconds more. Open the iron carefully. Loosen cookie with a narrow spatula; invert onto a wire rack. *Immediately* roll the cookie into a cone or cylinder, using a wooden or metal form. Let cool around the cone or cylinder till the cookie holds its shape.

Reheat iron and repeat with remaining batter. Cool rolled cookies on a wire

Mandoo (Korean Dumplings)

"In Hawaii, eating was always a good excuse for a family get-together. Christmas was no exception. The biggest treat was sampling Grandma Hong's Mandoo before everyone else arrived. I guess it would be the Korean equivalent of snitching a chocolate chip cookie straight from the oven."

—Brad Hong, Art Director

Mandoo (Korean Dumplings) ◆

rack. If desired, before serving, pipe or fill with whipped cream; top with chopped almonds or chocolate-flavored sprinkles. Serve with preserves. Makes 26 to 30 cookies.

To make ahead: Store unfilled krumkake, tightly covered, in a storage container up to 1 week in a cool, dry place. Or, freeze up to 2 months.

Nutrition information per cookie: 62 ca., 4 g fat, 34 mg chol., 1 g pro., 6 g carbo., 0 g fiber, 43 mg sodium.

Mandoo (Korean Dumplings)

1½ cups fresh bean sprouts
½ of a 10.5-ounce package extra-firm tofu
(fresh bean curd)
1 pound lean ground beef
3 green onions, finely chopped
2 cloves garlic, minced
2 tablespoons soy sauce
1 tablespoon cornstarch
¼ teaspoon pepper
1 10-ounce package (96 wrappers) round
mandoo, potsticker, or wonton wrappers
1 egg, slightly beaten
Cooking oil
Lettuce leaves (optional)
Mandoo Dipping Sauce

For filling, in a saucepan bring 3 cups *water* to boiling. Add bean sprouts; cook for 3 minutes. Drain; rinse in cold water. Drain again; dry with paper towels. Chop drained sprouts; set aside.

Place tofu in a double layer of 100% cotton cheesecloth; squeeze till dry. In a large mixing bowl use a fork to mash tofu. Add chopped sprouts, beef, green onions, garlic, soy sauce, cornstarch, and pepper; mix well.

Spoon *about 1 tablespoon* of the filling in the center of *each* wrapper. Moisten edges of rounds with beaten egg; fold in half, pressing to seal. If desired, fold small pleats along 1 edge to seal. Place, pleated side up, on a lightly floured baking sheet; cover with a slightly damp cloth till ready to use or freeze.

To freeze, arrange Mandoo in a single layer on baking sheets; freeze till firm. Transfer to a storage container; seal, label, and freeze for up to 3 months.

continued on page 206

Grandma Massa's Ravioli
♦ ♦ ♦
Grandma Massa's Red Meat Sauce

"Making ravioli was a long, involved process for my Italian Great-Grandma Massa. She would use a long rolling pin that Great-Grandpa had made especially for her. Now that she's gone, my mom, my aunts, and my wife continue her tradition. I'm not much help, except when it's time to eat them."——Mick Schnepf, Graphic Designer

♦ Grandma Massa's Ravioli, Grandma Massa's Red Meat Sauce
continued from page 205
Thaw in refrigerator overnight before using. Makes 48.

Mandoo Wontons: In a 3-quart heavy saucepan or deep-fat fryer heat *3 inches* cooking oil to 365°. Carefully fry Mandoo, 5 or 6 at a time, in hot oil for 1½ to 2 minutes or till golden brown, turning once. (Fat may spatter slightly because of the moisture in the wonton. Use a spatter cover.) With a slotted spoon, carefully remove wontons. Drain on paper towels. Keep warm in a 300° oven while frying remaining wontons. If desired, serve on lettuce leaves with Mandoo Dipping Sauce.

Nutrition information per wonton: 58 cal., 3 g fat, 15 mg chol., 3 g pro., 5 g carbo., 49 mg sodium, 0 g fiber.

Mandoo Potstickers: In a 10-inch nonstick skillet heat *2 tablespoons* cooking oil over medium-high heat. Arrange about 12 dumplings in the skillet, pleated side up. Cook, uncovered, for 1 to 2 minutes or till bottoms are light brown.

Reduce heat to low. Remove from heat; add ¼ cup *water* all at once near the edge of the skillet. Return to heat. Cover and cook for 10 minutes.

Increase heat to medium-high. Uncover; cook for 3 to 5 minutes or till water is evaporated. Add *2 teaspoons* cooking oil to skillet; tilt to coat bottom. Cook, uncovered, for 1 minute. If desired, serve on lettuce leaves with Mandoo Dipping Sauce.

Nutrition information per potsticker: 49 cal., 2 g fat, 15 mg chol., 3 g pro., 5 g carbo., 49 mg sodium, 0 g fiber.

Mandoo Dipping Sauce: In a small mixing bowl combine 2 tablespoons *Kochoochang* (Korean hot, spicy, fermented bean sauce) *or hot bean paste,* 2 tablespoons *honey,* 2 tablespoons *soy sauce,* 2 teaspoons *rice vinegar or white vinegar,* and 2 teaspoons toasted *seasme seed.* Makes about 1 cup.

Nutrition information per tablespoon: 15 cal., 0 g fat, 0 mg chol., 0 g pro., 3 g carbo., 130 mg sodium, 0 g fiber.

Grandma Massa's Ravioli

3⅓ to 3⅔ cups all-purpose flour
1 teaspoon salt
¾ cup water
1 egg
1 egg white
Spinach Filling
Grandma Massa's Red Meat Sauce
(see recipe, below) or spaghetti sauce
Grated Parmesan cheese

For ravioli dough, in a mixing bowl stir together *3 cups* of the flour and salt. Make a well in the center. In a mixing bowl combine water, egg, and egg white; add to flour mixture and mix well.

Turn dough out onto a lightly floured surface. Knead in enough of the remaining flour to make a dough that is smooth and elastic (8 to 10 minutes total). Divide into 8 portions. Cover; let rest for 10 minutes.

Use a pasta machine or rolling pin on a lightly floured surface to roll out each dough portion to a very thin 15x6-inch rectangle.

To cut ravioli by hand: Using a fluted pastry wheel or sharp knife, cut rolled dough lengthwise into 2-inch-wide strips. Place rounded teaspoons of Spinach Filling, 1 inch apart, on *half* of the strips. Moisten pasta around filling. Lay another strip atop each strip; seal edges. Cut into individual ravioli. Reroll any trimmings.

To cut ravioli with a ravioli frame: Lightly flour the hollows of the frame. Place a rectangle of pasta over the frame; fill each hole with a rounded teaspoon of filling. Moisten dough around filling. Top with a second sheet of pasta; roll a rolling pin over the top, pressing firmly to seal and score the ravioli. Trim excess

dough. Carefully invert the frame onto a lightly floured surface. Using a fluted pastry wheel or sharp knife, cut into individual ravioli. Reroll trimmings.

Freeze *half* of the ravioli for later use. To freeze, arrange in a single layer on baking sheets; freeze till firm. Transfer to a storage container; seal, label, and freeze for up to 3 months.

Cover and chill remaining ravioli. Within 2 days, cook the chilled ravioli in boiling salted water for 6 to 8 minutes or till *al dente* (tender but still firm). Drain immediately. Pour sauce over ravioli; toss gently to coat. Sprinkle with additional Parmesan cheese. Makes 96 ravioli.

Spinach Filling: Cook one 10-ounce package *frozen chopped spinach* according to package directions. Drain; cool slightly. Squeeze out excess liquid. In a medium mixing bowl combine spinach, 2 *eggs*, 1½ cups ground *fully cooked chicken and/or beef*, one 15-ounce carton *lower-fat ricotta cheese*, ½ cup *grated Parmesan cheese*, ½ teaspoon *garlic powder*, and ⅛ teaspoon *pepper*.

Nutrition information for 6 ravioli without sauce: 189 cal., 6 g fat, 60 mg chol., 11 g pro., 21 g carbo., 1 g fiber, 259 mg sodium. RDA: 18% calcium, 12% iron, 19% vit. A, 20% thiamine, 21% riboflavin, 14% niacin.

Grandma Massa's Red Meat Sauce

SPOON THIS ZESTY SAUCE OVER GRANDMA Massa's Ravioli or other pasta—

2-to 3-pounds trimmed boneless
beef chuck pot roast
1 to 2 tablespoons cooking oil
1 medium onion, chopped

1 stalk celery, chopped
1 small carrot, chopped
½ cup snipped parsley
3 cloves garlic, minced
2 pounds tomatoes, peeled and chopped
(about 4 cups), or two
14 ½-ounce cans tomatoes, cut up
1 15-ounce can tomato sauce
1 6-ounce can tomato paste
1 tablespoon dried oregano, crushed
½ teaspoon sugar (optional)
½ teaspoon salt
½ teaspoon dried rosemary, crushed
½ teaspoon pepper

In a Dutch oven brown meat in oil about 5 minutes on each side. Remove meat, reserving drippings. Cook onion, celery, carrot, parsley, and garlic in drippings till tender but not brown.

Stir in fresh tomatoes or *undrained* canned tomatoes, tomato sauce, tomato paste, oregano, sugar (if desired), salt, rosemary, and pepper. Return meat to pan. Bring to boiling; reduce heat. Cover and simmer over low heat for 2½ hours.

Uncover and simmer for 30 to 60 minutes or till meat is tender and sauce reaches the desired consistency, stirring occasionally. Slice meat; keep warm on a serving platter. (*Or*, chop meat and stir into sauce.)

If desired, strain the sauce; arrange meat and vegetables on a platter.

Serve sauce over ravioli or other pasta. Makes 8 (½ cup) servings.

Nutrition information per ½-cup sauce with meat: 316 cal., 11 g fat, 115 mg chol., 40 g pro., 15 g carbo., 3 g fiber, 716 mg sodium. RDA: 42% iron, 43% vit. A, 62% vit. C, 21% thiamine, 35% riboflavin, 41% niacin.

Prize Tested Recipes.

Chocolate Mousse Torte

DRESS UP A CHOCOLATE CAKE MIX WITH mousse, chocolate topping, and fresh raspberries—

*1 package 1-layer-size devil's
food cake mix
⅓ cup chocolate ice-cream topping
4 squares (4 ounces) semisweet chocolate
2 tablespoons powdered sugar
2 tablespoons coffee liqueur
2 egg yolks
½ cup whipping cream
1 tablespoon chocolate ice-cream topping
½ cup whipping cream
Fresh raspberries (optional)*

Prepare cake mix and bake according to package directions. Cool 10 minutes. Remove from pan; cool completely. Place on a serving platter. Spread cake with the ⅓ cup ice cream topping. Chill till needed. Set aside.

For mousse, in a small saucepan melt semisweet chocolate over low heat; remove from heat. Stir in powdered sugar, liqueur, and egg yolks. Cook and stir over medium heat for 2 minutes or till mixture just coats a metal spoon. Remove from heat; cool completely. Beat the first ½ cup whipping cream with an electric mixer to soft peaks. Stir *half* of the chocolate mixture into whipped cream. Fold in remaining chocolate. Cover; chill mixture just till it mounds. Spread onto cake to within 1 inch of edge. Chill the cake, covered, for several hours.

To serve, drizzle the cake with the 1 tablespoon topping. Beat the remaining whipping cream to stiff peaks. Using a pastry bag fitted with a large star tip, pipe whipped cream around cake edge. Garnish with raspberries, if desired. Makes 12 servings.

◆ Chocolate Mousse Torte

Nutrition information per serving: 258 cal., 14 g fat, 63 mg chol., 3 g pro., 32 g carbo., 0 g fiber, 200 mg sodium. RDA: 14% vit. A, 10% riboflavin.
$200 WINNER
Jennifer Don Apy, Winchester, Mass.

Scarlet Pears

'TIS THE SEASON FOR CRANBERRIES, which give these elegant pears their striking scarlet color—

1½ cups cranberries
¾ cup water
6 ripe medium pears
½ cup sugar
⅓ cup amaretto or hazelnut liqueur
1 cup whipping cream
2 tablespoons amaretto or hazelnut liqueur (optional)
Toasted sliced or slivered almonds
Fresh mint (optional)

In a large saucepan or Dutch oven combine cranberries and water; heat to boiling. Reduce heat and simmer, uncovered, about 5 minutes or till cranberry skins begin to pop. Cool slightly. Place mixture in a food processor bowl or blender container. Cover and process or blend till almost smooth; sieve mixture, if desired. Return mixture to saucepan or Dutch oven.

Meanwhile, peel and core pears, leaving stems intact. If necessary, cut a thin slice from bottom of pears so they stand upright. Add sugar and the ⅓ cup amaretto to cranberry mixture; bring to boiling. Add pears, turning to coat. Simmer, covered, for 10 to 15 minutes or till tender. Cool. Serve warm or chill, covered, till serving time.

To serve, in a mixing bowl beat whipping cream and the 2 tablespoons amaretto (if desired) on medium speed of an electric mixer till soft peaks form. Divide cranberry sauce among 6 dessert plates; place a pear on each plate. Serve with whipped cream and garnish with toasted almonds and mint, if desired. Makes 6 servings.

Nutrition information per serving: 372 cal., 18 g fat., 54 mg chol., 3 g pro., 50 g carbo., 5 g fiber, 17 mg sodium.

◆ Scarlet Pears. *left*
◆ Peppy Chick-Pea Dip. *above*

RDA: 22% vit. A, 18% vit. C, 12% riboflavin.
$100 WINNER
Geri Hupp, Brookeland, Tex.

Peppy Chick-Pea Dip

1 15-ounce can garbanzo beans, drained
½ cup plain yogurt
¼ cup buttermilk salad dressing
2 tablespoons fine dry seasoned bread crumbs
2 teaspoons lemon juice

continued on page 210

French-Style Cream Cheese Spread

HERBES DE PROVENCE, A BLEND OF herbs often used in French cooking, seasons this spread. You can find it in the spice section of your supermarket or make your own. You need only a little in this recipe, so use the extra herb blend to season meat, poultry, or vegetables—

1 8-ounce package cream cheese, softened
¼ cup margarine or butter, softened
1 clove garlic, minced
1 tablespoon snipped parsley
1 tablespoon water
2 teaspoons white wine vinegar
1 teaspoon Worcestershire sauce
1 teaspoon herbes de Provence, crushed
¼ teaspoon seasoned salt
Fresh thyme (optional)
Assorted crackers

In a medium bowl stir together cream cheese, margarine or butter, garlic, parsley, water, vinegar, Worcestershire sauce, herbes de Provence, and seasoned salt. Cover and refrigerate overnight. To serve, garnish with fresh thyme, if desired. Serve with crackers. Makes 1⅓ cups spread.

Herbes de Provence: In a small storage container combine 1 tablespoon dried *marjoram,* 1 tablespoon dried *thyme,* 1 tablespoon dried *savory,* 1 teaspoon dried *basil,* 1 teaspoon dried *rosemary,* ½ teaspoon dried *sage,* and ½ teaspoon *fennel seed.* Store in an airtight container. Crush before using.

Nutrition information per tablespoon spread: 58 cal., 6 g fat, 18 mg chol., 1 g pro., 0 g carbo., 0 g fiber, 72 mg sodium.
$100 WINNER
Mrs. Glo Hacker, Oroville, Calif.

◆ French-Style Cream Cheese Spread
continued from page 209

½ teaspoon crushed red pepper
2 tablespoons chopped pitted ripe olives
Radishes, thinly sliced (optional)
Assorted vegetable dippers or crackers

In food processor bowl or blender container combine garbanzo beans, yogurt, salad dressing, bread crumbs, lemon juice, and red pepper. Cover and process or blend till smooth. Stir in olives. Chill, covered, at least 1 hour.

Garnish with radishes, if desired. Serve with vegetable dippers or crackers. Makes about 1⅔ cups.

Nutrition information per tablespoon: 32 cal., 1 g fat, 0 mg chol., 1 g pro., 4 g carbo., 0 g fiber, 57 mg sodium.
$200 WINNER
Rosemarie Berger, Jamestown, N. C.

Index

A-B

Appetizers
  Black Bean Chili in Phyllo Cups, 176
  Buffalo Wings, 72
  Crispy Chicken Bites, 73
  Curried Crab Dip, 177
  Dried Tomato Crostini, 175
  French-Style Cream Cheese
    Spread, 210
  Garlic-Ginger Chicken Strips, 172
  Herb Crisps, 177
  Herbed Cheese and Greens, 173
  Peppy Chick-Pea Dip, 209
  Salmon-Dill Canapés, 170
  Shrimp Kabobs with Sesame Dipping
    Sauce, 172
  Spiced Pita Crisps with Creamy
    Strawberry Spread, 55
Apples
  Apple-and-Sweet-Pepper Slaw, 141
  Apple-Cranberry Deep-Dish Pie, 154
  Applesauce-Rhubarb Muffins, 54
  Applesauce-Walnut Biscuits, 163
  Brandied Date-Apple
    Dumplings, 157
  Cherry-Apple Cobbler, 8
  Fall Apple Cake, 42
  Heart-Healthy Apple Coffee
    Cake, 144
  Honey Apple Ribs, 107
Apricots
  Apricot-Pecan Hot Cross Buns, 53
  Apricot Icing, 54
  Brandied Apricot-Pear
    Dumplings, 156
  Cherry-Apricot Freezer Jam, 124
  Double Apricot Coolers, 112
  Double Apricot Margaritas, 112
Artichokes
  Artichoke and Basil Hero, 145
  Chicken-Artichoke Pizza, 18

Dill-Artichoke Potato Salad, 106
Beans
  Black Bean Chili in Phyllo Cups, 176
  Meatball and Bean Soup, 9
  Midwestern Baked Chili, 63
  Peppy Chick-Pea Dip, 209
  Potato-Bean Soup, 138
  Quick Veggie Chili con Queso, 167
  Sherried Black Bean Soup, 10
  South-of-the-Border Pie, 45
  Tex-Mex Chicken Tostadas, 68
  Tortilla-Black Bean Casserole, 88
Beef
  Beef-and-Noodle Stir-Fry, 137
  Beef Stew with Sour Cream
    Biscuits, 38
  Freezer Meatballs, 8
  Fruit-and-Nut Chili, 168
  Grandma Massa's Red Meat
    Sauce, 207
  Lemony Flank Steak, 140
  Mandoo (Korean Dumplings), 205
  Marinated Prime Rib, 192
  Meatball and Bean Soup, 9
  Oriental Meatballs and Vegetables, 6
  Spicy Beef Pitas, 146
  Taco Salad, 34
  Thai Steak and Pasta Salad with
    Peanut-Pepper Dressing, 111
  Tropical Fiesta Steak, 89
Beverages
  Double Apricot Coolers, 112
  Double Apricot Margaritas, 112
  Jule Glögg, 201
  Peach 'n' Yogurt Smoothie, 100
  State Fair Lemonade, 100
  Wet-and-Wild Berry Slush, 100
Biscuits
  Applesauce-Walnut Biscuits, 163
  Buttermilk Biscuits, 162
  Cornmeal Biscuits, 10
  Homemade Biscuit Mix, 9
  Sour Cream Biscuits, 39
Breads (see also Biscuits, Muffins, Pizza,
    Popovers, Tortillas)
  Apricot-Pecan Hot Cross Buns, 53
  Cheddar Batter Bread, 152
  Cherry Tea Ring, 198

Cloverleaf Rye Rolls, 193
Creamy Caramel-Pecan Rolls, 163
Crunchy Parmesan Corn Bread, 54
Cucumber Buns, 131
Currant-Orange Scones, 163
Dried Tomato Crostini, 175
Honey Anise Bread, 44
Jelly Doughnuts
  (Soofganyah), 197
Julekake (Norwegian Christmas
  Bread), 200
Lemon-Pepper Breadsticks, 114
Pagache (Polish Pizza), 202
Parmesan-Herb Sourdough
  Breadsticks, 152
Pear Buttermilk Scones, 57
Pineapple-Carrot Tea Bread, 56
Sourdough Breadsticks, 151
Spiced Pita Crisps with Creamy
  Strawberry Spread, 55
Walnut Easter Bread, 53
Walnut Rolls, 202
Wheat Swirl Bread, 45
Whole Wheat Brick Alley Bread, 12
Whole Wheat Sourdough Bread, 148
Broccoli
  Broccoli-Noodle Stir-Fry, 19
  Broccoli-Sausage Quiche, 20

C

Cakes
  Bittersweet Chocolate Torte with
    Raspberries, 28
  Chocolate Mousse Torte, 208
  Fall Apple Cake, 42
  Fresh Raspberry Kuchen, 178
  Gingerbread Pound Cake, 59
  Graham-Streusel Coffee Cake, 145
  Heart-Healthy Apple
    Coffee Cake, 144
  Lemon Tea Cakes, 25
  Old Fashioned Pumpkin
    Gingerbread, 180
  Pecan Cake with Tangerine
    Cream Filling, 27
  Pound Cake with Raspberries, 144

Pumpkin-Pear Cake, 186
Cakes *continued*
    Royal Christmas Cake, 194
    Sherry-Almond Sponge Cake, 60
Candies
    Martha Washingtons, 195
    Marzipan Treasures, 25
    Phenomenal Fudge, 201
    Rum Truffles, 23
Carrots
    Carrot Cups with Summer
        Sauce, 119
    Carrot-Raisin Muffins, 43
    Pineapple-Carrot Tea Bread, 56
Cheese
    Cheddar Batter Bread, 152
    Cheesy Mashed Potatoes, 192
    Chocolate-Mint Cheesecake, 31
    Creamy Pesto Pasta, 187
    Crunchy Parmesan Corn Bread, 54
    Four-Cheese and Peppers Pizza, 18
    French-Style Cream Cheese
        Spread, 210
    Herbed Cheese and Greens, 173
    Honey-Nut Cheesecake, 159
    Parmesan-Herb Sourdough
        Breadsticks, 152
    Pecan Rice and Feta Salad, 89
    Quick Veggie Chili con Queso, 167
    Spinach-Feta Tart, 48
    Tofu-Cheese-Stuffed Shells, 15
    Very Berry Cheesecake, 123
    Wisconsin Cheese-Stuffed Chicken
        Rolls, 76
Cherries
    Cherry-Apple Cobbler, 8
    Cherry-Apricot Freezer Jam, 124
    Cherry-Champagne Ice, 22
    Cherry-Chocolate Cookies, 80
    Cherry Tea Ring, 198
    Fresh Fruit with Cherry Cream, 114
    Michigan Cherry Dipping Sauce, 73
Chicken (see Poultry)
Chocolate
    Bittersweet Chocolate Torte with
        Raspberries, 28
    Candy Bar Pie, 195

Cherry-Chocolate Cookies, 80
Chocolate and Pear Bread
    Pudding, 167
Chocolate Hazelnut Meringue
    Torte, 183
Chocolate-Mint Cheesecake, 31
Chocolate Mousse Torte, 208
Chocolate-Peanut Butter
    Pudding, 17
Chocolate Pumpkin Brownies, 181
Chocolate Truffle Tarts, 60
Creamy, Fudgy, and Nutty
    Brownies, 157
Martha Washingtons, 195
Mocha Truffle Cookies, 79
Phenomenal Fudge, 201
Rum Truffles, 23
Sky-High Brownie Pie, 96
S'Mores Sundae, 98
Cookies
    Brown Sugar Spritz, 203
    Cherry-Chocolate Cookies, 80
    Fairy Drops, 199
    Ginger Shortbread, 153
    Krumkake (Cone Cookies), 204
    Mocha Truffle Cookies, 79
    Orange-Poppy-Seed Shortbread, 153
    Shortbread Cookies, 153
    Shortbread Wedges, 153
Cranberries
    Apple-Cranberry Deep-Dish Pie, 154
    Cranberry-Pear Pie, 166
    Fresh Cranberry Relish, 193
    Scarlet Pears, 209

D-E

Desserts (see also Cakes, Candies,
Cookies, Pies, and Tarts)
    All-American Berries and
        Cream, 104
    Banana Crunch Pops, 105
    Blackberry Frozen Yogurt, 30
    Brandied Apricot-Pear
        Dumplings, 156
    Brandied Date-Apple
        Dumplings, 157

Cherry-Apple Cobbler, 8
Cherry-Champagne Ice, 22
Chocolate and Pear Bread
    Pudding, 167
Chocolate Hazelnut Meringue
    Torte, 183
Chocolate-Mint Cheesecake, 31
Chocolate-Peanut Butter
    Pudding, 17
Chocolate-Pumpkin Brownies, 181
Creamy, Fudgy, and Nutty
    Brownies, 157
Fresh Fruit with Cherry Cream, 114
Fried Strawberries with Honey
    Cream, 93
Gingerbread Lemon Terrine, 58
Honey-Nut Cheesecake, 159
Ice Cream on a Stick, 98
Lemon Yogurt Creme, 181
Lime and Lemon Ice Cream, 90
Orange and Rice Custard, 185
Party-Size Banana Split, 96
Pumpkin Flan, 186
Scarlet Pears, 209
Sky-High Brownie Pie, 96
S'Mores Sundae, 98
Sweet-Potato-Banana Custards, 184
Tortilla Fruit Cups, 101
Tropical Cream in a Coconut
    Puff, 120
Very Berry Cheesecake, 123
Eggs
    Breakfast Casserole, 39
    Broccoli-Sausage Quiche, 20
    Carrot Cups with Summer
        Sauce, 119
    Greek Spanakopita, 36
    Orange and Rice Custard, 185
    Pumpkin Flan, 186
    Scrambled Eggs with Smoked
        Salmon, 50
    Spinach-Feta Tart, 48
    Sweet-Potato-Banana Custards, 184

F-H

Fish
  Fish Fillets with Ginger-Dill
    Sauce, 92
  Island Swordfish, 31
  Orange-Tarragon Fish, 135
  Salmon and Lemon-Caper
    Cream, 56
  Salmon-Dill Canapés, 170
  Scrambled Eggs with Smoked
    Salmon, 50
  Seafood Enchiladas, 92
Frostings
  Almond Frosting, 199
  Apricot Icing, 54
  Lemon Satin Icing, 26
  Royal Icing, 195
  Vanilla Glaze, 199
  Whipped Cream Frosting, 28
Fruits (see also Individual Fruits)
  All-American Berries and
    Cream, 104
  Almond-Melon Tart, 122
  Applesauce-Rhubarb Muffins, 54
  Banana Crunch Pops, 105
  Blackberry Frozen Yogurt, 30
  Fresh Fruit with Cherry Cream, 114
  Fruit and Honey-Bran Muffins, 161
  Fruit-and-Nut Chili, 168
  Golden Fruit Conserve, 130
  Kiwi Sauce, 58
  Lime and Lemon Ice Cream, 90
  Party-Size Banana Split, 96
  Peach 'n' Yogurt Smoothie, 100
  Peaches-and-Cream Tart, 86
  Pear-Persimmon Deep-Dish Pie, 154
  Pineapple-Carrot Tea Bread, 56
  Strawberry-Melon Soup with Ginger
    Melon Balls, 48
  Tortilla Fruit Cups, 101
  Very Berry Cheesecake, 123
Herbes de Provence, 210

I-N

Lemon
  Fennel-Lemon Roasted
    Vegetables, 117
  Gingerbread Lemon Terrine, 58
  Lemon-Pepper Breadsticks, 114
  Lemon Satin Icing, 26
  Lemon Tea Cakes, 25
  Lemon Yogurt Creme, 181
  Lemony Flank Steak, 140
  Lime and Lemon Ice Cream, 90
  Salmon and Lemon-Caper Cream, 56
  State Fair Lemonade, 100
Meatballs
  Freezer Meatballs, 8
  Meatball and Bean Soup, 9
  Oriental Meatballs with Vegetables, 6
Muffins
  Applesauce-Rhubarb Muffins, 54
  Carrot-Raisin Muffins, 43
  Fruit and Honey-Bran Muffins, 161
  Pumpkin-Nut Muffins, 162
Nuts
  Almond-Melon Tart, 122
  Applesauce-Walnut Biscuits, 163
  Apricot-Pecan Hot Cross Buns, 53
  Cauliflower Toss with Pecan
    Dressing, 115
  Chicken-Cashew Curry, 56
  Chocolate Hazelnut Meringue
    Torte, 183
  Creamy Caramel-Pecan Rolls, 163
  Creamy, Fudgy, and Nutty
    Brownies, 157
  Fruit-and-Nut Chili, 168
  Honey-Nut Cheesecake, 159
  Mideastern Cashew Salad Pitas, 46
  Pecan Cake with Tangerine Cream
    Filling, 27
  Pecan Rice and Feta Salad, 89
  Pumpkin-Nut Muffins, 162
  Romaine and Walnut Salad, 17
  Royal Christmas Cake, 194
  Sherry-Almond Sponge Cake, 60
  Thai Steak and Pasta Salad with
    Peanut-Pepper Dressing, 111

Vegetables with Macadamia
    Nut Butter, 118
  Walnut Crust, 195
  Walnut Easter Bread, 53
  Walnut Rolls, 202

O-Q

Oranges
  Citrus-Greens Salad, 8
  Currant-Orange Scones, 163
  Orange and Beet Spinach Salad, 144
  Orange and Rice Custard, 185
  Orange-Poppy-Seed Shortbread, 153
  Orange-Tarragon Fish, 135
  Pecan Cake with Tangerine
    Cream Filling, 27
Pasta
  Beef-and-Noodle Stir-Fry, 137
  Broccoli-Noodle Stir-Fry, 19
  Chicken Provençale, 12
  Citrus Chicken, 67
  Creamy Pesto Pasta, 187
  Grandma Massa's Ravioli, 207
  Greek Tortellini Salad, 106
  Mediterranean Pasta Salad, 15
  Pasta with Red Clam Sauce, 188
  Spaghetti Alla Carbonara, 35
  Thai Steak and Pasta Salad with
    Peanut-Pepper Dressing, 111
  Tofu-Cheese-Stuffed Shells, 15
  Vegetarian Pasta, 114
Pears
  Brandied Apricot-Pear
    Dumplings, 156
  Chocolate and Pear Bread
    Pudding, 167
  Cranberry-Pear Pie, 166
  Pear Buttermilk Scones, 57
  Pear-Persimmon Deep-Dish Pie, 154
  Pork and Pear Stir-Fry, 78
  Pumpkin-Pear Cake, 186
  Scarlet Pears, 209
Pepper Jelly, Western-Style, 130
Pepper Slaw, Apple-and-Sweet-, 141
Phyllo
  Greek Spanakopita, 36
  Honey-Nut Cheesecake, 159
  Phyllo Cups, 176

Pies and Tarts
    Almond-Melon Tart, 122
    Apple-Cranberry Deep-Dish Pie, 154
    Berry Meringue Pie, 94
    Broccoli Sausage Quiche, 20
    Candy Bar Pie, 195
    Chocolate Truffle Tarts, 60
    Cranberry-Pear Pie, 166
    Peaches-and-Cream Tart, 86
    Pear-Persimmon Deep-Dish Pie, 154
    Single-Crust Pastry, 154
    South-of-the-Border Pie, 45
    Spinach-Feta Tart, 48
    Walnut Crust, 195
Pizza
    Chicken-Artichoke Pizza, 18
    Four-Cheese and Peppers Pizza, 18
    Grilled Pizza, 102
    Pagache (Polish Pizza), 202
    Ratatouille Pizza, 110
Popovers
    Caraway Rye Popovers, 161
    Eggnog Popovers, 161
    Old-Fashioned Popovers, 160
Pork (see also Sausage)
    Hawaiian Hoagies, 103
    Honey Apple Ribs, 107
    Marvelous Mustard Ribs, 108
    Pacific Rim Grilled Pork Salad, 84
    Pork and Pear Stir-Fry, 78
    Sherried Black Bean Soup, 10
    Spinach and Lentil Soup, 138
Potatoes
    Basil-Potato Soup, 40
    Cheesy Mashed Potatoes, 192
    Creamy Potluck Potatoes, 42
    Dill-Artichoke Potato Salad, 106
    Hot Mexican Potato Salad, 63
    New-Style Potato Salad, 117
    Pagache (Polish Pizza), 202
    Potato-Bean Soup, 138
    Potato Latkes, 197
    Rosemary Roasted New Potatoes, 51
    Scalloped Potatoes and Spinach, 64
    Sweet-Potato-Banana Custards, 184
    Warm Dilled Potato Salad, 132
Potstickers, Mandoo, 206

Poultry
    All-American Barbecued Chicken, 71
    Black Bean Chili in Phyllo Cups, 176
    Breakfast Casserole, 39
    Buffalo Wings, 72
    California Chicken Salad, 67
    Chicken-Artichoke Pizza, 18
    Chicken-Cashew Curry, 56
    Chicken Provençale, 12
    Chicken Salad with Tahini Sauce, 79
    Citrus Chicken, 67
    Country Captain, 74
    Crispy Chicken Bites, 73
    Garlic-Ginger Chicken Strips, 172
    Grilled Chicken Salad with Plum
        Vinaigrette, 116
    Grilled Honey-Soy Chicken
        Sandwiches, 14
    Hawaiian Chicken Burgers, 75
    Honolulu Chicken Salad, 67
    Maryland Fried Chicken, 76
    Midwestern Baked Chili, 63
    Minnesota Wild Rice
        Stuffed Chicken, 71
    Northwestern Chicken Salad, 66
    Pacific Rim Stir-Fry, 69
    Peanut-Ginger Chicken with
        California Salsa, 83
    Portuguese-Style Turkey Steaks, 62
    Skillet Chicken Paella, 142
    Southwestern-Style Burgers, 74
    Spaghetti Alla Carbonara, 35
    Spicy Ginger-Garlic Chicken, 32
    Tex-Mex Chicken Tostadas, 68
    Turkey Enchiladas, 37
    Turkey-Berry Club, 103
    Wisconsin Cheese-Stuffed Chicken
        Rolls, 76
Preserves
    Cherry-Apricot Freezer Jam, 124
    Golden Fruit Conserve, 130
    Western-Style Pepper Jelly, 130
Pumpkin
    Chocolate Pumpkin Brownies, 181
    Double Mushroom-Pumpkin
        Soup, 190
    Pumpkin Flan, 186

    Old-Fashioned Pumpkin
        Gingerbread, 180
    Pumpkin-Nut Muffins, 162
    Pumpkin-Pear Cake, 186

R-S

Raspberries
    Bittersweet Chocolate Torte with
        Raspberries, 28
    Fresh Raspberry Kuchen, 178
    Pound Cake with Raspberries, 144
    Raspberry Sauce, 58
    Raspberry Sauce, 184
Rice
    Minnesota Wild Rice Stuffed
        Chicken, 71
    Orange and Rice Custard, 185
    Pecan Rice and Feta Salad, 89
    South-of-the-Border Pie, 45
Salad Dressings
    Cauliflower Toss with Pecan
        Dressing, 115
    Cilantro Vinaigrette, 71
    Fresh Greens with Honey-Jalapeño
        Dressing, 10
    Grilled Chicken Salad with Plum
        Vinaigrette, 116
    Papaya Vinaigrette, 70
    Raspberry Vinaigrette, 70
    Thai Steak and Pasta Salad with
        Peanut-Pepper Dressing, 111
Salads, Main-Dish
    California Chicken Salad, 67
    Chicken Salad with Tahini Sauce, 79
    Grilled Chicken Salad with Plum
        Vinaigrette, 116
    Honolulu Chicken Salad, 67
    Northwestern Chicken Salad, 66
    Pacific Rim Grilled Pork Salad, 84
    Taco Salad, 34
    Thai Steak and Pasta Salad with
        Peanut-Pepper Dressing, 111
Salads, Side-Dish
    Apple-and-Sweet-Pepper Slaw, 141
    Cauliflower Toss with Pecan
        Dressing, 115
    Citrus-Greens Salad, 8
    Dill-Artichoke Potato Salad, 106

Fresh Greens with Honey-Jalapeño
    Dressing, 10
Greek Tortellini Salad, 106
Hot Mexican Potato Salad, 63
Mediterranean Pasta Salad, 15
New-Style Potato Salad, 117
Orange and Beet Spinach Salad, 144
Pecan Rice and Feta Salad, 89
Romaine and Walnut Salad, 17
Warm Dilled Potato Salad, 132
Sandwiches
    Artichoke and Basil Hero, 145
    Chicken-Cashew Curry, 56
    Grilled Honey-Soy Chicken
        Sandwiches, 14
    Hawaiian Chicken Burgers, 75
    Hawaiian Hoagies, 103
    Honey-Vegetable Vinaigrette, 55
    Mideastern Cashew Salad Pita, 46
    Peanut Butter Triple Decker, 103
    Salmon and Lemon-Caper Cream, 56
    Southwestern-Style Burgers, 74
    Spicy Beef Pitas, 146
    Tea Sandwiches, 55
    Turkey-Berry Club, 103
    Vegetarian, The, 103
Sauces and Dips
    Blue Cheese Dip, 72
    Cajun Dipping Sauce, 73
    Carrot Cups with Summer
        Sauce, 119
    Chicken Salad with Tahini Sauce, 79
    Classic Barbecue Sauce, 71
    Cream Gravy, 77
    Curried Crab Dip, 177
    Fish Fillets with Ginger-Dill
        Sauce, 92
    French-Style Cream Cheese
        Spread, 210
    Grandma Massa's Red Meat Sauce, 207
    Honey Cream, 93
    Kiwi Sauce, 58
    Mandoo Dipping Sauce, 206
    Michigan Cherry Dipping Sauce, 73
    Ohio-Style Barbecue Sauce, 71
    Pasta with Red Clam Sauce, 188
    Peanut-Ginger Chicken with
    California Salsa, 83
    Peppy Chick-Pea Dip, 209

Pineapple-Mustard Sauce, 90
Raspberry Sauce, 58
Raspberry Sauce, 184
Sesame Dipping Sauce, 173
Southwestern Mole Dipping
    Sauce, 73
Spiced Pita Crisps with Creamy
    Strawberry Spread, 55
Texas-Style Barbecue Sauce, 71
Tomatillo Guacamole, 35
Sausage
    Breakfast Casserole, 39
    Broccoli-Sausage Quiche, 20
Shellfish
    Curried Crab Dip, 177
    Fish Fillets with Ginger-Dill
        Sauce, 92
    Pasta with Red Clam Sauce, 188
    Seafood Enchiladas, 92
    Shrimp Curry, 40
    Shrimp Kabobs with Sesame Dipping
        Sauce, 172
Soups, Main Dish
    Basil-Potato Soup, 40
    Beef Stew with Sour Cream
        Biscuits, 38
    Fruit-and-Nut Chili, 168
    Meatball and Bean Soup, 9
    Potato-Bean Soup, 138
    Quick Veggie Chili con Queso, 167
    Sherried Black Bean Soup, 10
    Spinach and Lentil Soup, 138
Soups, Side-Dish
    Double Mushroom-Pumpkin
        Soup, 190
    Strawberry-Melon Soup with Ginger
        Melon Balls, 48
Spinach
    Greek Spanakopita, 36
    Orange and Beet Spinach Salad, 144
    Scalloped Potatoes and Spinach, 64
    Spinach and Lentil Soup, 138
    Spinach-Feta Tart, 48
Stir-Fries
    Beef-and-Noodle Stir-Fry, 137
    Broccoli-Noodle Stir-Fry, 19
    Pacific Rim Stir-Fry, 69
    Pork and Pear Stir-Fry, 78

Strawberries
    All-American Berries and Cream, 104
    Berry Meringue Pie, 94
    Fried Strawberries with Honey
        Cream, 93
    Spiced Pita Crisps with Creamy
        Strawberry Spread, 55
    Strawberry-Melon Soup with
        Ginger Melon Balls, 48
    Turkey-Berry Club, 103
    Wet-and-Wild Berry Slush, 100

T-Z

Tofu-Cheese-Stuffed Shells, 15
Tortillas
    Seafood Enchiladas, 92
    Spiced Pita Crisps with Creamy
        Strawberry Spread, 55
    Taco Salad, 34
    Tex-Mex Chicken Tostadas, 68
    Tortilla-Black Bean Casserole, 88
    Tortilla Cups, 34
    Tortilla Fruit Cups, 101
    Turkey Enchiladas, 37
Turkey (see Poultry)
Vegetables (see also Broccoli, Carrots,
        Potatoes, Spinach)
    Cauliflower Toss with Pecan
        Dressing, 115
    Cucumber Buns, 131
    Dried Tomato Crostini, 175
    Fennel-Lemon Roasted
        Vegetables, 117
    Grilled Tomatoes with Pesto, 85
    Honey-Vegetable Vinaigrette, 55
    Orange and Beet Spinach Salad, 144
    Oriental Meatballs and Vegetables, 6
    Quick Veggie Chili con Queso, 167
    Ratatouille Pizza, 110
    Steamed Asparagus Bundles, 51
    Sweet-and-Sour Red Cabbage, 193
    Tomatillo Guacamole, 35
    Vegetables with Macadamia Nut
        Butter, 118
    Vegetarian Pasta, 114
Wontons, Mandoo, 206
Zany-Zoo Mix, 99

Metric Cooking Hints

By making a few conversions, cooks in Australia, Canada, and the United Kingdom can use the recipes in Better Homes and Gardens® *1993 Best Recipes Yearbook* with confidence. The charts on this page provide a guide for converting measurements from the U.S. customary system, which is used throughout this book, to the imperial and metric systems. There also is a conversion table for oven temperatures to accommodate the differences in oven calibrations.

Volume and Weight: Americans traditionally use cup measures for liquid and solid ingredients. The chart (top right) shows the approximate imperial and metric equivalents. If you are accustomed to weighing solid ingredients, here are some helpful approximate equivalents.
- 1 cup butter, caster sugar, or rice = 8 ounces = about 250 grams
- 1 cup flour = 4 ounces = about 125 grams
- 1 cup icing sugar = 5 ounces = about 150 grams

Spoon measures are used for smaller amounts of ingredients. Although the size of the tablespoon varies slightly among countries, for practical purposes and for recipes in this book, a straight substitution is all that's necessary.

Measurements made using cups or spoons should always be level, unless stated otherwise.

Product Differences: Most of the ingredients called for in the recipes in this book are available in English-speaking countries. However, some are known by different names. Here are some common American ingredients and their possible counterparts:
- Sugar is granulated or caster sugar.
- Powdered sugar is icing sugar.
- All-purpose flour is plain household flour or white flour. When self-rising flour is used in place of all-purpose flour in a recipe that calls for leavening, omit the leavening agent (baking soda or baking powder) and salt.
- Light corn syrup is golden syrup.
- Cornstarch is cornflour.
- Baking soda is bicarbonate of soda.
- Vanilla is vanilla essence.

Useful Equivalents

⅛ teaspoon = 0.5ml	⅔ cup = 5 fluid ounces = 150ml
¼ teaspoon = 1ml	¾ cup = 6 fluid ounces = 175ml
½ teaspoon = 2 ml	1 cup = 8 fluid ounces = 250ml
1 teaspoon = 5 ml	2 cups = 1 pint
¼ cup = 2 fluid ounces = 50ml	2 pints = 1 litre
⅓ cup = 3 fluid ounces = 75ml	½ inch =1 centimetre
½ cup = 4 fluid ounces = 125ml	1 inch = 2 centimetres

Baking Pan Sizes

American	Metric
8x1½-inch round baking pan	20x4-centimetre sandwich or cake tin
9x1½-inch round baking pan	23x3.5-centimetre sandwich or cake
11x7x1½-inch baking pan	28x18x4-centimetre baking pan
13x9x2-inch baking pan	32.5x23x5-centimetre baking pan
2-quart rectangular baking dish	30x19x5-centimetre baking pan
15x10x2-inch baking pan	38x25.5x2.5-centimetre baking pan (Swiss roll tin)
9-inch pie plate	22x4- or 23x4-centimetre pie plate
7- or 8-inch springform pan	18- or 20-centimetre springform or loose-bottom cake tin
9x5x3-inch loaf pan	23x13x6-centimetre or 2-pound narrow loaf pan or paté tin
1½-quart casserole	1.5-litre casserole
2-quart casserole	2-litre casserole

Oven Temperature Equivalents

Farenheit Setting	Celsius Setting*	Gas Setting
300°F	150°C	Gas Mark 2
325°F	160°C	Gas Mark 3
350°F	180°C	Gas Mark 4
375°F	190°C	Gas Mark 5
400°F	200°C	Gas Mark 6
425°F	220°C	Gas Mark 7
450°F	230°C	Gas Mark 8
Broil		Grill

Electric and gas ovens may be calibrated using Celsius. However, increase the Celsius setting 10 to 20 degrees when cooking above 160°C with an electric oven. For convection or forced-air ovens (gas or electric), lower the temperature setting 10°C when cooking at all heat levels.